原　著：【明】罗贯中
主　编：史　迹　黎　明
副主编：齐燕荣　全彩宜
编　者：马　郡　王文理　蒋维维
　　　　李　裴　陶梦然　陈恺熙

1500 words
Level 5

三国演义

Romance of the Three Kingdoms

(Abridged)

罗贯中 原著
史 迹 黎 明 主编
薛彧威 闫传海 翻译

MP3
Download Online

SinolinguA
华语教学出版社

First Edition 2019

ISBN 978-7-5138-1646-5

Published by Sinolingua Co., Ltd
24 Baiwanzhuang Road, Beijing 100037, China
Tel: (86) 10-68320585 68997826
Fax: (86) 10-68997826 68326333
http://www.sinolingua.com.cn
E-mail: hyjx@sinolingua.com.cn
Facebook: www.facebook.com/sinolingua
Printed by Beijing Jinghua Hucais Printing Co., Ltd

Printed in the People's Republic of China

编者的话

对于广大汉语学习者来说，要想快速提高汉语水平，扩大阅读量是很有必要的。“彩虹桥”汉语分级读物为汉语学习者提供了一系列有趣、有用的汉语阅读材料。本系列读物按照词汇量进行分级，力求用限定的词汇讲述精彩的故事。本套读物主要有以下特点：

一、分级精准，循序渐进。我们参考“新汉语水平考试（HSK）词汇表”（2012 年修订版）、《汉语国际教育用音节汉字词汇等级划分（国家标准）》和《常用汉语 1500 高频词语表》等词汇分级标准，结合《欧洲语言教学与评估框架性共同标准》（CEFR），设计了一套适合汉语学习者的“彩虹桥”词汇分级标准。本系列读物分为 7 个级别（入门级*、1 级、2 级、3 级、4 级、5 级、6 级），供不同水平的汉语学习者选择，每个级别故事的生词数量不超过本级别对应词汇量的 20%。随着级别的升高，故事的篇幅逐渐加长。本系列读物与 HSK、CEFR 的对应级别，各级词汇量以及每本书的字数详见下表。

---

* 入门级（Starter）在封底用 S 标识。

级别	入门级	1级	2级	3级	4级	5级	6级
对应级别	HSK1 CEFR A1	HSK1-2 CEFR A1-A2	HSK2-3 CEFR A2-B1	HSK3 CEFR A2-B1	HSK3-4 CEFR B1	HSK4 CEFR B1-B2	HSK5 CEFR B2-C1
词汇量	150	300	500	750	1 000	1 500	2 500
字数	1 000	2 500	5 000	7 500	10 000	15 000	25 000

二、故事精彩，题材多样。本套读物选材的标准就是“精彩”，所选的故事要么曲折离奇，要么感人至深，对读者构成奇妙的吸引力。选题广泛取材于中国的神话传说、民间故事、文学名著、名人传记和历史故事等，让汉语学习者在阅读中潜移默化地了解中国的文化和历史。

三、结构合理，实用性强。“彩虹桥”系列读物的每一本书中，除了中文故事正文之外，都配有主要人物的中英文介绍、生词英文注释及例句、故事正文的英文翻译、练习题和生词表，方便读者阅读和理解故事内容，提升汉语阅读能力。练习题主要采用客观题，题型多样，难度适中，并附有参考答案，既可供汉语教师在课堂上教学使用，又可供汉语学习者进行自我水平检测。

如果您对本系列读物有什么想法，比如推荐精彩故事、提出改进意见等，请发邮件到 hyjx@sinolingua.com.cn，与我们交流探讨。也可以关注我们的微信公众号 CHQRainbowBridge，随时与我们交流互动。同时，微信公众号会不定期发布有关“彩虹桥”的出版信息，以及汉语阅读、中国文化小知识等。

韩 颖 刘小琳

Preface

For students who study Chinese as a foreign language, it's crucial for them to enlarge the scope of their reading to improve their comprehension skills. The "Rainbow Bridge" Graded Chinese Reader series is designed to provide a collection of interesting and useful Chinese reading materials. This series grades each volume by its vocabulary level and brings the learners into every scene through vivid storytelling. The series has the following features:

I. A gradual approach by grading the volumes based on vocabulary levels. We have consulted the New HSK Vocabulary (2012 Revised Edition), the *Graded Chinese Syllables, Characters and Words for the Application of Teaching Chinese to the Speakers of Other Languages (National Standard)* and the 1,500 Commonly Used High Frequency Chinese Vocabulary, along with the Common European Framework of Reference for Languages (CEFR) to design the "Rainbow Bridge" vocabulary grading standard. The series is divided into seven levels (Starter*, Level 1, Level 2, Level 3, Level 4, Level 5 and Level 6) for students at different stages in their Chinese education to choose from. For each level, new words are no more than 20% of the vocabulary amount as specified in the corresponding HSK and CEFR levels. As the levels progress, the passage length will in turn increase. The following table indicates the corresponding "Rainbow Bridge" level, HSK and CEFR levels, the vocabulary amount, and number of characters.

* Represented by "S" on the back cover.

Level	Starter	1	2	3	4	5	6
HSK/ CEFR Level	HSK1 CEFR A1	HSK1-2 CEFR A1-A2	HSK2-3 CEFR A2-B1	HSK3 CEFR A2-B1	HSK3-4 CEFR B1	HSK4 CEFR B1-B2	HSK5 CEFR B2-C1
Vocabulary	150	300	500	750	1,000	1,500	2,500
Characters	1,000	2,500	5,000	7,500	10,000	15,000	25,000

II. Intriguing stories on various themes. The series features engaging stories known for their twists and turns as well as deeply touching plots. The readers will find it a joyful experience to read the stories. The topics are selected from Chinese mythology, legends, folklore, literary classics, biographies of renowned people and historical tales. Such wide-ranging topics exert an invisible, yet formative, influence on readers' understanding of Chinese culture and history.

III. Reasonably structured and easy to use. For each volume of the "Rainbow Bridge" series, apart from a Chinese story, we also provide an introduction to the main characters in Chinese and English, new words with English explanations and sample sentences, and an English translation of the story, followed by comprehension exercises and a vocabulary list to help users read and understand the story and improve their Chinese reading skills. The exercises are mainly presented as objective questions that take on various forms with moderate difficulty. Moreover, keys to the exercises are also provided. The series can be used by teachers in class or by students for self-study.

If you have any questions, comments or suggestions about the series, please email us at hyjx@sinolingua.com.cn. You can also exchange ideas with us via our WeChat account: CHQRainbowBridge. This account will provide updates on the series along with Chinese reading materials and cultural tips.

Han Ying and Liu Xiaolin

目　录
Contents

1. 桃园结义[1]

主要人物和地点：
Main Characters and Places

刘备（Liú Bèi）(161–223)：字玄德，汉朝皇室后代。他建立了蜀国，成了蜀国的皇帝，一心想恢复汉室，统一全国。

Liu Bei (161–223): Courtesy name Xuande, one of the descendants of the Han royal family. He founded the Kingdom of Shu (221–263) and became its emperor. He was devoted to revitalizing the Han Dynasty and reunifying the whole country.

关羽（Guān Yǔ）(?–220)：字云长，蜀国大将军。他武艺高强，忠诚重情义。

Guan Yu (?–220): Courtesy name Yunchang, a major Shu general. He excelled at martial arts, was loyal and valued friendship.

张飞（Zhāng Fēi）(?–221)：字翼德，蜀国大将军。他武艺高强，十分勇敢，但有时做事鲁莽。

Zhang Fei (?–221): Courtesy name Yide, a major Shu general. He excelled at martial arts and was brave, but sometimes he acted recklessly.

张角（Zhāng Jiǎo）（？–184）：东汉末年农民起义军"黄巾军"的首领。

Zhang Jiao (?–184): Head of the "Yellow Turban Army" who led the Yellow Turban Uprising, a large-scale peasant uprising at the close of the Eastern Han Dynasty (25–220).

刘焉（Liú Yān）（？–194）：汉朝皇室后代，管辖益州（今四川、重庆、陕西南部、云南西北部等地）的地方官。

Liu Yan (?–194): One of the descendants of the Han royal family. He was a local official who governed Yizhou, which covered the areas of present-day Sichuan, Chongqing, southern Shaanxi and northwestern Yunnan.

幽州（Yōuzhōu）：中国古代地名，主要包括今北京市、河北北部、辽宁南部等地。

Youzhou: A place in ancient China that covered the areas of present-day Beijing, northern Hebei and southern Liaoning.

东汉末年[2]，皇帝①年纪小，不能管理国家。朝廷②腐败③，年轻人都去打仗④了。这一年，很久没有下雨了。因为没有雨水，到了秋天，农民没有收获⑤，没有饭吃，生活非常困难。因为没法生活，百姓⑥都起来反对朝廷。

有一个农民叫张角，他组织了一支黄巾起义军[3]反对朝廷，得到了百姓的支持。一个月之内，全国各地都在反对朝廷，到处都在打仗，人们生活在战乱⑦之中。

幽州的地方官叫刘焉。他看见黄巾起义军发展得很快，非常害怕，就贴出征兵⑧告示⑨，准备跟黄巾起

① 皇帝 (huángdì)
n. emperor
e.g. 汉献帝是东汉的最后一个皇帝。

② 朝廷 (cháotíng)
n. royal court
e.g. 朝廷是皇帝处理国家大事的地方。

③ 腐败 (fǔbài)
adj. corrupt
e.g. 东汉末年的朝廷非常腐败。

④ 打仗 (dǎzhàng)
v. fight in a battle
e.g. 很多年轻人都去打仗了，只有很少的人种地。

⑤ 收获 (shōuhuò)
n. harvest
e.g. 秋天是一个收获的季节。

⑥ 百姓 (bǎixìng)
n. common people; ordinary people
e.g. 百姓们希望过上好日子。

⑦ 战乱 (zhànluàn)
n. turmoil of war
e.g. 战乱给人们的生活带来很多灾难。

⑧ 征兵 (zhēngbīng)
v. recruit soldiers; conscript
e,g. 每年国家都要征兵。

⑨ 告示 (gàoshì)
n. official notice
e.g. 墙上贴着一张告示。

义军打仗，保护幽州。

一位英雄[1]站在征兵告示前看告示。这位英雄看上去高大，英俊[2]。他的耳朵很长，他的眼睛能看到他长长的耳朵。他的胳膊和手也很长。他就是刘备，是汉朝[3]皇室[4]的后代[5]。

刘备家里很穷，他跟母亲生活在一起。他非常爱他的母亲，对母亲非常孝顺[6]。他喜欢读书，从小就有远大的理想，特别喜欢跟天下英雄交朋友。

刘备从征兵告示想到百姓生活在战乱之中，自己又没有能力匡扶天下[4]，让百姓过上好日子，心里很难过。他一边看一边叹气。

① 英雄 (yīngxióng)
n. hero
e.g. 关羽是中国古代的英雄。

② 英俊 (yīngjùn)
adj. handsome
e.g. 这位年轻人很英俊。

③ 汉朝 (Hàncháo)
n. Han Dynasty (206 BC-220 AD)
e.g. 汉朝分为西汉和东汉，有四百多年的历史。

④ 皇室 (huángshì)
n. royal family
e.g. 汉朝皇室姓刘，有很多后代。

⑤ 后代 (hòudài)
n. descendant; offspring
e.g. 为了我们的后代，我们要保护好环境。

⑥ 孝顺 (xiàoshùn)
v. be filially pious; be dutiful
e.g. 孝顺父母是一种美德。

① 胡子 (húzi)
n. beard
e.g. 张飞脸上长着黑黑的胡子。

② 打天下 (dǎ tiānxià) seize state power by armed force;
天下 (tiānxià) land under heaven; the country
e.g. 东汉末年，很多英雄都想打天下，建立新的朝代。

突然，刘备听到一个人大声说："国难当头[5]，你却在这里叹气，怎么能算是一个大英雄呢？"刘备回头一看，这个人又高又大，眼睛圆圆的，脸上胡子①黑黑的。他说话声音很大，一看就是一位英雄。

这个人说："我姓张，叫张飞，字翼德，喜欢跟天下英雄交朋友。我看见你一边看征兵告示一边在那儿叹气，所以我这样问你。"

刘备告诉张飞，因为自己没有能力帮助天下人，心里很难过，所以才叹气。张飞听了之后，说："我有点儿钱，可以找一些英雄。我跟你一起打天下②，怎么样？”刘备听了非常高兴，两个人来到一个酒馆[①]，一边喝酒一边商量。

就在这个时候，走进来一个人。刘备仔细看了看，这个人比自己和张飞还高，长长的胡子，红红的脸，长得十分英俊。刘备马上站起来，请他过来一起喝酒，并问他叫什么名字。

这个人说：“我姓关，叫关羽，字云长。我听说这里有征兵告示，就过来看看。”他们三人互相认识之后，一边喝酒一边商量。刘备、张飞把他们治国安民[6]的打算告诉了关羽，关羽听了非常高兴，决定跟他们一起打天下。

① 酒馆 (jiǔguǎn)
n. pub
e.g. 刘备和张飞在酒馆认识了关羽。

张飞说："我家后面有一个桃园，明天我们就在桃园里结拜为兄弟[7]，一起打天下！"刘备和关羽高兴地同意了。

第二天，刘备、关羽、张飞三个人来到张飞家的桃园举行结拜仪式。他们说："我们三个人姓名不同，

出生的年月日不同，今天结为兄弟，一起打天下，治国安民。”于是，三个人从此结成了兄弟。

刘备年纪最大，被称为大哥。关羽年纪比刘备小，被称为二哥。张飞年纪最小，被称为三弟。这就是《三国演义》中“桃园三结义”的故事。

刘备他们结拜兄弟之后，举办了一个酒宴[1]庆祝[2]，找来了三百多名英雄。他们还收到了人们送给他们的一些兵器[3]，但是没有马。打仗不能没有马啊！这时候，有两个卖马的人听说了他们的事，就送给他们很多马，还送给他们很多钱，另加一千斤铁[4]做

① 酒宴 (jiǔyàn)
n. banquet
e.g. 他见到老朋友非常高兴，摆了一桌酒宴。

② 庆祝 (qìngzhù)
v. celebrate
e.g. 他们打败了敌人，喝酒庆祝胜利。

③ 兵器 (bīngqì)
n. arms；weaponry
e.g. 关羽的兵器非常重，叫青龙偃月刀。

④ 铁 (tiě) *n.* iron
e.g. 张飞的兵器是用铁做的，叫丈八长矛。

兵器。他们兄弟三人请人为他们做了兵器。有了兵器之后，他们又找来了更多的英雄。最后，他们带着五百多位英雄去幽州见地方官刘焉。

到了幽州，因为刘备是皇室的后代，所以刘焉收留了刘备等人。就这样，刘备、关羽、张飞在东汉末年朝廷腐败、天下大乱的时候，开始打天下了。

[1] 桃园结义（táoyuán-jiéyì）Oath of the Peach Orchard
《三国演义》中，刘备、关羽、张飞在一个桃园结为兄弟，他们发誓要平定天下，为百姓带来和平安康，彼此忠诚、仗义。在中国传统文化中，这个习语代表了儒家道德的忠义。
In *Romance of the Three Kingdoms*, Liu Bei, Guan Yu and Zhang Fei decide to be sworn brothers in a peach orchard. They vow to bring peace to their country, provide the people with security, and maintain loyalty to each other. In traditional Chinese culture, this phrase is an idiom that represents the combination of loyalty and righteousness in Confucian ethics.

[2] 东汉末年（Dōnghàn mònián）late Eastern Han Dynasty
一般指公元 184 年—220 年，东汉灭亡前的这段时间。在这期间，中国各地战乱四起，政治混乱。
Approximately 184-220, the period before the collapse of the Eastern Han Dynasty, during which there were wars and political chaos in various parts of China.

[3] 黄巾起义军（Huángjīn Qǐyìjūn）Yellow Turban Army
东汉末年农民自己组织的反抗朝廷暴政的军队。士兵的头上包着黄巾，所以叫黄巾军。起义于公元 184 年开始，一年后失败。
The army of a large-scale peasant uprising at the close of the Eastern Han Dynasty. The participants wore yellow turbans, hence the name. They rebelled against despotic rule. The uprising started in the year 184 and ended in failure one year later.

[4] 匡扶天下（kuāngfú tiānxià）assist the country
帮扶国家。战乱的年代里涌现出了很多英雄，他们立志要匡扶天下，比如东汉末年出现的刘备、张飞和关羽这些英雄。
In turbulent times, heroes came out to assist the country. In the late Eastern Han Dynasty, heroes like Liu Bei, Zhang Fei, and Guan Yu appeared to assist the Han Dynasty.

[5] 国难当头（guónàn-dāngtóu）the country is in a state of crisis
在东汉末年，因为朝廷腐败、连年征战及饥荒，整个国家都面临着巨大的危难，像刘备、关羽、张飞这样的英雄都出来帮扶国家。这个成语现在被用来描述整个国家面临危机。
In the late Eastern Han Dynasty, the entire country was in a serious crisis due to the corruption of the imperial court and successive years of war and famine. Heroes, like Liu Bei, Guan Yu, and Zhang Fei, emerged to assist the country. This phrase is an idiom used to describe the crisis a country faces.

[6] 治国安民（zhìguó-ānmín）govern the country and bring peace to the people
在封建社会，皇帝的最终目标是管理国家，安抚人民。
During the period of feudalism, the ultimate goals of the emperor were governing the country and bringing peace to the people.

[7] 结拜兄弟（jié bài xiōngdì）become sworn brothers
在中国传统习俗中，没有亲戚关系的人因为感情好或者因为共同的个人利益，通过发誓、喝酒等形式形成利益关系，互相用兄弟来称呼。
It is a Chinese social custom for some men who do not have kinship to become sworn brothers for common beliefs and benefits, etc. The ceremonies involve taking oaths, drinking wine, etc.

练习题 Reading exercises

一、选词填空。Fill in the blanks with the given words.

反对　　打仗　　理想　　桃园

1. 东汉末年，年轻人都去（　　）了。
2. 刘备、关羽、张飞三个人在（　　）结拜为兄弟。
3. 两个卖马的人知道他们三人的（　　）后，送给他们很多马、很多钱。

二、判断正误。Read the following sentences and decide whether the statements are true or false.

1. 东汉末年，朝廷腐败，人们没有饭吃，生活十分困难。（　）
2. 关羽、张飞和刘备三个人在桃园结拜兄弟，准备去卖马。（　）
3. 关羽、张飞和刘备带着五百多人去幽州找刘焉，准备打天下。（　）

答案：

一、1. 打仗　2. 桃园　3. 理想

二、1. 正　2. 误　3. 正

2. 曹操献刀

主要人物和地点：
Main Characters and Places

董卓（Dǒng Zhuó）(?–192)：东汉末年的地方军阀。他带领军队占据了东汉都城洛阳，控制了皇帝，掌握了朝廷大权，为人荒淫。

Dong Zhuo (?–192): A local warlord during the late Eastern Han Dynasty. He commanded his army to capture Luoyang, the capital of the Eastern Han Dynasty. Then he controlled the emperor and state power. He was cruel and lived a dissipated life.

王允（Wáng Yǔn）(137–192)：东汉末年汉朝大臣。他与其他大臣密谋刺杀董卓，但没有成功。后来他用美人计离间董卓和吕布，唆使吕布杀了董卓。

Wang Yun (137–192): A minister during the late Eastern Han Dynasty. He made a secret plan together with other ministers to assassinate Dong Zhuo, but failed in their attempt. Afterwards, he used a woman to sow discord between Dong Zhuo and his adopted son, Lü Bu, which led to Dong's death.

曹操（Cáo Cāo）(155–220)：字孟德，东汉末年的丞相。董卓死后，他控制了汉献帝，掌握了朝廷大权，占据了北方，建立了政权。

Cao Cao (155–220): Courtesy name Mengde, the Prime Minister during the late Eastern Han Dynasty. He took control of Emperor Xiandi after Dong Zhuo's death. He then gradually seized state power and occupied northern China.

吕布（Lǚ Bù）(?–198)：三国时期的名将，武艺高强。他是董卓的义子，后被曹操所杀。

Lü Bu (?–198): A famous general during the Three Kingdoms Period (220–280) who excelled at martial arts. He was Dong Zhuo's adopted son and was later killed by Cao Cao.

汉献帝（Hàn Xiàndì）(181–234)：东汉最后一位皇帝（189–220年在位）。他最初被董卓控制，后来受曹操控制。

Emperor Xiandi (181–234): The last emperor of the Eastern Han Dynasty whose reign spanned from 189 to 220. As a young emperor, he was first controlled by Dong Zhuo and then became the puppet of Cao Cao.

洛阳（Luòyáng）：中国古代的地名，今河南省洛阳市。洛阳是东汉末年的都城。公元220年，曹操的儿子曹丕(187–226)在洛阳建立了三国时期的魏国。

Luoyang: A place in ancient China which is present-day Luoyang City, Henan Province. It was the capital of the late Eastern Han Dynasty. In 220, Cao Pi (187–226), one of Cao Cao's sons, established the Kingdom of Wei there.

① 吃喝玩乐 (chīhē-wánlè) indulge in eating, drinking, and pleasure-seeking
e.g. 董卓控制了朝廷，整天吃喝玩乐。

② 军阀 (jūnfá)
n. warlord
e.g. 东汉末年，很多军阀都想当皇帝。

③ 军队 (jūnduì)
n. army; troops
e.g. 这支军队要去打仗了。

④ 大权 (dàquán)
n. great power; authority
e.g. 汉献帝应该掌握朝廷大权，但是实际上他没有权。

⑤ 大臣 (dàchén)
n. court official; minister
e.g. 董卓控制着朝廷，大臣们都听从董卓的。

汉朝的皇帝汉灵帝每天吃喝玩乐①，不管国家大事。公元189年他去世后，他的儿子当了皇帝，被称为汉少帝。当时汉少帝只有14岁，不会管理国家大事，国家一片混乱。

有一个军阀②叫董卓。他带着军队③进入了都城洛阳。董卓废了汉少帝，让汉少帝的弟弟当了皇帝，也就是汉献帝。虽然汉献帝是皇帝，但整个朝廷都听董卓的。就这样，董卓掌握了汉朝大权④。

董卓掌握了朝廷大权之后，欺君害民[1]，吃喝玩乐，生活腐败。大臣⑤和百姓都恨他。

一些大臣想杀了董卓，

可是董卓身边有很多士兵保护他，大臣们没有机会杀他。有一个大臣叫王允，他一直在考虑杀死董卓的计划。

一天，王允在家里摆了酒宴，请了一些朝廷大臣来庆祝他的生日。王允和朋友们喝了几杯酒之后，突然大哭起来。他说："其实今天不是我的生日。我是请大家来商量一件事，因为害怕被董卓怀疑，所以就说是我过生日。"大家听完都不说话了。

王允接着说："现在董卓掌握着朝廷大权，汉朝已经非常危险。我一想到这些，就想哭。"大臣们听到这里，都大声哭了起来。

① 回报 (huíbào)
v. requite; repay
e.g. 他成功后，想要回报帮助过他的人。

② 计谋 (jìmóu)
n. scheme; stratagem
e.g. 曹操想了一个杀董卓的计谋。

③ 锋利 (fēnglì)
adj. sharp
e.g. 皇帝用的这把剑非常锋利。

大家一起骂董卓，可谁也想不出杀董卓的好办法。

就在这个时候，忽然曹操拍着手，大笑着说："看看我们这些满朝文武[2]，像女人一样在哭，难道我们能哭死董卓吗？我愿意去杀董卓，回报①天下。"

王允忙问："你有什么计谋②？"

曹操对王允说："这些日子，我在董卓身边做事，他很信任我。我听说您有一把七星宝刀，非常锋利③，能不能借给我，我拿着它去杀董卓。"

王允看见曹操这么勇敢，又足智多谋[3]，非常高兴，立刻把七星宝刀交给了曹操。

第二天，曹操带着七星宝刀来到董卓住的相府[4]，拜见①董卓。董卓这时候坐在床上，好像要睡觉。他的义子[5]吕布站在他的后面。

曹操说因为自己的马跑得慢，所以来晚了。董卓知道曹操很有能力，想让曹操为他做事，就想给曹操一点儿好处。董卓说要送给曹操一匹②好马，然后让吕布去为曹操挑马，于是吕布出去了。董卓因为太胖，不能长时间坐着，就躺在了床上。

曹操心里想：现在吕布不在，正是杀董卓的好机会。他立刻拿出七星宝刀。可是没想到，董卓忽

① 拜见 (bàijiàn)
v. pay a formal visit
e.g 大臣们要去朝廷拜见皇帝。

② 匹 (pǐ) *m.w.* (for horses, mules, etc.)
e.g 吕布有一匹红色的马，跑得非常快。

然从床上的镜子中看到了曹操拿刀。董卓非常吃惊，一下子从床上跳了起来，大声说："曹操，你要干什么？"正在这时候，吕布已经带着马来到门外了。

曹操见吕布回来了，知道失去了杀董卓的机会，因为他打不过吕布。在这危险的时刻，曹操马上想出了一个计谋，赶忙跪[1]在地上，骗董卓说："我想把七星宝刀献给[2]您。"董卓听了，接过了七星宝刀。他看见这把刀十分锋利，上面还有七颗宝石[3]，确实是一把宝刀，非常高兴地收下了。曹操害怕董卓杀他，就对董卓说："我想出去试试马。"

① 跪 (guì) *v.* kneel
e.g. 大臣们跪着拜见皇帝。

② 献给 (xiàn gěi) *v.* give; present sth. to sb.
e.g. 他献给女朋友一束鲜花。

③ 宝石 (bǎoshí) *n.* gem
e,g. 这颗蓝宝石非常贵。

得到董卓同意以后，曹操出门骑上马跑了，离开了董卓的相府。

[1] 欺君害民（qījūn-hàimín）deceive the emperor and bring disasters to the people

表示某人欺骗君王，给百姓带来灾难。在《三国演义》中，董卓势力非常强大，欺君害民，给人们带来了巨大的灾难。

In *Romance of the Three Kingdoms*, Dong Zhuo, who is very powerful, deceives and rides roughshod over the emperor of the Han Dynasty and its people. Dong brings great disasters to the people.

[2] 满朝文武（mǎncháo wénwǔ）all the civilian and military officials

朝廷上的所有文官和武将。在封建王朝，文官和武将协同工作，帮助皇帝治理国家。在这个故事中，董卓篡夺权力，压制百姓，于是朝廷的文官和武将都秘谋刺杀董卓。在封建社会，皇帝是国家的最高权威，像董卓这样篡夺皇帝权力的人是大家心中的叛贼。

In the feudal dynasties, civil ministers and military generals worked together to help the emperor run the country. In the story, Dong Zhuo usurps the power of the emperor of the Han Dynasty and oppresses the people, so the ministers and generals secretly discuss a scheme to kill Dong. In the feudal dynasties, the emperor was the supreme authority of the country. Anyone who usurped the power of the emperor was regarded as a traitor like Dong Zhuo.

[3] 足智多谋（zúzhì-duōmóu）clever and resourceful

指人聪明、机智，有计谋。在《三国演义》中，诸葛亮、曹操、司马懿、周瑜都是足智多谋的人。

In *Romance of the Three Kingdoms*, characters like Zhuge Liang, Cao Cao, Sima Yi, and Zhou Yu are all described as resourceful and intelligent figures.

[4] 相府（xiàngfǔ）prime minister's residence

古时候丞相居住的宫殿称为相府。相：丞相；府：（古词）高官居住的地方。在这个故事中，相府指董卓居住的地方。

相 (xiàng): prime minister; 府 (fǔ): (*old word*) residence of a high-ranking official. In the story, 相府 refers to the palace where Dong Zhuo lives.

[5] 义子（yìzǐ）adopted son

收认的儿子。汉语里的义父、义母是拜认的父亲和母亲，义子、义女是收认的儿子、女儿。人们通常会举行一个仪式来拜认和收认某人为义父（义母，义子、义女）。在《三国演义》中，吕布是董卓收认的义子。

Chinese words like 义父, 义母, 义子, 义女 refer to adoptive father, adoptive mother, adoptive son, and adoptive daughter. People usually hold a ceremony to acknowledge somebody as one's adoptive father (mother, son, or daughter). In *Romance of the Three Kingdoms*, Lü Bu is the adopted son of Dong Zhuo.

练习题 Reading exercises

一、选择填空。Choose proper words to fill in the blanks.

1. 董卓带着军队进入了洛阳，掌握了朝廷大权。一些大臣（　　）他，想杀他，可是没有好的办法。

A. 爱　　B. 帮

C. 跟　　D. 恨

2. 七星宝刀非常（　　）。

A. 锋利　　B. 明亮

C. 宝贵　　D. 沉重

3. 吕布为曹操（　　）了一匹好马。

A. 买　　B. 挑

C. 跪　　D. 献

二、根据故事，给下面的句子排序。Put the following statements in order according to the story.

1. 董卓带着军队进入洛阳，掌握了汉朝的大权。他欺君害民，吃喝玩乐。
2. 曹操向王允要了他的七星宝刀，准备去杀董卓。
3. 曹操连忙说要把宝刀送给董卓。
4. 曹操在拿出宝刀时，被董卓在镜子中看见了。

答案：

一、1.D　2.A　3.B

二、1-2-4-3

3. 三英战吕布

主要人物和地点：
Main Characters and Places

袁绍（Yuán Shào）（？–202）：东汉末年的一个地方诸侯和军阀。他被各地诸侯选为讨伐董卓联军的首领，后来被曹操打败。

Yuan Shao (?–202): A duke and warlord during the late Eastern Han Dynasty, who was elected as the head of the allied forces by other warlords to send a punitive expedition against Dong Zhuo. He was later defeated by Cao Cao when the two fought for dominance in northern China.

公孙瓒（Gōngsūn Zàn）（？–199）：东汉末年的一个地方诸侯和军阀，加入了讨伐董卓的联军，后与袁绍作战，被袁绍打败。

Gongsun Zan (?–199): A duke and warlord during the late Eastern Han Dynasty, who joined the allied forces to fight Dong Zhuo. He later went to war against Yuan Shao and was defeated.

虎牢关（Hǔláo Guān）：中国古代地名，也称汜水关。在今河南省荥阳市西北汜水镇境内，是通往洛阳东边的重要关隘。

Hulao Pass: An important pass in ancient China that led to the east of Luoyang, also known as Sishui Pass. It was situated in present-day Sishui Town in the northwest of Xingyang City, Henan Province.

曹操刺杀董卓失败后，召集①天下的诸侯②和英雄，共同讨伐③董卓。不久，很多诸侯来到了洛阳附近。诸侯们选了声望④最高的袁绍当联军⑤的首领⑥，刘备、关羽、张飞三人也加入了这支联军，一起讨伐董卓。

联军来到了河南的虎牢关，准备攻打⑦董卓的军队。董卓也带领⑧吕布和五十万军队来到虎牢关。袁绍派公孙瓒带领军队在虎牢关迎战董卓。

董卓派出吕布打头阵[1]。英俊的吕布骑着一匹红马，身上挂着弓箭⑨，手里拿着方天画戟[2]，这就是人们常说的"人中吕布，马中赤兔[3]"！吕布带着三千

① 召集 (zhàojí)
v. call together; rally
e.g. 他召集了很多歌手，准备举办演唱会。

② 诸侯 (zhūhóu)
n. dukes or princes under an empire
e.g. 各地诸侯都有自己的军队和地盘。

③ 讨伐 (tǎofá)
v. send a punitive expedition against
e.g. 曹操召集诸侯们准备讨伐董卓。

④ 声望 (shēngwàng)
n. reputation; fame
e.g. 这位科学家在世界上有很高的声望。

⑤ 联军 (liánjūn)
n. allied troops; united army
e.g. 各地诸侯们组成了一支联军攻打董卓。

⑥ 首领 (shǒulǐng)
n. leader; head
e.g. 张角是黄巾起义军的首领。

⑦ 攻打 (gōngdǎ)
v. attack; assault
e.g. 这支联军来到汜水关，准备攻打洛阳。

⑧ 带领 (dàilǐng)
v. lead; command
e.g. 公孙瓒带领军队准备攻打虎牢关。

⑨ 弓箭 (gōngjiàn)
n. bow and arrows
e.g. 吕布打仗除了用兵器，还要用弓箭。

骑兵①，飞快地跑过来挑战②。

袁绍联军的一位将军③骑着马去迎战吕布。他们打了不到五个回合④，吕布用方天画戟刺向这位将军，把他刺下了马。由于吕布非常厉害，袁绍的联军死了很多人。袁绍急忙跟大家商量，派谁去迎战吕布。

大家正在商量，一个士兵跑来，说："吕布又在外面挑战了。"袁绍联军的穆顺和武安国两位将军立刻骑着马冲出去迎战，可是他们很快又被吕布打败⑤了。于是，袁绍的各路联军一起冲出去。

吕布见联军一起朝着自己冲来，想到自己的士

① 骑兵 (qíbīng)
n. cavalrymen
e.g. 这些骑兵非常勇敢，特别能打仗。

② 挑战 (tiǎozhàn)
v. challenge in battle
e.g. 吕布向袁绍联军挑战。

③ 将军 (jiāngjūn)
n. general
e.g. 人们常说，不想当将军的士兵不是好士兵。

④ 回合 (huíhé)
n. round; bout
e.g. 张飞跟吕布打了五十几个回合，也没打败吕布。

⑤ 打败 (dǎbài)
v. defeat
e.g. 吕布武艺高强，袁绍联军的将军们没有打败吕布。

① 命令 (mìnglìng)
v. command; order
e.g. 这位将军命令骑兵往前冲。

兵少，打不过，赶紧命令[1]自己的士兵往回跑。袁绍和诸侯们看见吕布跑了，也没让联军继续追。然后，他们继续商量打败吕布的办法。

没过多久，吕布带着士兵又来挑战，公孙瓒立刻带着士兵出去迎战。没打几个回合，公孙瓒也被吕布打败了。这时，从公孙瓒旁边冲出一位将军，这位将军就是张飞。张飞骑着马大声向吕布喊道："三姓家奴[4]不要跑，我张飞在这里！"吕布听到张飞骂他，十分生气，转过来跟张飞打了起来。两个人打了五十多个回合，谁也没输，谁也没赢。

关羽见张飞一个人很难打败吕布，就骑着马冲上去帮助张飞。三匹马打在一起。张飞、关羽、吕布三个人打了三十个回合。刘备见关羽和张飞两个人仍然没有打败吕布，也骑着马冲过来，帮助关羽、张飞打吕布。

吕布感觉到自己一个人很难打败关羽、张飞、刘备三个人，于是向刘备的方向刺了一刀，转身就

① 射 (shè) *v.* shoot at e.g. 董卓在山上命令士兵向张飞射箭。

跑。关羽、张飞、刘备三兄弟骑着马在后面追，一直追到一座山下。张飞抬头往山上看，看见了一辆马车。张飞大声喊道："坐在马车上的肯定是董卓，追吕布有什么用，还不如把董卓抓起来，斩草除根[5]！"于是他骑着马往山上跑，要去抓董卓。想不到，山上飞下来很多石头和箭，像雨点一样射①向张飞。张飞没有办法继续前进，只好骑着马回来了。这时，吕布抓住这个机会，回到了董卓的身边。

虽然刘备、关羽、张飞三兄弟没有抓住董卓和吕布，但是这三位英雄表现出了他们的勇敢和能力。

这就是《三国演义》中著名的“三英战吕布”的故事。联军也慢慢认识了刘备三兄弟。

由于董卓继续欺君害民，天下的英雄们仍然在想办法讨伐董卓。

[1] 打头阵（dǎ tóuzhèn）lead the charge in battle
在战斗中带领军队冲锋陷阵的人。在这个故事中，董卓派吕布打头阵袭击袁绍的联军。在《三国演义》中，吕布是在战场上最著名的、最勇猛的将领之一。
In the story, Dong Zhuo sends Lü Bu to spearhead the attack on Yuan Shao's allied troops. In battle, Lü is one of the most famous and valiant generals in *Romance of the Three Kingdoms*.

[2] 方天画戟（fāngtiānhuàjǐ）a special halberd used by Lü Bu
吕布使用的一种特殊的兵器。“戟”是一种古代兵器的名称，在长柄的一端装有青铜或铁制成的枪尖，旁边附有月牙形锋刃。
戟 is an ancient weapon with a pointed bronze or iron head and a sharp crescent blade fitted on one end of a long handle.

[3] 人中吕布，马中赤兔（rén zhōng Lǚ Bù，mǎ zhōng chìtù）Lü Bu stands out among men; the Red Hare stands out among horses
人们认为三国时的吕布是武艺高强、最有实力的英雄，并且认为他的赤兔马是最快、最强壮、最忠诚的战马。现在，这个习语用来描述能力超强的人。
Lü Bu was akin to a superhero during the Three Kingdoms Period. People considered him to be the person who excelled at martial arts and was invincible, and considered his horse, the Red Hare, the fastest, strongest, and most loyal horse. Now this phrase is used to describe an outstanding person.

[4] 三姓家奴（sān xìng jiānú）domestic servant with three surnames
在《三国演义》中，吕布本来姓吕，后来他当了丁原的义子，改姓丁。最后

他又当了董卓的义子，又改姓董，所以说吕布有三姓。“三姓家奴”带有讽刺意味，是说吕布虽然是义子，但其实就是别人家的奴仆。张飞看不起吕布，他用这句话来讽刺吕布不忠不义，为了利益反复无常。
In the story, Lü Bu has three family names: his original surname of Lü, the surname of Ding (which has been used ever since he was adopted by Ding Yuan), and the surname of Dong (which has been used ever since he was adopted by Dong Zhuo). Zhang Fei looks down on Lü Bu because he has changed his family names repeatedly for his personal interests, and the term is used to ridicule Lü Bu's disloyalty.

[5] 斩草除根（zhǎncǎo-chúgēn）when cutting weeds, remove the roots as well
这个成语的字面意思是割除杂草的时候，应该连杂草的根一起除去，比喻彻底消灭和清除。在本故事中，袁绍的联军非常憎恨董卓。在战斗中，当张飞看见敌军首领董卓坐在马车上，就想杀掉他。
This proverb means to root something out. In this story, Dong Zhuo is hated by Yuan Shao's allied troops. In battle, when Zhang Fei sees Dong Zhuo sitting in the carriage on the hill, he wants to kill Dong Zhuo, the head of the enemy.

练习题 Reading exercises

一、选择填空。Choose proper words to fill in the blanks.

1. 曹操杀董卓失败之后，召集天下的英雄共同（　　）董卓。

A. 联合　　B. 憎恨

C. 挑战　　D. 讨伐

2. 吕布打仗非常厉害，袁绍的联军一起商量派谁去（　　）吕布。

A. 召集　　B. 迎战

C. 讨伐　　　　D. 冲向

3. 关羽、张飞和刘备三人没有打败吕布，因为吕布一看打不过，就（　　）了。

A. 躲藏　　　　B. 埋伏

C. 逃跑　　　　D. 突围

二、判断正误。Read the following sentences and decide whether the statements are true or false.

1. 天下的英雄豪杰准备一起讨伐董卓，推举了刘备为首领。（　）

2. 张飞在追吕布时，发现董卓坐在马车上，立刻去追马车。（　）

3. 关羽、张飞和刘备终于打败了吕布。（　）

答案：

一、1.D　2.B　3.C

二、1.误　2.正　3.误

4. 美人计 [1]

主要人物和地点：
Main Characters and Places

貂蝉（Diāo Chán）：王允的义女，中国历史上的“四大美女”之一。王允把貂蝉先嫁给吕布，后又嫁给董卓，最后唆使吕布杀了董卓。

Diao Chan: Wang Yun's adopted daughter, one of the "Four Great Beauties" of ancient China. Wang married her first to Lü Bu, and then to Dong Zhuo. In the end, this motivated Lü Bu to kill his adoptive father.

长安（Cháng'ān）：中国古代地名，今陕西省西安。长安曾经是西汉、东汉、西晋、隋、唐等朝代的都城。

Chang'an: A place in ancient China which is present-day Xi'an, Shaanxi Province. It was the capital of several imperial dynasties such as Western Han (206 BC–25 AD), Eastern Han, Western Jin (265–317), Sui (581–618) and Tang (618–907).

郿坞（Méiwù）：中国古代地名，今陕西省眉县东北。董卓把东汉都城从洛阳迁到长安（今陕西省西安）后，又在长安以西二百五十里的郿坞修建了宫殿。

Meiwu: A place in ancient China that was located in the northeast of present-day Meixian County, Shaanxi Province. Dong Zhuo moved the capital of the Eastern Han Dynasty from Luoyang to Chang'an. Afterwards, he had a palace built at Meiwu, 125 km west of Chang'an.

白门楼（Báimén Lóu）：中国古代地名，今江苏省徐州市古邳镇境内。吕布在白门楼被曹操杀害。

Baimenlou Gate Tower: A place in ancient China that was located in present-day Gupi Town, Xuzhou City, Jiangsu Province. Cao Cao had Lü Bu executed there.

董卓掌握着朝廷大权，他决定把都城从洛阳搬到长安。在离开洛阳的时候，他下令杀了很多富人，抢①走了很多钱。董卓到了新都城长安之后，继续过着吃喝玩乐的生活，整天做着当皇帝的美梦②，百姓生活得非常苦。

董卓权力很大，吕布又非常厉害，没有人能打败他们。大臣王允一直为朝廷担忧③，但是始终没有找到杀董卓的机会。

王允慢慢观察，发现董卓和吕布有一个共同的特点：喜欢漂亮的女人。王允想，董卓是朝廷的敌人④，如果能让吕布去杀董卓就容易多了。

① 抢 (qiǎng) *v.* rob; grab
e.g. 这位老人的钱包被人抢走了。

② 美梦 (měimèng) *n.* happy dream
e.g. 董卓一直做着当皇帝的美梦。

③ 担忧 (dānyōu) *v.* worry about
e.g. 儿子去打仗了，母亲整天为儿子担忧。

④ 敌人 (dírén) *n.* enemy; foe
e.g. 这位将军打败了很多敌人。

① 义女 (yìnǚ)
n. adoptive daughter
e.g. 王允让貂蝉做了自己的义女。

② 仇恨 (chóuhèn)
v. feel great hatred toward
e.g. 大臣和百姓对董卓都充满了仇恨。

③ 保卫 (bǎowèi)
v. protect; defend
e.g. 朝廷的大臣们想杀了董卓，保卫汉朝。

④ 小妾 (xiǎoqiè)
n. concubine
e.g. 为了杀董卓，貂蝉当了董卓的小妾。

王允的家里有一个美女叫貂蝉[2]。貂蝉十分漂亮，唱歌唱得好，跳舞也跳得好。王允突然有了一个主意：先让貂蝉做自己的义女①，把她送给吕布当小妾，然后再把她送给董卓，让董卓与吕布互相仇恨②，最后让吕布杀掉董卓。

王允决定用“美人计”杀死董卓，保卫③汉朝。

王允把自己的计谋告诉了貂蝉，貂蝉也非常恨董卓，她愿意做王允的义女，帮助他杀董卓。

王允先用计谋把吕布请到他的家里，把貂蝉送给他当小妾④。几天后，王允又请董卓来到自己的家里喝酒。王允告诉董卓，漂亮的貂蝉是自己的义女，他想把貂蝉送给董卓。董卓听了非常高兴，就把貂蝉带回了自己的相府。然后，王允又找来吕布，跟他说："你的义父今天来到我家，把貂蝉带走了。"

第二天，吕布听说董卓和貂蝉一直在一起，就来到董卓的相府。听说董卓和貂蝉还没有起床，他非常生气，于是跑到董卓的卧室外偷看。貂蝉在窗户前看见了吕布，故意假装[1]擦眼泪。吕布看了很久才离开。董卓起床之后，吕布才走进去见董卓。貂蝉在旁边向吕布秋波送情[3]。董卓看到了很不高兴，开始怀疑他们。

① 假装 (jiǎzhuāng)
v. pretend
e.g. 貂蝉假装流泪，表示她爱吕布。

有一次，董卓得了小病，吕布去看望董卓。刚好董卓在睡觉，吕布看见了站在床后面的貂蝉。因为吕布一直想着、爱着貂蝉，所以他心里的怒气上升，特别憎恨董卓。

一天，董卓离开相府去了朝廷。吕布抓住这个机会，去相府与貂蝉偷偷

约会。貂蝉告诉吕布，她不愿意跟董卓在一起，还说她不想活了，说完就要往旁边的荷花池[1]里跳。吕布赶紧抱住了貂蝉，然后两人抱在一起哭了起来。

这时候，他们听到一声大喊，吓得赶紧分开。原来董卓在朝廷没见到吕布，心中怀疑，决定回相府看看，没想到正好看到吕布和貂蝉抱在一起。吕布见到董卓回来，非常吃惊，赶紧离开了。吕布走得太快，董卓因为身体太胖没追上。董卓问貂蝉为什么和吕布抱在一起。貂蝉哭着说，是吕布偷偷找她约会的。董卓试探貂蝉，说想把她送给吕布。貂蝉

① 荷花池 (héhuāchí)
n. lotus pool
e.g. 公园里有一个荷花池。

① 宫殿 (gōngdiàn)
n. palace
e.g. 董卓在郿坞建造了很多宫殿。

② 奸污 (jiānwū)
v. rape
e.g. 吕布认为董卓奸污了貂蝉，就把董卓杀了。

显得很吃惊，拿起一把刀对董卓说，她是爱董卓的，要是董卓把她送给吕布，她就自杀。董卓看到貂蝉这么爱自己，非常高兴，就不再怀疑她了。

后来，董卓要带着貂蝉离开长安，去郿坞的宫殿①。满朝文武大臣都来送行。貂蝉坐在车上，假装流眼泪。吕布站在很远的地方看着，心里非常痛苦。这时候王允走过来跟吕布聊天，吕布就把自己跟貂蝉的事情告诉了王允。王允连忙请吕布到家里，对他说："董卓奸污②了我的女儿，抢走了您的貂蝉，实在是太可恨了。"吕布告诉王允，他决定杀死董卓。

王允立刻请大臣们来商量杀董卓的计谋。他们派一个将军带着骑兵去郿坞，骗董卓说皇帝准备把皇位让给他，让他赶紧回长安。董卓听说自己要当皇帝了，非常高兴，当天就从郿坞赶回到长安。

第二天早上，董卓去了朝廷，大臣们都来欢迎他。当董卓的车走到宫门外时，董卓身边的士兵都被留在了外边。到了宫殿门口，王允大喊一声："奸贼[1]来了！"董卓的两边突然出现了一百多个人，这些人都拿着兵器刺向董卓。

董卓大叫："我的儿子吕布呢？"

吕布从车后面冲出来，

① 奸贼 (jiānzéi)
n. conspirator
e.g. 董卓控制皇帝，命令大臣，被认为是奸贼。

① 尸体 (shītǐ)
n. corpse
e.g. 董卓死了，百姓们都恨他，打他的尸体。

② 控制 (kòngzhì)
v. control
e.g. 董卓控制朝廷，想自己当皇帝。

③ 丞相 (chéngxiàng)
n. prime minister
e.g. 董卓虽然是丞相，但掌握了朝廷大权。

说："我奉旨讨伐[4]奸贼！"然后，他拿着方天画戟直接刺向董卓，杀死了他。董卓的尸体①被扔在街上，百姓们都恨董卓，一起打他的尸体。

董卓死了以后，他的将军李傕、郭汜带着士兵攻打长安。他们进入长安之后，杀死了王允。吕布带着貂蝉跑出了长安城。后来，吕布在白门楼被曹操杀死了。在战乱之中，汉献帝也逃出了长安，被曹操找到。曹操控制②了汉献帝，当了丞相③，掌握了朝廷的大权。曹操通过皇帝给各地的诸侯下命令，这就是"挟天子以令诸侯"[5]的著名故事。

[1] 美人计（měirénjì）beauty trap
在军事行动中，当敌军难以征服时，用送美女的方式来引诱敌军将领进圈套的计谋。先用此计从心理上让敌军将领放松，使其内部丧失战斗力，然后再进行军事进攻，从而达到取得战斗胜利的目的。
In military affairs, when it is difficult to conquer the enemy, the trap of sending a beautiful woman is used to ensnare the head of the enemy. This will help to weaken the morale of the enemy and finally win the battle.

[2] 貂蝉（Diāo Chán）Diao Chan
传说貂蝉是中国古代四大美人之一，她的美貌胜过月亮，能让月亮羞愧地躲进云中。在这个故事中，董卓势力太过强大，没人能够杀死他。大臣王允用了美人计，把貂蝉先嫁给吕布，再嫁给董卓，然后让貂蝉煽动吕布反叛董卓。最后，吕布中计，杀死了董卓。在除掉董卓的过程中，貂蝉发挥了至关重要的作用。
She was said to be one of the four great beauties of ancient China, whose beauty could outshine even the moon to make it hide in the clouds. In the story, Dong Zhuo is so powerful that nobody can kill him. Wang Yun, the minster, uses the beauty trap, a stratagem that sees Diao marry Lü Bu first and then Dong, to incite Lü against Dong. In the end, Lü traps and kills Dong. Diao plays a vital part in killing Dong.

[3] 秋波送情（qiūbō-sòngqíng）throw amorous glances at someone
向某人传递情感的目光。秋波：比喻女子传情的目光。在这个故事中，貂蝉将传情的目光投向吕布来引诱他。这一举动让吕布更爱貂蝉，并使他与义父董卓反目成仇。
秋 波 (qiubo)：the bright, clear eyes of a beauty. In the story, Diao Chan throws amorous glances at Lü Bu to seduce him. This action makes Lü lose his heart to Diao and sets him against his adoptive father, Dong Zhuo.

[4] 奉旨讨伐（fèngzhǐ tǎofá）send armed forces to suppress the enemy under the emperor's edict
按照皇帝的指令派遣军队镇压敌人。在这个故事中，吕布声称自己奉皇帝旨令杀死董卓。
In the story, Lü Bu proclaims that he followed the emperor's edict to kill Dong Zhuo.

[5] 挟天子以令诸侯（xié tiānzǐ yǐ lìng zhūhóu）Cao Cao controls the emperor and commands the warlords in his name
东汉末年，董卓被吕布杀死，朝廷处于混乱之中。这时，曹操控制住了皇帝，并且以皇帝的名义指挥各位诸侯。现在这句话被用来比喻一个人冒名发号施令。
At the end of the Eastern Han Dynasty, Dong Zhuo was killed by Lü Bu. The imperial court was in chaos. At the time, Cao Cao controlled the emperor and commanded the warlords in the name of the emperor. Now, this idiom is used to describe someone giving orders under the guise of someone else.

练习题 Reading exercises

一、选词填空。Choose proper words to fill in the blanks.

美梦　　痛苦　　义女　　仇恨　　宫殿

1. 王允让貂蝉当自己的（　　），然后把她送给了吕布和董卓，让吕布恨董卓。
2. 吕布和董卓都喜欢貂蝉，他们互相（　　）。
3. 董卓到了长安以后，一直做着当皇帝的（　　）。
4. 董卓抢走了貂蝉，吕布感到十分（　　）。

二、判断正误。Read the following sentences and decide whether the statements are true or false.

1. 王允的计谋是让董卓与吕布互相仇恨，然后让吕布杀死董卓。（　）
2. 王允最后杀死了董卓。（　）
3. 董卓的将军杀了王允，汉献帝被曹操控制，最后曹操掌握了大权。（　）

答案：

一、1. 义女　2. 仇恨　3. 美梦　4. 痛苦

二、1. 正　2. 误　3. 正

5. 煮酒论英雄

主要人物和地点：
Main Characters and Places

董承（Dǒng Chéng）（?–200）：东汉汉献帝的妃子董贵人的父亲。

Dong Cheng (?–200): Father-in-law of Emperor Xiandi of the Eastern Han Dynasty. His daughter was one of the emperor's concubines.

袁术（Yuán Shù）（?–199）：东汉末年朝廷的将军，后占领扬州。他是袁绍的弟弟。

Yuan Shu (?–199): A general of the late Eastern Han Dynasty, who once occupied Yangzhou. Yuan Shao was his elder brother.

孙策（Sūn Cè）（175–200）：东汉末年的贵族，占领江东一带（今中国长江中下游地区）。

Sun Ce (175–200): An aristocrat of the late Eastern Han Dynasty, who occupied the Jiangdong region (present-day middle and lower reaches of the Yangtze River).

刘璋（Liú Zhāng）（?–220）：刘焉的儿子，汉朝皇室后代。他继承了父亲刘焉的官职。

Liu Zhang (?–220): A descendant of the royal family of the Eastern Han Dynasty, Liu Yan's son. He succeeded to his father's official position.

徐州（Xúzhōu）：中国古代地名，今江苏省徐州市。

Xuzhou: A place in ancient China (present-day Xuzhou City, Jiangsu Province).

① 皇叔 (huángshū)
n. uncle of the emperor
e.g. 因为刘备是汉朝皇室后代，被称为"刘皇叔"。

② 看作 (kànzuò)
v. regard…as
e.g. 这家公司把顾客看作上帝。

③ 奸臣 (jiānchén)
n. wicked minister
e.g. 对皇帝不忠诚的大臣被看作是奸臣。

④ 仁义 (rényì)
adj. amiable and upright
e.g. 他的朋友挺仁义，给了他很多帮助。

曹操杀了吕布之后，就把刘备、关羽、张飞介绍给汉献帝。汉献帝知道刘备也是皇室的后代以后，想利用刘备控制曹操，就称刘备为皇叔①。于是，人们都称刘备为"刘皇叔"。

曹操做了丞相以后，不把汉献帝放在眼里，朝廷的大臣们都把曹操看作②是奸臣③。有一个大臣叫董承，他看到这种情况，就召集刘备等人商量要讨伐曹操。刘备答应了董承和他一起讨伐曹操。

因为天下人都说刘备仁义④，关羽、张飞又是刘备的虎狼之将[1]，所以曹操身边的人担心刘备今后会控制朝廷，于是劝曹操把刘备杀了。曹操也怀疑刘备，就决定试试刘备的能力如何。

刘备虽然答应了董承讨伐曹操，但是又怕曹操知道了会杀了自己，于是就在家里学种菜，假装不关心外面的事。关羽、张飞觉得非常奇怪，刘备也不告诉他们自己为什么学种菜。

有一天，刘备正在种菜，一位大臣突然来到刘备家中，请刘备去见曹操。这时关羽、张飞都不在，刘备又不能不去，就只好一个人去拜见曹操。

曹操看见刘备来了，笑着说："你在家做大事啊！"这句话把刘备吓坏

① 青梅 (qīngméi)
n. green plum
e.g. 青梅也叫梅子，味道是酸的。

了。他以为曹操知道了自己答应董承讨伐曹操的事，心想，这次一定是凶多吉少[2]了。

可是曹操却拉着刘备的手，说："你学种菜很辛苦啊！"刘备听了这句话才放心，回答说："我在家没事儿干，才学着种菜的。"

曹操说："我刚才看见树上的青梅[①]，忽然想起一件事。有一次，我的军队在路上走了很久，因为没有水，所以士兵们非常渴，都走不动了。我对士兵们说，'前面有很多树，树上有很多青梅。'士兵们听我这么一说就不渴了，继续行进。我今天看见这些青梅，就想请你过来和我一起喝青梅酒，聊聊天。”听曹操讲了望梅止渴[3]的故事之后，刘备更放心了。

桌子上放了一盘青梅、一壶酒和两个酒杯。曹操请刘备坐下来，两个人在院子里一边慢慢地喝酒一边聊天。

忽然，他们看见远处刮起了龙卷风[①]。曹操问刘备：“你知道龙[②]的变化

① 龙卷风
(lóngjuǎnfēng)
n. tornado
e.g. 曹操看见龙卷风，就想起了龙。

② 龙 (lóng)
n. dragon
e.g. 在中国古代，龙是帝王的象征。

① 遮天蔽日 (zhētiān-bìrì) blot out the sun and the sky
e.g. 天上乌云遮天蔽日，要下雨了。

② 比作 (bǐzuò) compare to
e.g 曹操把自己比作龙。

③ 粮草 (liángcǎo) *n.* army provision
e.g. 军队打仗必须要准备好粮草。

吗？”刘备说：“我愿意听听您对‘龙’的看法。”

曹操说：“龙的变化很多。龙变大的时候能够遮天蔽日[1]，变小的时候你根本看不见它在哪里。你走过很多地方，见过很多人。如果我们把今天的英雄比作[2]龙，你一定知道有哪些英雄是龙。”

刘备回答说：“我只在朝廷中做事，不知道天下有哪些英雄。”

曹操说：“你虽然不认识全天下的英雄，但至少听说过他们的名字吧！”

刘备听到曹操这样说，只好回答：“淮南有个袁术，他有很多将军和士兵，也有很多粮草[3]，他可以算是英雄吗？”

曹操笑着说：“袁术已经不行了。”

刘备说：“河北的袁绍声望很高，可以算是英雄吧？”

曹操大笑说：“袁绍胆子[1]很小，算不上英雄。”

刘备又接着说了刘表、孙策、刘璋等人，曹操认为这些人都不能算作英雄。

刘备只好问曹操：“除了这些人以外，我真不知道谁可以算得上是英雄。”

曹操说道：“能成为英雄的人，应该有远大的理想。”

刘备又问：“那么您觉得谁有远大的理想，能算是英雄呢？”

① 胆子 (dǎnzi)
n. courage
e.g. 刘备假装自己是一个胆子小的人。

① 打雷 (dǎléi)
v. thunder
e.g. 远处传来了打雷的声音，要下雨了。

② 圣人 (shèngrén)
n. sage
e.g. 孔子被看作是一位圣人。

③ 试探 (shìtàn)
v. test; probe
e.g. 曹操想试探刘备有没有打天下的理想。

曹操指指刘备，然后又指向自己，说："天下能算得上英雄的，只有你和我呀！"

刘备一听，心中十分吃惊，手里的筷子一下子掉在了地上。这时，天上突然打雷了①，下起了大雨。刘备慢慢地从地上捡起筷子，向曹操道歉说："不好意思，我害怕打雷，这个雷把我吓着了。"

曹操笑着说："你这位大英雄也怕打雷吗？"

刘备说："圣人②都尊敬雷，害怕雷，我怎能不害怕？"

其实，刘备心里明白曹操怀疑他，跟他讨论龙和天下英雄都是在试探③他呢，所以他假装害怕打雷，让曹操认为他胆子小。曹操以为刘备真是胆小，就不再怀疑他了。

曹操掌握着朝廷大权，刘备感到跟曹操在一起不安全，后来就借着攻打徐州的机会，带着关羽和张飞离开了曹操。

[1] 虎狼之将（hǔ láng zhī jiàng）ferocious general
形容将军勇猛，善于作战，不怕死，像虎和狼一样，比如关羽和张飞。
A general as ferocious and ruthless as a tiger or wolf, such as Guan Yu or Zhang Fei.

[2] 凶多吉少（xiōngduō-jíshǎo）bode ill rather than well
指不好的可能性大于好的可能性，凶险多，吉利少。在本故事中，曹操邀请刘备来自己的住所喝酒，刘备担心曹操可能会杀了自己。
This idiom means more ominous than propitious, or the odds are against one rather than in one's favor. In the story, Liu Bei is invited to Cao Cao's residence to drink alcohol and he fears that Cao will kill him.

[3] 望梅止渴（wàngméi-zhǐkě）quench one's thirst by thinking of green plums
原指通过想象吃梅子来止渴，后来比喻用空想来安慰自己。
This idiom is used nowadays to describe someone who consoles himself or herself with a false hope.

练习题 Reading exercises

一、选词填空。Choose proper words to fill in the blanks.

仁义　　种　　比作　　胆子　　试探

1. 曹操把英雄（　　）龙。
2. 一天刘备正在（　　）菜，有人请他去见曹操。
3. 刘备假装害怕打雷，让曹操以为他（　　）小，不让曹操怀疑他。

二、根据故事，给下面的句子排序。Put the following sentences in order according to the story.

1. 刘备答应讨伐曹操，又害怕被曹操杀害，就假装在家种菜。一天，一位大臣来邀请他去见曹操，刘备不得不去。
2. 曹操和刘备一边喝酒一边讨论天下的英雄。刘备假装害怕打雷，让曹操以为他胆子小。后来刘备带着士兵跑到徐州，离开了曹操。
3. 曹操杀了吕布之后当上了丞相，不把皇帝放在眼里。董承召集了很多人，准备讨伐曹操。

答案：

一、1. 比作　2. 种　3. 胆子

二、3-1-2

6. 千里走单骑[1]

主要人物和地点：
Main Characters and Places

孔秀（Kǒng Xiù）：曹操手下的将军，因阻拦关羽出关，被关羽斩杀。
Kong Xiu: One of Cao Cao's generals. He was killed by Guan Yu for not allowing him to exit the pass.

韩福（Hán Fú）：曹操手下管辖洛阳的将军，因阻拦关羽离开洛阳，被关羽斩杀。
Han Fu: One of Cao Cao's generals. He governed Luoyang and tried to stop Guan Yu from leaving the city but was killed by him.

孟坦（Mèng Tǎn）：曹操手下的将军，韩福的部下，因阻拦关羽出关，被关羽斩杀。
Meng Tan: One of Cao Cao's generals under the command of Han Fu. He was killed by Guan Yu for not allowing him to exit the pass.

卞喜（Biàn Xǐ）：曹操手下的将军，因阻拦关羽出关，被关羽斩杀。
Bian Xi: One of Cao Cao's generals. He was killed by Guan Yu for not allowing him to exit the pass.

王植（Wáng Zhí）：曹操手下的将军，因阻拦关羽出关，被关羽斩杀。
Wang Zhi: One of Cao Cao's generals. He was killed by Guan Yu for not allowing him to exit the pass.

秦琪（Qín Qí）：曹操手下的将军，因阻拦关羽出关，被关羽斩杀。

Qin Qi: One of Cao Cao's generals. He was killed by Guan Yu for not allowing him to exit the pass.

东岭关（Dōnglǐng Guān）：古地名。
Dongling Pass: A strategic pass in the novel.

荥阳（Xíngyáng）：中国古代地名，今河南省郑州市西。
Xingyang: A place in ancient China that was located to the west of present-day Zhengzhou City, Henan Province.

黄河渡口（Huáng Hé dùkǒu）：古代的黄河渡口。黄河从古至今有很多渡口。
Yellow River Crossing: A crossing on the Yellow River. There have been many crossings on the Yellow River since ancient times.

刘备一直有“兴复汉室[2]”的理想。他知道，如果曹操知道了他的理想，肯定会杀了他。于是，借着打徐州的机会，刘备带着关羽和张飞离开了。

可是，在打徐州的过程中，刘备、关羽、张飞三人被打散了。关羽不知道刘备去哪儿了，可是他知道刘备的两位夫人还在曹操的军营[①]中。这两位夫人一位是甘夫人，一位是糜夫人。所以，关羽就留在曹操的军营里照顾她们。

曹操喜欢有才能的人，他送给关羽很多钱财[②]和一匹好马，还给关羽封官加爵[3]，希望关羽能够为自己打仗。可是关羽是一个重

① 军营 (jūnyíng)
n. barracks; military camp
e.g. 刘备感觉在曹操的军营里不安全，就离开了。

② 钱财 (qiáncái)
n. money; wealth
e.g. 曹操给了关羽很多钱财，想让关羽为自己打仗。

① 情义 (qíngyì)
n. friendship; brotherhood
e.g. 为了兄弟情义，关羽拒绝了曹操。

② 忠诚 (zhōngchéng)
adj. loyal
e.g. 关羽对刘备非常忠诚。

③ 关 (guān)
n. strategic pass
e.g. 关羽过了五关才找到刘备。

情义①的人，他对刘备非常忠诚②。他一直在等着刘备，打算一听到刘备的消息，就离开曹操的军营。

一天，关羽终于打听到了刘备的消息，他立刻带着刘备的两位夫人准备离开。可是曹操拒绝给关羽手谕[4]，不让他走。在曹操控制的地方，如果没有曹操的手谕，就过不了关③，也就没有办法离开。但是关羽还是坚持要走，他一定要去找大哥刘备。

关羽他们来到第一关——东岭关，曹操手下的将军孔秀向关羽要手谕。

关羽骗孔秀说："时间紧，没有来得及要。"

孔秀一听就知道关羽

在骗他，不让关羽过关。

关羽非常生气地说：“你真的不让我们过关吗？你可不要耽误[1]了我的时间。”

孔秀听了也很生气，他觉得关羽太放肆[2]了，就对关羽说：“要过去可以，你把刘备的两位夫人留下。”

关羽一听非常生气，拿起大刀骑马上前，一刀下去就把孔秀杀了，过了第一关。

关羽他们来到第二关——洛阳。曹操手下的将军韩福听说关羽杀了孔秀，就跟他的手下大将孟坦商量，要把关羽杀了。

韩福问关羽：“你有没有曹丞相的手谕呀？”

① 耽误 (dānwu)
v. delay
e.g. 路上车太多，耽误了上班的时间。

② 放肆 (fàngsì)
adj. presumptuous; rude
e.g. 关羽觉得孔秀说话太放肆，就把他杀了。

关羽回答：“没有。”

韩福说：“没有手谕就不能过关。”

关羽说：“孔秀不让我过关，我把他杀了。你们不怕死吗？”说完就跟他们打了起来。

孟坦先上前跟关羽打。可是关羽实在是太厉害了，他一刀就把孟坦杀了。这

时，一只箭射过来，正射在关羽左臂上①。关羽忍住疼，仍然骑着马追过去，举起刀把韩福杀了。

之后，关羽带着刘备的两位夫人过了第二关。

关羽他们来到第三关——汜水关。曹操的将军卞喜听说关羽已经杀了三位将军，于是，他决定先把关羽骗到一个寺庙②里，然后再杀他。

卞喜微笑着欢迎关羽。他把关羽请到寺庙里，安排他住了下来。没想到，寺庙里的僧人③十分仰慕④关羽，他知道卞喜的计谋后，告诉了关羽。关羽听了非常生气，杀了卞喜，过了第三关。

① 左臂 (zuǒ bì)
n. left arm
e.g. 虽然关羽的左臂受伤了，但他还是打败了敌人。

② 寺庙 (sìmiào)
n. temple
e.g. 山上有一座古老的寺庙。

③ 僧人 (sēngrén)
n. Buddhist monk
e.g 寺庙里的僧人帮助了关羽。

④ 仰慕 (yǎngmù)
v. admire
e.g. 很多人都仰慕关羽这位大英雄。

① 烧 (shāo)
v. burn; set fire
e.g. 敌人放火烧了军营。

接着，关羽来到了第四关——荥阳，这里的将军叫王植。王植知道关羽很厉害，他打不过关羽，于是想烧死关羽。

王植见到关羽后态度很好。他请关羽先住下来，休息好以后再出发。关羽一路上很累，就同意了。

王植军营里有一个人叫胡班，他早就听说关羽是一位大英雄，一直仰慕关羽，可从没有见过，这次终于见到了这位大英雄。胡班听说王植要放火烧①死关羽，就把王植的计谋告诉了关羽。关羽一听，赶紧带着夫人们离开了。

王植发现关羽他们跑了，立刻去追。关羽等王植追上来，很轻松地把他杀了。就这样，关羽过了第四关。

关羽继续往前走，来到了第五关——黄河渡口。第五关的将军叫秦琪。秦琪性格火爆[1]，他一看到关羽就大声喊道："你是谁？要去哪儿？你有曹丞相的手谕吗？"

关羽说："我是关羽，要去找我的大哥刘备，没有手谕。"

秦琪说："没有手谕就别想走！看刀！"秦琪说着就冲了上去。

关羽一点儿都不紧张，他举起刀，一刀下去就把秦琪杀了。然后，关羽等人上了船，过了黄河。

① 火爆 (huǒbào)
adj. hot-tempered
e.g. 张飞非常勇敢，但脾气火爆。

就这样，关羽过五关斩六将[5]，离开了曹操的军营。在找刘备的路上，关羽在砼砀山遇到了张飞，然后跟张飞一起在袁绍那儿找到了刘备，把两位夫人交给了刘备。

后来，刘备他们又离开了袁绍。三兄弟到荆州暂时住下来，等待兴复汉室的机会。

[1] 千里走单骑（qiānlǐ zǒu dān jì）ride on a solitary journey
这是一个关于关羽的故事。关羽放弃了曹操给他的好处，独自一人骑着马，带着刘备的两位夫人行走了数千里，从曹操的军营回到刘备的军营。后来比喻行动无人帮助，独自勇往直前。
A story about Guan Yu who gives up the official position, money and wealth offered by Cao Cao and rides alone for thousands of miles with the two wives of Liu Bei from Cao Cao's barracks to Liu Bei's camp by overcoming various difficulties and obstacles. The idiom is later used to describe someone who forges ahead without relying on others' help.

[2] 兴复汉室（xīngfù Hànshì）revitalize the Han Dynasty
本书中指让东汉重新强大起来，让所有的军阀都停止战争，听从东汉皇帝的命令。
In the novel, this phrase refers to revitalizing the Eastern Han Dynasty and bringing an end to the wars among the warlords so that all of them would obey the emperor's orders.

[3] 封官加爵（fēngguān-jiājué）promote someone to a higher position and rank
授予官职，晋升爵位。"官"指的是"官职"，即具有确切责任与政治权利的具体职位。"爵"指的是中国古代贵族的等级，象征着荣耀。这些职位都只能由皇帝授予。曹操授予关羽很高的职位，希望关羽成为自己人，但是关羽始终忠于刘备，最终还是离开了曹操。
官 means "official position", which is a specific position with certain responsibilities and political powers. 爵 refers to the rank of Chinese nobility, which symbolizes honor. These titles could only be granted by the emperor. Cao Cao offers Guan Yu a high official position, hoping Guan will obey him. But Guan is loyal to Liu Bei, and leaves Cao in the end.

[4] 手谕（shǒuyù）handwritten directive of a high-ranking official
上级官员或尊长亲笔写的指令。在这个故事中，关羽在没有拿到曹操手谕的情况下离开曹操的军营，曹操的部下没有见到曹操的手谕，所以不让关羽离开。
In this story, Guan Yu decides to leave Cao Cao's troops without his handwritten directive. Without seeing Cao's personal handwritten directive, the generals prevent Guan from leaving Cao's camp.

[5] 过五关斩六将（guò wǔ guān zhǎn liù jiāng）pass through five passes and kill six generals
这是一个关于关羽的故事。关羽英勇无比，杀死了六名曹操手下的将领，通过了曹操的五个关卡。现在这个成语比喻某人克服重重困难完成某事。
A story about Guan Yu, an intrepid general, passing through five passes and killing six of Cao Cao's generals. Now we use this idiom to describe someone overcoming all difficulties to complete a task.

练习题 Reading exercises

一、选择填空。Choose proper words to fill in the blanks.

1. 关羽是一个非常重（　　）的人，他带着刘备的夫人们历经艰难找到了刘备。

A. 爱情　　B. 忠心

C. 情义　　D. 心情

2. 一支箭（　　）中关羽的左臂，但是他还是把韩福杀了。

A. 打　　B. 射

C. 击　　D. 杀

3. 王植的军队里有一个人一直（　　）关羽，不想让王植杀害关羽，就把王植的计谋告诉了关羽。

A. 大学　　B. 大声

C. 大小　　D. 仰慕

二、判断正误。Read the following sentences and decide whether the statements are true or false.

1. 走到第二关（洛阳）的时候，关羽没有受伤，轻松过关了。（　）

2. 走到第五关（黄河渡口）的时候，关羽杀了曹操的将军，坐船过了黄河。（　）

3. 关羽带着刘备的夫人们，过五关斩六将，终于找到了刘备。（　）

答案：

一、1. C　2. B　3. D

二、1. 误　2. 正　3. 误

7. 刘备三顾茅庐 [1]

主要人物和地点：
Main Characters and Places

徐庶（Xú Shù）：诸葛亮的朋友。他之前是刘备的军师，后来曹操扣留了他的母亲，他被迫离开刘备。离开的时候，他向刘备推荐了诸葛亮。

Xu Shu: A friend of Zhuge Liang. He once served as Liu Bei's military advisor, but later left Liu's camp because his mother was put under house arrest by Cao Cao. He then recommended Zhuge to Liu.

诸葛亮（Zhūgě Liàng）(181–234)：字孔明，刘备的军师，蜀国的开国丞相。他上知天文，下知地理，精通兵法，才智过人。

Zhuge Liang (181–234): Courtesy name Kongming. He served as Liu Bei's military advisor and later became the Prime Minister of the Kingdom of Shu (221–263) founded by Liu. As a wise person, he was well-versed in astronomy, geography and military tactics.

新野（Xīnyě）：中国古代地名，今河南省南阳市境内。东汉末年，刘备在诸葛亮的帮助下，在新野聚集军队，奠定了蜀国政权的基础。

Xinye: A place in ancient China that was located in present-day Nanyang City, Henan Province. During the late Eastern Han Dynasty, Liu Bei assembled troops there with the help of Zhuge Liang, which laid the foundation for the Kingdom of Shu.

隆中（Lóngzhōng）：中国古代地名，今湖北省襄阳市襄城区。诸葛亮出山之前的居住地。

Longzhong: A place in ancient China that was located in present-day Xiangcheng District, Xiangyang City, Hubei Province. It was here that Zhuge Liang lived before he took up an official position.

荆州（Jīngzhōu）：中国古代地名，今湖北省荆州市。长江边的重要城市。
Jingzhou: A place in ancient China that was located in present-day Jingzhou City, Hubei Province. It has been a city of strategic importance along the Yangtze River.

益州（Yìzhōu）：中国古代地名，今四川、重庆、云南等地。
Yizhou: A region in ancient China that covered present-day Sichuan, Chongqing, and Yunnan.

曹操在北方打败了袁绍，占领[1]了北方。刘备不想再回到曹操的军队，就去找住在新野的汉朝皇室的后代刘表。

刘备有一个军师[2]叫徐庶，很有才智[3]。曹操为了得到徐庶，就派人告诉徐庶说他的母亲病了，让徐庶立刻回家见他的母亲。徐庶非常孝顺，为了母亲，他只好离开刘备回老家了。

徐庶知道，离开刘备之后曹操不会让他回来了。徐庶在离开之前对刘备说："隆中有一个卧龙先生[2]叫诸葛亮，他是一位奇才[4]。如果你能得到他的帮助，就可以兴复汉室，得到天下，统一[5]国家。"刘备听

① 占领 (zhànlǐng)
v. occupy
e.g. 曹操占领了北方之后，还想统一南方。

② 军师 (jūnshī)
n. military counselor
e.g. 刘备请诸葛亮做自己的军师。

③ 才智 (cáizhì)
n. intelligence; wisdom
e.g. 他在工作中表现出了聪明才智。

④ 奇才 (qícái)
n. rare talent
e.g. 诸葛亮才智超过很多人，被称为奇才。

⑤ 统一 (tǒngyī)
v. reunify
e.g. 曹操和刘备都想统一天下。

①茅庐 (máolú)
n. thatched cottage
e.g. 诸葛亮在山中的茅庐里过着安静的生活。

了之后非常高兴。

徐庶走后，刘备带着礼物，跟关羽、张飞一起去隆中拜见诸葛亮。半路上，他们遇到一个农民。刘备向农民问了诸葛亮的地址，原来，诸葛亮住在山里的一个茅庐①里。

到了诸葛亮家门口，刘备下马敲门。门开了，开门的人说诸葛亮出远门了，不在家，不知道什么时候回来。刘备没有办法，只好回去了。

刘备回到新野后，经常派人到隆中打听诸葛亮回来没有。一天，刘备听说诸葛亮已经回家了，马上决定再次去拜见诸葛亮。于是，他们兄弟三人骑着马又去了隆中。

当他们再次来到诸葛亮的茅庐时，却发现里面的人不是诸葛亮，而是诸葛亮的弟弟。刘备给诸葛亮留下一封信后，带着关羽、张飞又回到了新野。

第二年春天，刘备做好了准备，决定第三次去拜见诸葛亮。这一次，张飞和关羽都很不高兴，劝刘备别去找诸葛亮了。可是刘备还是坚持去。

刘备说："没有诚意①哪能得到天下奇才呢？这次你们别去了，我自己去就行了。"关羽和张飞见刘备坚持要去，只好跟着他去。这是他们第三次去拜见诸葛亮。

① 诚意 (chéngyì)
n. sincerity
e.g. 诸葛亮被刘备的诚意感动了，答应帮助他。

刘备三人骑着马来到诸葛亮的茅庐。诸葛亮正在睡觉，刘备安静地站在门外等诸葛亮醒来。过了好长时间，诸葛亮还没醒。张飞十分生气，想放火烧了诸葛亮的茅庐。刘备让张飞安静地等着，不允许他做不礼貌的事。

他们在诸葛亮门前安静地等啊等啊。又过了两个小时，诸葛亮终于醒了，把他们请进屋里。

刘备一见到诸葛亮就说："我听说先生的大名已经很久了，今天终于见到先生了！我想兴复汉室，匡扶天下。可是我没有才智，希望先生多多指教。"

诸葛亮说："你们三次来到我的茅庐，我非常感动。可是我不想出山，我喜欢在山里过安静的生活。"

刘备哭着说："请先生想想天下百姓的生活，为了百姓帮助我吧！"

诸葛亮被刘备的诚意感动了，答应帮助他。

刘备继续问："根据现

① 争夺 (zhēngduó)
v. contend for
e.g. 军阀们打仗是为了争夺土地和钱财。

② 地势 (dìshì)
n. terrain
e.g 打仗之前，将军们都要观察地势。

③ 险要 (xiǎnyào)
adj. strategic and inaccessible
e.g. 军队打仗都要占领险要的地势。

④ 联合 (liánhé)
v. unite; ally with
e.g. 诸葛亮建议刘备联合孙权，对抗曹操。

⑤ 运输 (yùnshū)
v. transport
e.g. 前面的军队打仗，后面的军队运输粮草。

在天下的形势，先生认为我应该怎么做？”

诸葛亮分析了当时社会的各种情况，向刘备提了五点建议：

“第一，曹操占领着北方，拥有一百万军队。他控制着皇帝，现在您还不能与曹操争夺①北方。

“第二，孙权占领着江东，那里地势②险要③。孙权喜欢有能力的人，江东百姓都支持他。他的军队没有曹操多，您可以联合④孙权一起反对曹操。

“第三，荆州这个地方很重要。荆州北边的两条河是运输⑤粮草的重要通道。荆州的东面连接着孙权的吴郡，您可以跟孙权联合。荆州的西边是蜀郡，是非常重要的地方，但是蜀郡的主人没有能力管理，您可以占领蜀郡。

“第四，益州也是一个重要的地方。益州地势险要，土地肥沃[1]，自然条件好。可是益州的刘璋没有能力，胆子又小。您是汉朝皇室的后代，而且有很高的声望，又召集了很多英雄，为什么不占领益州呢？

“第五，您把西南各个少数民族[2]收服[3]，再联合孙权一起反对曹操。这样一来，老百姓都会欢迎您，您就可以兴复汉室，天下就又会变成汉朝的天下了。”

诸葛亮从天时、地利、人和[3]几个方面为刘备做了

① 肥沃 (féiwò)
adj. fertile
e.g. 长江两边的土地很肥沃。

② 少数民族 (shǎoshù mínzú)
n. ethnic minority group
e.g. 中国云南省有很多少数民族。

③ 收服 (shōufú)
v. subdue; bring under control
e.g. 诸葛亮建议刘备收服西南的少数民族首领。

① 佩服 (pèifú)
v. admire
e.g. 人们佩服关羽的忠诚，诸葛亮的才智。

② 局面 (júmiàn)
n. situation
e.g. 这个国家的政治局面很稳定。

③ 形成 (xíngchéng)
v. form
e.g. 刘备有了军队之后，三国鼎立的局面开始形成。

完整的计划。这就是著名的"隆中对"[4]。刘备听后十分佩服①他的才智，采用了他的计划。

刘备三顾茅庐之后，诸葛亮做了刘备的军师。在诸葛亮的帮助下，刘备建立了自己的军队，三国鼎立[5]的局面②开始形成③。

[1] 三顾茅庐（sāngù-máolú）paying three visits at the thatched cottage
茅庐：茅草屋。东汉末年，诸葛亮居住在隆中（今湖北襄阳西部）乡村的一个茅草屋内。刘备为兴复汉室，三次前往隆中拜访诸葛亮，寻求诸葛亮的帮助。最终诸葛亮被刘备的真诚打动，同意辅佐他。现在，这个成语用来表示渴望寻求智者的帮助，或者真诚急切地拜访某人。
During the late Eastern Han Dynasty, Zhuge Liang lived in a thatched cottage in the countryside of Longzhong (located in the west of present-day Xiangyang, Hubei Province). Intent on revitalizing the Han Dynasty, Liu visited Zhuge three times to ask for his help. Zhuge was finally moved by Liu's sincerity and agreed to assist him. Now this idiom means to eagerly seek someone for their talents, or to visit someone in all sincerity and eagerness.
茅庐：thatched cottage

[2] 卧龙先生（Wòlóng xiānsheng）Mr. Crouching Dragon
指诸葛亮。传说诸葛亮在隆中居住的地方叫"卧龙岗"，所以人们叫他"卧龙先生"。
Honorary name for Zhuge Liang. It is said that Zhuge Liang's residence was named "Crouching Dragon Ridge", hence the name.

[3] 天时、地利、人和（tiānshí, dìlì, rénhé）favorable timing, geography and human conditions
指自然气候条件、地形环境及人心所向。
This idiom denotes favorable climates, geographical convenience, and good human relations. It refers to an ancient war situation in which the natural climatic conditions, geographical circumstances, and will of the people are all in a favorable state.

[4] "隆中对"（Lóngzhōngduì）Longzhong Plan
指诸葛亮在隆中跟刘备的对话内容，主要谈的是关于政治、军事或经济方面的谋略。在这次交谈中，诸葛亮分析了当时天下的形势，并提出了统一全国的策略。
The strategies Zhuge Liang mapped out for Liu Bei at Longzhong, which mainly involved politics, the military and the economy. It describes the conversation between Liu Bei and Zhuge Liang during which Zhuge Liang analyzed the country's situation and proposed relevant strategies to reunify the nation.

[5] 三国鼎立（sānguó dǐnglì）tripartite confrontation among three kingdoms
东汉末年魏（220-265)、蜀 (221-263)、吴 (222-280) 三个势力对峙的局面。
A phrase which refers to the triangular balance of power among the kingdoms of Wei (220-265), Shu (221-263) and Wu (222-280) during the late Eastern Han Dynasty.

练习题 Reading exercises

一、选择填空。Choose proper words to fill in the blanks.

1. 徐庶让刘备去（　　）诸葛亮。

A. 拜见　　B. 说

C. 佩服　　D. 联合

2. 刘备三顾茅庐之前，张飞和关羽（　　）刘备，让他不要去了。

A. 关心　　B. 问

C. 劝　　　　　　　　D. 支持

3. 诸葛亮帮助刘备之后，三国鼎立的（　　）开始形成。

A. 国家　　　　　　　B. 方面

C. 时候　　　　　　　D. 局面

二、判断正误。Read the following sentences and decide whether the statements are true or false.

1. 刘备第一次拜见诸葛亮就成功地请到他来帮助自己。（　）
2. 诸葛亮分析了情况，认为刘备要联合孙权，反对曹操，并且要占据荆州、益州，收服西南的少数民族。（　）
3. “隆中对”是刘备对当时情况的分析。（　）

答案：

一、1. A　2. C　3. D

二、1. 误　2. 正　3. 误

8. 赵云单骑救主[1]，张飞吓退[①]曹军

主要人物和地点：
Main Characters and Places

刘琮（Liú Cóng）：刘表的儿子，汉朝皇室后代。刘表死后，刘琮接管荆州，后来投降了曹操。

Liu Cong: One of Liu Biao's sons, a descendant of the Han royal family. After Liu Biao's death, Liu Cong took over Jingzhou and then surrendered to Cao Cao.

赵云（Zhào Yún）（？–229）：蜀国大将军，武艺高强，才智双全，终生帮助刘备兴复汉室。

Zhao Yun: (?–229)：Major General of the Kingdom of Shu, He excelled at martial arts and had great wisdom. He assisted Liu Bei in revitalizing the Han Dynasty all his life.

糜夫人（Mí fūrén）：刘备的妻子。

Lady Mi: One of Liu Bei's wives.

阿斗（Ādǒu）（207–271）：即刘禅，阿斗是他的小名。刘备死后，他成了蜀国的皇帝，被称为蜀国的"后主"。

Liu Edou (207–271)：Liu Shan (pet name, Edou) was Liu Bei's son. After Liu Bei's death, he ascended to the throne and was called "last emperor" of the Kingdom of Shu.

张郃（Zhāng Hé）（？–231）：曹操军队中的著名将领。

Zhang He (?–231)：A famous general in Cao Cao's army.

① 退 (tuì) *v.* retreat
e.g. 曹操害怕前面有埋伏，就带着士兵后退了。

樊城（Fánchéng）：中国古代地名，今湖北省襄阳市境内。

Fancheng: A place in ancient China that was located in present-day Xiangyang City, Hubei Province.

长坂坡（Chángbǎn Pō）：中国古代地名，今湖北省当阳市境内。

The Long Slope: A place in ancient China that was located in present-day Dangyang City, Hubei Province.

江陵（Jiānglíng）：中国古代地名，也叫“荆州”，今湖北省荆州市。

Jiangling: A place in ancient China (also called Jingzhou) that was located in present-day Jingzhou City, Hubei Province.

公元208年，北方的曹操带着军队到南方攻打荆州。当年八月，刘表得了重病，不久就去世了。刘表的小儿子刘琮当了荆州的地方官。他害怕曹操的军队，就投降[1]了曹操。刘备当时在樊城，不知道刘琮已经投降。

曹操的军队打到樊城的时候，刘备立刻迎战。这时，刘备才得到刘琮投降的消息。他非常吃惊，也非常生气。刘备的军队没有曹操多，如果没有刘琮的支持，肯定打不过曹操。现在刘琮投降了，刘备只好带着军队和百姓逃跑[2]，离开了樊城。

刘备的军队与百姓

① 投降 (tóuxiáng)
v. surrender
e.g. 刘琮害怕曹操，就投降了。

② 逃跑 (táopǎo)
v. escape; flee
e.g. 刘备带着百姓一起逃跑。

① 阻挡 (zǔdǎng)
v. obstruct; stop
e.g. 为了阻挡曹操前进，张飞把桥拆了。

② 撤退 (chètuì)
v. retreat
e.g. 敌人的军队开始撤退了。

③ 树枝 (shùzhī)
n. branch
e.g. 可爱的小鸟落在树枝上。

④ 捆 (kǔn)
v. bind; tie
e.g. 要搬家了，他把书捆在一起。

⑤ 树林 (shùlín)
n. woods; grove
e.g. 山上有一片树林。

⑥ 尘土 (chéntǔ)
n. dust
e.g. 汽车经过之后，尘土都飞起来了。

⑦ 飞扬 (fēiyáng)
v. fly upward
e.g 骑兵经过之后，到处尘土飞扬。

一共有十万多人，车和马都很多，走得很慢。曹军在长坂坡这个地方追上了刘备。刘备命令张飞召集二十多名士兵骑着马去长坂桥阻挡①曹军，自己带着军队和百姓撤退②。

张飞来到长坂桥后，命令士兵们把树枝③捆④起来让马拖着，然后让士兵骑着马在树林⑤里来回跑。树林里尘土⑥飞扬⑦，从远处看，就像有一支大部队。张飞骑着马站在桥上，让曹军以为刘备的军队都在长坂坡。

刘备撤退时，他的家人和他的一位将军赵云跟他们走散了。赵云被打散之后，从早上就开始与曹军交战[①]。他到处找刘备的夫人们，终于在一群百姓中找到了甘夫人。这时候，他听到百姓们大喊：曹军来了。糜夫人的哥哥被捆在一匹马上，后面跟着一千多名曹军士兵。

赵云大喊一声，骑着马，拿着枪[②]，一枪把曹军的将领[③]从马上刺了下来，救[④]下了糜夫人的哥哥。赵云杀开一条路，把甘夫人直接送到长坂桥，然后又冲了回来。

曹军大将夏侯恩正带着士兵抢百姓的钱财。他一看见赵云，就带着十几名骑兵冲了过来。赵云立刻迎战，直接把枪刺向夏侯恩。赵云跟夏侯恩只打

① 交战 (jiāozhàn)
v. fight; battle
e.g. 刘备的军队准备跟曹操的军队交战。

② 枪 (qiāng)
n. spear; pike
e.g. 赵云用枪杀了很多曹军。

③ 将领 (jiànglǐng)
n. general
e.g. 赵云一个人杀死了几十个曹军的将领。

④ 救 (jiù)
v. save; rescue
e.g. 赵云救了刘备的儿子。

了一个回合，夏侯恩就被赵云从马上刺下来死了。赵云提着枪，继续迎战曹军。

赵云终于在一座院子里找到了糜夫人，糜夫人抱着刘备的儿子阿斗正坐在水井①旁边哭。

赵云立刻下马，请糜夫人上马，他要带着糜夫人冲出去。糜夫人怕连累赵云，她把阿斗交给赵云，请他把阿斗送到刘备那里，说完就跳进了水井。

糜夫人死了，赵云非常难过。他怕曹军动糜夫人的尸体，就把水井旁边的墙推倒，盖住了水井。

赵云把阿斗小心地包好，放在自己的怀里，然

① 水井 (shuǐjǐng)
n. well
e.g. 这口水井早就没有水了。

后骑上马去找刘备。

这时，曹军士兵冲了过来。赵云勇敢地冲杀过去，终于杀出了一条路。接着，前面又出现了很多曹军，将领叫张郃。赵云立刻与张郃打在一起。

赵云和张郃打了大约十个回合。赵云身上带着阿斗，又急着去找刘备，不想再跟张郃打了，于是骑着马转身就跑。张郃在后面追。

突然，赵云连人带马掉进了一个土坑[1]里，张郃拿着枪刺向赵云。在这个危急[2]关头，突然一道红光，赵云的红马从土坑里跳了出来。张郃十分吃惊，赶紧逃跑。

① 土坑 (tǔkēng)
n. pit
e.g. 大雨之后，地上的土坑里都是水。

② 危急 (wēijí)
adj. critical
e.g. 赵云前后都是曹军，情况十分危急。

① 血 (xuè) *n.* blood e.g. 他的左臂受伤，流血了。

赵云正准备离开，又冲出了钟缙、钟绅两兄弟，他们都是曹操手下的将领。赵云跟钟缙、钟绅打了很多回合，全身上下到处是血[①]，终于杀出一条血路冲了出来。钟缙、钟绅带着士兵再次冲上来，赵云拿着枪又刺过去。打了几个回合之后，赵云把这两兄弟都杀死了。趁这个机会，赵云立刻往长坂桥的方向跑。

赵云在前面跑，曹军在后面追。赵云终于跑到了长坂桥。他一看见张飞就大声喊："翼德帮我！"张飞看见赵云跑过来，赶紧冲过去保护赵云。

赵云骑着马冲过长坂

桥，见到了刘备。赵云把糜夫人的事告诉了刘备，然后从衣服里面抱出了阿斗，没想到这孩子还在睡觉呢。赵云把阿斗交给刘备，刘备接过阿斗后，生气地把儿子扔在地上，说："为了你这孩子，差点儿失去我的大将军赵云！"

赵云赶紧从地上抱起阿斗，一边哭一边跪下，对刘备说："您这样做，我就算肝脑涂地[2]，也不能报答您啊！"

曹军追到长坂桥，看到树林里面尘土飞扬，怀疑这里有很多刘备的军队。曹军看见张飞瞪[1]着大眼睛、骑着马站在桥上，以为这是诸葛亮的计谋，吓

① 瞪 (dèng)
v. stare; glare
e.g. 张飞一生气就瞪眼睛。

① 决一死战
(juéyìsǐzhàn)
fight to the death
e.g. 曹军没有人敢跟张飞决一死战。

得不敢靠近。

曹操得到消息后也赶了过来。张飞看到曹操来了，大声喊：“我是张飞张翼德！谁敢和我决一死战[1]？”曹操听了也吓坏了。

曹操说：“我听说张飞能轻松地从百万大军里杀死首领，拿到首领的头，

今天我们可要小心啊！”

曹操的话还没有说完，张飞瞪着大眼睛又大声喊道：“张翼德在这儿！谁敢来决一死战？”曹操害怕了，准备撤退。

这时候，张飞又大喊：“你们为什么不敢过来？你们为什么还站在那里？”

当张飞在大声喊叫时，曹操身边的将军夏侯杰被吓得从马上掉了下来。曹操更害怕了，立刻带着曹军撤退。曹军士兵被吓得丢了枪、刀等兵器，四处逃跑。没想到，张飞用喊声吓退了曹操和众多曹军。

张飞看到曹操带着曹军撤退了，赶紧命令士兵们把长坂桥拆①了。

① 拆 (chāi)
v. dismantle; pull down
e.g. 工人们把旧房子拆了。

① 中……计谋
(zhòng…jìmóu)
v. be caught in (a scheme)
e.g. 曹操中了诸葛亮的计谋。

张飞骑着马回来向刘备报告。刘备说："你把桥拆了，曹操肯定会猜到我们没有军队，一定会追上来。"于是，刘备赶紧带着军队和百姓从小路逃跑。

曹操听说张飞拆了长坂桥，知道被张飞骗了，赶紧带着曹军又追了回来。眼看曹操就要追上刘备了，这时候，刘备看见前面有一条江。刘备过不去江，后面曹军又快追上了，情况十分危急。突然，从山后面冲出来一支军队——关羽带着士兵来救刘备了！原来，关羽被诸葛亮安排在这里等着接应刘备。曹操一看见关羽，知道中①了诸葛亮的计谋，只好赶紧撤退。

这次跟曹操交战，赵云杀了曹操五十多名大将，还救出了刘备的儿子阿斗。从此，赵云名震天下[1]。

刘备虽然失去了很多士兵，但是关羽、张飞、赵云等大将军还在，他决定去找刘表的大儿子刘琦。

曹操这次虽然没有抓到刘备，但是他占领了很多地方，比如江陵、荆州等。

① 名震天下 (míngzhèn-tiānxià) become well-known all over the world e.g. 赵云与曹军交战之后，名震天下。

[1] 单骑救主（dānjì-jiùzhǔ）save the lord by oneself
《三国演义》里的一个著名的故事。赵云是一个非常勇猛的将领，为了救出刘备的儿子刘禅，他独自一人骑着马穿过曹操的军队，杀死了无数的敌人。此典故现常用来比喻主人深陷危难之中，部下单人独骑拯救主人。
A famous story in *Romance of the Three Kingdoms*. Zhao Yun, a courageous general, rides his battle steed and fights Cao Cao's troops on his own to rescue Liu Bei's son, Liu Shan. He kills a lot of enemies in the battle. This idiom tells about a subordinate whose master is in a dire situation, so the subordinate sets out on horse to save the master.

[2] 肝脑涂地（gānnǎo-túdì）have one's liver and brains smeared on the ground
指竭尽全力侍奉某人，不惜以自己的生命为代价。在这个故事中，赵云对刘备非常忠诚，救了刘备的儿子。赵云用这个成语表达他对刘备的忠诚。
This idiom means trying one's very best to serve someone, even at the expense of one's own life. In the story, Zhao Yun risks his own life and saves Liu Bei's son, which demonstrates his loyalty to Liu Bei.

练习题 Reading exercises

一、选择填空。Choose proper words to fill in the blanks.

1. 刘琮由于害怕曹操大军，（　　）了曹操，使刘备没有了支持。

A. 降服　　B. 降落
C. 下降　　D. 投降

2. 张飞让士兵把（　　）捆起来让马拖着，然后让士兵骑着马在树林里来回地跑，好像有很多军队在这儿的样子。

A. 树枝　　B. 树皮
C. 树林　　D. 树苗

3. 张飞用计谋吓退了曹操的军队，曹操的士兵四处（　　　）。

A. 跑步　　　　B. 交战

C. 逃跑　　　　D. 投降

二、根据故事，将下面的句子排序。Put the following sentences in order according to the story.

1. 虽然曹操的将领被杀死，也没有抓到刘备，但是他占据了很多地方。
2. 张飞、诸葛亮用计谋打赢了曹操，杀掉了曹操的很多将领。
3. 曹操带领军队攻打荆州，刘琮投降了曹操。刘备失去了支持，带着将士和百姓逃跑了。

答案：

一、1. D　2. A　3. C

二、3-2-1

9. 诸葛亮舌战群儒[1]

主要人物和地点：
Main Characters and Places

孙权（Sūn Quán）(182–252)：吴国的第一个皇帝，孙策的弟弟。孙权占领了长江以南地区，公元229年建立吴国。

Sun Quan (182–252): The first emperor of the Kingdom of Wu and Sun Ce's younger brother. He occupied the regions south of the Yangtze River and founded the Kingdom of Wu in 229.

周瑜（Zhōu Yú）(175–210)：字公瑾，吴国的大将军。他年轻英俊，武艺高强，才智双全，但心胸狭窄。

Zhou Yu (175–210): Courtesy name Gongjin. As a major general of the Kingdom of Wu, he was young and handsome and excelled at martial arts. He had great wisdom, but was rather narrow-minded.

鲁肃（Lǔ Sù）(172–217)：吴国的军师、谋士、外交家。

Lu Su (172–217): A great diplomat who was also a military advisor and counselor of the Kingdom of Wu.

张昭（Zhāng Zhāo）(156–236)：吴国的谋士、大臣。

Zhang Zhao (156–236): A counselor and minister of the Kingdom of Wu.

虞翻（Yú Fān）(164–233)：吴国的谋士、大臣。

Yu Fan (164–233): A counselor and minister of the Kingdom of Wu.

薛综（Xuē Zōng）(?–243)：吴国的谋士、大臣。

Xue Zong (?–243): A counselor and minister of the Kingdom of Wu.

陆绩（Lù Jì）（188–219）：吴国的谋士、大臣。
Lu Ji (188–219): A counselor and minister of the Kingdom of Wu.

黄盖（Huáng Gài）：吴国的老将军。为了打败曹操，他和周瑜设计了"苦肉计"，假装投降曹操，帮吴国赢得了"赤壁之战"。
Huang Gai: A senior general of the Kingdom of Wu. To defeat Cao Cao, he and Zhou Yu designed a "self-injury ruse" in which he feigned surrender to Cao and helped his side win the "Battle of Red Cliffs".

东吴（Dōngwú）：也称吴国（222–280）。三国时期，孙权建立了吴国，历史上也称之为孙吴。
Eastern Wu: Also known as the Kingdom of Wu (222–280), it was established by Sun Quan during the Three Kingdoms Period. Historically, it was also called Sun Wu.

长江（Cháng Jiāng）：中国第一大河，全长 6300 公里，流经西藏、四川、云南、重庆、湖北、湖南、江西、安徽、江苏等省、市、自治区，最后在上海流入东海。
Yangtze River: China's longest river with a total length of 6,300 kilometers. It flows through the Tibet Autonomous Region, Sichuan Province, Yunnan Province, Chongqing Municipality, Hubei Province, Hunan Province, Jiangxi Province, Anhui Province and Jiangsu Province. It flows into the East China Sea at Shanghai.

曹操占领了荆州之后，拥有百万大军。他带领百万大军南下，来到长江边上，想要占领东吴。东吴的主人叫孙权，曹操给孙权写了一封信，劝他投降。曹操在信里说，如果孙权不投降，他就带兵攻打东吴。

曹军很强大，东吴的很多大臣和谋士[2]十分害怕曹操，都劝说孙权投降。周瑜是孙权的大将军，他年轻、英俊，足智多谋，坚决反对投降。军师鲁肃也反对投降。

孙权一直在思考是否投降。鲁肃劝孙权联合刘备一起阻挡曹操，于是孙权派鲁肃去找刘备商量。刘备同意与孙权一起攻打曹操，就派诸葛亮来到东吴，与孙权商量攻打曹操的计谋。

孙权让诸葛亮先和东吴的谋士们见面。这些谋士都想投降曹操，他们提了很多问题跟诸葛亮辩论[1]。

[1] 辩论 (biànlùn)
v. debate
e.g. 他不同意这个意见，就跟朋友辩论起来了。

谋士张昭首先问诸葛亮："听说先生住在隆中，把自己比作管仲[3]、乐毅[4]这样的好大臣。刘备三次请您出山帮助他，他有了您如鱼得水[5]。你们想要得到荆州，可是刘琮投降了曹操，现在曹操占领了荆州，您怎么看？"

诸葛亮说："荆州是汉朝王室的后代刘表的地方。刘备不想占领刘表的地方，所以才没有占领荆州。刘表的儿子刘琮投降了曹操，把荆州献给了曹操。现在我们退守江夏，这是我们的计谋，你们是不会懂的。"

张昭又问："您的话自相矛盾[6]。您把自己比作管仲、乐毅。可是您没有帮助刘备时，刘备还能和曹操对抗①；为什么您帮了刘备，当曹操攻打刘备时，刘备却逃跑了呢？可见刘备不如以前了。您真的是管仲、乐毅这样的人才吗？"

诸葛亮笑着说："如果一个人得了重病，首先要给病人用温和②的药。等到病人身体慢慢好转，再用猛烈③的药，这样病人才能好起来。如果不等病人身体变好，就用猛烈的药来治病④，病人会死的。刘备刚打了败仗⑤，军队还不到一千人，将领也只有关羽、张飞和赵云，没有兵器，也没有粮草。如果现在与曹操交战，那就像得重病

① 对抗 (duìkàng)
v. resist; oppose
e.g. 刘备和孙权联合对抗曹操。

② 温和 (wēnhé)
adj. moderate; mild
e.g. 老师的态度很温和。

③ 猛烈 (měngliè)
adj. strong; violent
e.g. 他们这一仗打得非常猛烈。

④ 治病 (zhìbìng)
v. treat an illness
e.g. 曹操请华佗为他治病。

⑤ 败仗 (bàizhàng)
n. lost battle
e.g. 刘备的军队士兵少，打了败仗。

的人吃猛药一样，非常危险。刘表的儿子把荆州献给了曹操，可数十万百姓都跟着刘备。刘备不愿意丢下百姓，军队因为照顾百姓，所以才走得很慢。这次打了败仗也是很正常的事情。”张昭听了以后就不说话了。

谋士虞翻又接着问：“曹操的军队很强大，您怎么看？”

诸葛亮笑着说：“虽然曹操有百万大军，我们却不用害怕。”

虞翻冷笑着问：“刘备打了败仗，现在想让我们救他，您还敢说不害怕曹操？”

诸葛亮答道：“我们只是在等待机会。你们既有士兵，又有将领，还有长江阻挡，却想投降曹操，真是让人感到好笑。看来，刘备才是真正不怕曹操的人。”虞翻听了以后也不说话了。

谋士薛综问：“您认为曹操是什么样的人？”

诸葛亮回答：“曹操的父亲曹嵩是汉朝的丞相，而他现在挟天子以令诸侯，是背叛[1]朝廷的小人。”

谋士薛综又问：“汉朝要灭亡[2]了，刘备却非要抗击[3]曹操，怎么会不失败呢？”

诸葛亮说：“曹操谋反[4]，这是天下人都感到愤怒[5]的事情。你怎么提这样的问题！我不愿跟你这种人辩论！”薛综感觉非常

① 背叛 (bèipàn)
v. betray
e.g. 他不应该背叛他的朋友。

② 灭亡 (mièwáng)
v. perish
e.g. 皇帝都不希望自己的朝代灭亡。

③ 抗击 (kàngjī)
v. fight against
e.g. 孙权同意和刘备一起抗击曹操。

④ 谋反 (móufǎn)
v. conspire against the court
e.g. 皇帝最担心有人谋反。

⑤ 愤怒 (fènnù)
adj. angry; indignant
e.g. 张飞骑上马，愤怒地冲向吕布。

① 惭愧 (cánkuì)
adj. ashamed
e.g. 他对自己的错误感到惭愧。

② 草鞋 (cǎoxié)
n. straw sandals
e.g. 刘备以前家里很穷，卖过草鞋。

③ 耻辱 (chǐrǔ)
n. disgrace; humiliation
e.g. 关羽认为投降是耻辱的行为。

惭愧[①]，不再问了。

谋士陆绩又问："曹操的爷爷以前是汉朝的丞相，可是刘备却是个卖草鞋[②]的人，怎么能和曹操比呢？"

诸葛亮笑着说："曹操虽然是汉朝丞相的后代，可是他谋反，那他就是朝廷的奸臣。当今的皇帝可是称刘备为皇叔的。再说，汉朝开国皇帝[7]刘邦本来也是一个很小的官，最后却得到了天下。刘备卖草鞋怎么能算是耻辱[③]呢？"陆绩也没有话说了。

这时，东吴的老将军黄盖突然走进来，生气地说："曹操大军就在长江对面，你们不想着怎样打败曹操，却一直在这里辩论！”大家这才停止了辩论。

诸葛亮的聪明才智让东吴的谋士们心服口服①。这就是著名的“舌战群儒”的故事。

① 心服口服
(xīnfú-kǒufú)
be sincerely convinced
e.g. 谋士们对诸葛亮的才智心服口服。

[1] 舌战群儒 (shézhàn-qúnrú) have a heated debate with a group of scholars
这个故事讲述了诸葛亮与吴国谋士辩论，并一个一个地说服他们与刘备军队联盟抗击曹操军队。现在这个成语用来描述一个人具有与众人雄辩的口才。
This is a story about Zhuge Liang arguing with the counselors of the Kingdom of Wu and persuading them one by one to ally with Liu Bei's army for the sake of fighting Cao Cao's army. Now this is an idiom used to describe someone who is talented at debating.

[2] 谋士 (móushì) counselor
为主人提供计谋和执行艰难任务的人。在大多数情况下，谋士没有官职。
A person who provides strategies and performs difficult tasks for his master. Usually the person doesn't hold an official position.

[3] 管仲 (Guǎn Zhòng) Guan Zhong (?-645 BC)
春秋时期一个非常著名的政治人物。他非常有才能，积极帮助齐国的国王齐桓公进行政治和经济改革，增强了齐国的实力，使齐国成为春秋时期的强国。
A famous politician in the Spring and Autumn Period (770-476 BC). He has great wisdom, and he helped Duke Huan of the State of Qi launch political and economic reforms, augmenting the strength of the State of Qi. As a result, Qi became a powerful state.

[4] 乐毅 (Yuè Yì) Yue Yi
战国时期燕国杰出的军事家。他帮助燕国的燕昭王振兴了燕国。公元前 284 年，他统帅燕国等五国联军攻打齐国，连下七十余城，创造了中国古代战争史上以弱胜强的著名战例。
A military strategist and a general of the State of Yan during the Warring States Period (475-221 BC). He helped the King of Yanzhao rejuvenate the State of Yan. In 284 BC, he commanded the allied troops of Yan and the other four states, defeated the State of Qi and conquered about 70 cities.

This is a famous battle in Chinese history and an example of the weak triumphing over the strong.

[5] 如鱼得水 (rúyú-déshuǐ) be in one's element
在《三国演义》中，刘备三次拜访诸葛亮，寻求他的帮助。吴国的一个名叫张昭的谋士说：有了诸葛亮的帮助，刘备就像鱼儿在水中游一样顺利。这个成语用来形容某人遇见了意气相投的朋友或者处于一个非常合适的环境中。
In *Romance of the Three Kingdoms*, Liu Bei visits Zhuge Liang three times to seek Zhuge's assistance. Zhang Zhao, one of Wu's counselors, says with irony that Liu is like a fish in the water with the help of Zhuge Liang. This idiom is used to indicate that someone meets a congenial person or is in a favorable condition.

[6] 自相矛盾 (zìxiāng-máodùn) be self-contradictory
这是中国古代的一个故事。从前有个商人在卖矛和盾，他称赞自己的矛能够刺穿世界上所有的东西，而世界上没有什么东西能够刺穿自己的盾。有人就问他："如果用你的矛刺你的盾，那会怎么样呢？"这个商人什么都没说就离开了。这个成语用来比喻一个人说话、行动前后抵触，不一致。
This is an old Chinese story about a person selling spears and shields. He claims that his spears can pierce anything in the world, and his shields cannot be pierced by any spear in the world. Someone asks him what will happen if he uses one of his spears to pierce one of his shields. The man leaves without any answer. So the idiom often refers to contradictions or contradictory factors.

[7] 开国皇帝 (kāiguó huángdì) founding emperor
一个王朝的创立者。如曹丕是魏国的开国皇帝，刘备是蜀汉的开国皇帝，孙权是东吴的开国皇帝。
An emperor who founded a new dynasty. For example, Cao Pi, the founding emperor of the Kingdom of Wei; Liu Bei, the founding emperor of the Kingdom of Shu; and Sun Quan, the founding emperor of the Kingdom of Wu.

练习题 Reading exercises

一、选择填空。Choose proper words to fill in the blanks.

1. 曹操（　　）了荆州。

A. 没有　　　　B. 战胜

C. 占领 　　　　D. 打败

2. 诸葛亮说："如果一个人得了重病，首先要用（　　）的药"。

A. 温和 　　　　B. 缓慢

C. 严重 　　　　D. 温柔

3. 黄盖看到大家不想办法打败曹操，反而在（　　），非常生气。

A. 聊天 　　　　B. 说话

C. 辩论 　　　　D. 理论

二、根据故事，给下面的句子排序。Put the following sentences in order according to the story.

1. 曹操准备攻打东吴，东吴的孙权请诸葛亮来商量抗击曹操的计谋。
2. 诸葛亮一一回答了张昭、虞翻、薛综等东吴谋士的提问，让他们心服口服。
3. 诸葛亮说服了孙权和刘备一起抗击曹操。

答案：

一、1. C　2. A　3. C

二、1-2-3

10. 草船借箭

① 嫉妒 (jídù)
v. envy; be jealous of
e.g. 周瑜总是输给诸葛亮，因此非常嫉妒诸葛亮。

诸葛亮在东吴舌战群儒之后，见到了孙权。诸葛亮劝孙权抵抗曹操大军，孙权终于同意了。周瑜听说了诸葛亮的才智，非常嫉妒①。他觉得诸葛亮太聪明，对东吴不利，想杀掉诸葛亮。

一天，周瑜把诸葛亮请来，说要跟他商量做箭的事。周瑜对诸葛亮说："在长江上交战，弓箭是最好的兵器。可是现在我们缺少箭，请先生想办法在十天之内做十万支箭。"

诸葛亮知道周瑜这么做是想杀他，于是说："如果等十天，一定会耽误了大事，我只需要三天！我愿意写下军令状[1]，如果三天做不出来，我愿意接受惩罚①。”

周瑜听了十分高兴，心想，这次诸葛亮肯定逃不了死罪②了，因为他在三天内不可能做出十万支箭。

周瑜命令部下③不要给诸葛亮做箭的材料，让诸葛亮自己找材料，还让士兵故意做箭做得慢一点儿，同时又派军师鲁肃去诸葛亮那里打听情况。

诸葛亮见到鲁肃，对他说：“请你借给我六百名士兵，二十条小船，在每条船的两边捆上草人④。这件事，一定不要告诉周瑜。你如果告诉周瑜，我就会被他杀了。”鲁肃答应了。

① 惩罚 (chéngfá)
v. punish
e.g. 周瑜想用计谋惩罚诸葛亮，结果失败了。

② 死罪 (sǐzuì)
n. capital offence
e.g. 军队最严重的惩罚是死罪。

③ 部下 (bùxià)
n. subordinate
e.g. 曹操的部下想杀刘备。

④ 草人 (cǎorén)
n. scarecrow
e.g. 雾太大，曹操的士兵把箭都射到草人上了。

① 莫名其妙 (mòmíngqímiào) be baffled; be perplexed
e.g. 诸葛亮经常有一些莫名其妙的举动。

② 雾 (wù) *n.* fog
e.g. 江面上出现了大雾。

③ 水寨 (shuǐzhài) *n.* naval camp
e.g. 曹操在长江边上建立了水寨。

④ 船头 (chuántóu) *n.* bow (of a boat)
e.g. 一个士兵站在船头观察情况。

⑤ 船尾 (chuánwěi) *n.* stern
e.g. 士兵们把箭放在船尾。

⑥ 擂鼓 (léi gǔ) beat drums
e.g. 擂鼓的声音像打雷一样，吓坏了曹军。

周瑜问鲁肃，诸葛亮有什么计谋，鲁肃只对周瑜说诸葛亮做箭不用材料。周瑜一听，觉得莫名其妙①，只好等着看诸葛亮到底会怎么做。

两天过去了，诸葛亮什么也没有做。第三天夜里，诸葛亮请鲁肃和他一起去取箭。鲁肃感到十分奇怪，不相信诸葛亮已经完成了任务。

这天夜里，长江上的雾②很大。诸葛亮的二十条小船在大雾中慢慢地靠近曹操的水寨③。快到曹军水寨的时候，诸葛亮叫二十条小船停下来，船头④向东，船尾⑤向西，一字排开，然后让士兵们擂鼓⑥

呐喊[1]。鲁肃担心曹操军队打过来，那他们就危险了，诸葛亮却笑着说："这么大的雾，曹操一定不敢出来。我们喝酒吧，等雾散了我们就回去。"

曹操听见鼓声和呐喊声，十分吃惊。江上雾大，什么也看不清楚。曹操以为是东吴的军队来了，但

① 呐喊 (nàhǎn)
v. shout loudly
e.g. 人们一边看足球赛一边大声呐喊。

① 恍然大悟
(huǎngrán-dàwù)
suddenly realize
e.g. 雾散了，曹操恍然大悟，原来中了诸葛亮的计谋。

又害怕这是诸葛亮的计谋，就命令一万多名士兵一起向江面上射箭，大部分的箭都射在了草人上。

不一会儿，二十条船的草人身上都是箭。这时，诸葛亮命令士兵调整船的方向，船头向西，船尾向东，继续让士兵擂鼓呐喊，于是又有很多箭射到草人上。

天快亮了，江上的雾也快散了，诸葛亮命令士兵收船回营。他让士兵在船上大声喊："谢谢曹丞相送的箭！"曹操这才恍然大悟①，原来是中了诸葛亮的计，白白浪费了十万支箭！

诸葛亮对鲁肃说："我

们喝酒聊天，就得了这十万多支箭，以后就用这些箭来攻打曹操。”

鲁肃说：“先生真是奇才啊！”

诸葛亮说：“周瑜叫我十天内做完箭，却不给我安排工人，也不给我材料，他就是想杀我。三天前我就算好今天有大雾，所以我才想出这个计谋。”

回来后，诸葛亮命令士兵把草人上的箭拿下来一数，差不多有十五六万支箭。诸葛亮让士兵们把箭交给周瑜。鲁肃见到周瑜，把事情的经过告诉了他。周瑜十分吃惊，感叹说：“诸葛亮真是神机妙算[3]，我不如他啊！”

① 对峙 (duìzhì)
v. confront each other
e.g. 双方对峙了很久，最后刘备和孙权的联军赢了。

之后，曹操带领八十万军队在长江北边，准备攻打东吴。长江南边的孙权和刘备联军只有五万人，两军对峙①。双方都在积极准备打仗。

[1] 军令状（jūnlìngzhuàng）military pledge
中国古代戏曲和旧小说中所说接受军令后写的保证书，表示如不能完成任务，愿依军法处罚，借指接受任务时所做的按时完成任务的保证。在这个故事中，诸葛亮立下军令状，保证在三天内造出十万支箭。
In ancient China, this term meant the pledge written by a general after he accepted a military order, which demonstrated that if he could not fulfill the military task, he would be punished according to military laws. In this story, Zhuge Liang writes this pledge to promise that he will finish making 100,000 arrows within only three days.

[2] 神机妙算（shénjī-miàosuàn）miraculous strategy and foresight
惊人的机智，巧妙的谋划，形容某人有预见性，善于估计客观形势，决定策略。在《三国演义》中，诸葛亮神机妙算，擅长制定精密的军事战术，并具有非凡的预测能力。
This idiom is used to describe someone with divine strategy and shrewd military tactics. In *Romance of Three Kingdoms*, Zhuge Liang is always described for his ingenious stratagem and shrewd predictions.

练习题 Reading exercises

一、选择填空。Choose proper words to fill in the blanks.

才能　　恍然大悟　　惩罚　　军令状　　江面

1. 诸葛亮让士兵们把船在（　　）上排开。
2. 曹操听到士兵大喊“谢谢曹丞相的箭”才（　　），自己中计了。
3. 诸葛亮通过草船借箭再次显示了他非凡的（　　）。

二、判断正误。Read the following sentences and decide whether the statements are true or false.

1. 周瑜让诸葛亮做十万只箭，并且派士兵帮助他。（　）
2. 诸葛亮让鲁肃借给他二十只船，在晚上的江上假装攻打曹操。（　）
3. 诸葛亮成功向曹操借到了十万只箭。（　）

答案：

一、1. 江面　2. 恍然大悟　3. 才能

二、1. 误　2. 正　3. 正

11. 赤壁之战[1]

主要人物和地点：
Main Characters and Places

庞统（Páng Tǒng）(179–214)：刘备军中的谋士。他设计了连环计，帮助刘备和孙权的联军取得了赤壁之战的胜利。

Pang Tong (179–214): A military advisor to Liu Bei. With his interlocking stratagems, he helped the allied forces of Liu Bei and Sun Quan win the Battle of the Red Cliffs.

阚泽（Kàn Zé）(?–243)：三国时期孙权军中的学者、大臣。他给曹操送去了黄盖诈降的密信，是苦肉计中的关键人物。

Kan Ze (?–243): A scholar and minister in Sun Quan's camp. Delivering to Cao Cao Huang Gai's confidential letter of feigned surrender, he played a key role in the self-injury trick.

赤壁（Chìbì）：中国古代地名，今湖北武汉市赤矶山，一说今湖北省赤壁市西北。三国时期著名的"赤壁之战"的古战场。

Chibi (The Red Cliffs): A place in ancient China located at present-day Chiji Hill in Wuhan City, Hubei Province. Some alternatively believe that its location is in the northwest of Chibi City, Hubei Province. It is here that the well-known Battle of the Red Cliffs during the Three Kingdoms Period took place.

曹操带领百万大军南下，来到长江边上的赤壁，准备攻打东吴。面对强大的曹军，刘备和孙权组成联军共同抵抗[1]曹操。

一天夜里，老将军黄盖来看周瑜。黄盖对周瑜说："敌人的人数多，我们的人数少，不适合长期作战。不如用火攻曹军，怎么样？"

周瑜说："这确实是个好办法，我也是这么想的。我想要派人假装向曹操投降，可是不知道让谁去。"

黄盖说："我愿意去完成这个任务！"

周瑜非常感动，连忙跪在地上对黄盖说："看来我们只有用苦肉计[2]了。老将军真是帮了我的大忙啊！"

① 抵抗 (dǐkàng)
v. resist
e.g. 孙权只有五万军队，没有办法抵抗曹操的百万大军。

① 扰乱 (rǎoluàn)
v. disturb; disrupt
e.g. 这些麻烦事扰乱了他的正常生活。

② 军心 (jūnxīn)
n. morale of troops
e.g. 打仗前，军心一定要稳定。

③ 求情 (qiúqíng)
v. beg for leniency
e.g. 周瑜命令打黄盖，将军们都为黄盖求情。

第二天，周瑜召集将领们说："曹操军队很强大。黄盖，你去准备三个月的粮草，做好长期打仗的准备。"

黄盖大声说："曹操那么强大，我们投降吧！"

周瑜听了，假装愤怒地说："你竟然扰乱①军心②！来人，把他拉出去杀了！"

黄盖听了，大声骂周瑜："我跟你父亲一起打仗的时候，你这个小孩子还不知道在什么地方呢，你竟然敢杀我！"

周瑜听了，假装更加生气，命令士兵赶快把黄盖杀了。将军们赶忙为黄盖求情③。最后周瑜对黄盖说："既然大家都在为你求情，这次就不杀你了，但是得打你一百军棍[1]！”

士兵打了不到五十军棍，黄盖已经被打得满身是血。将军们看黄盖年纪大，有点儿受不了了，又去为黄盖求情。周瑜命令士兵：“停下！剩下的五十军棍以后再说！”

黄盖的好朋友阚泽看出来黄盖和周瑜是在演一出苦肉计，周瑜打黄盖是给曹操的密探[2]看的。阚泽向周瑜表示，他愿意去给曹操送黄盖的投降信，周瑜同意了。当天夜里，阚泽划着小船去见曹操。

阚泽对曹操说，黄盖非常恨周瑜，想向曹操投降，然后帮助曹操打东吴。曹操读了黄盖的投降信，

① 军棍 (jūngùn)
n. rod of birch used for corporal punishment in an army
e.g. 以前士兵违反了军法，都用军棍惩罚。

② 密探 (mìtàn)
n. spy
e.g. 曹操派密探观察周瑜军营中的情况。

还是不太相信。这时，曹操在东吴的密探也送来了一封密信[1]，信中详细地说了黄盖被周瑜打军棍的经过。曹操高兴极了，不再怀疑黄盖，就等着黄盖来投降。

谋士庞统对鲁肃说，曹操有很多船，很难一次全部烧掉。庞统说自己可以去曹操的军营中当说客[2]，想办法劝曹操把所有的船连在一起，这样就可以用火攻[3]的办法把曹军的船全部烧掉。鲁肃把庞统的计谋告诉了周瑜，周瑜听了之后非常高兴，同意了庞统的计谋。

庞统假装投降曹操，来到曹操军营中。曹操的

① 密信 (mìxìn)
n. confidential letter
e.g. 曹操收到了黄盖的密信，但没想到黄盖是假投降。

② 说客（shuìkè）
n. lobbyist
e.g. 庞统愿意当说客，说服曹操用铁链把船连在一起。

③ 火攻 (huǒgōng)
n. fire attack
e.g. 曹操把船连起来，没想到火攻会把船烧了。

士兵大部分是北方人，平时很少坐船，一上船就晕船[1]，接着就生病，曹操很着急。这时庞统给曹操出了一个主意，建议曹操把所有的船连在一起，然后再在船上放上木板，这样士兵在船上走路就像在平地上一样，不会晕船了。曹操听了赶紧命令士兵把船都连了起来。他很高兴曹军可以像在陆地上一样打仗了。

周瑜做好了火攻曹操的各种准备，但是要想让火攻顺利，就需要刮东风！周瑜等了好几天，还是没刮东风。周瑜很着急，一下子病倒了。

诸葛亮去看周瑜，给

① 晕船 (yūnchuán)
v. be seasick
e.g. 曹操的士兵晕船，不能打仗。

① 吹牛 (chuīniú)
v. boast; brag
e.g. 他爱吹牛，朋友们都不信他的话。

他写了一张纸条，上面有十六个字："欲破曹操，宜用火攻。万事俱备，只欠东风[3]。"

周瑜看了纸条，对诸葛亮说："先生真聪明，我就是担心这个。现在怎么办呢？"

诸葛亮说："没问题，三天后，我帮你借东风[4]。"

周瑜心里想，诸葛亮说能"借"东风，一定是在吹牛[①]。

过了三天，江上刮起了很大的西北风，周瑜更加着急。如果到了晚上还刮西北风的话，就没有办法火攻曹操了。他既希望诸葛亮能借到东风，打败曹操，又怕诸葛亮真的借到东风，把自己比下去。诸葛亮却一点儿也不急。

到了晚上，诸葛亮开始借东风。只见诸葛亮走上一个高台，嘴里低声说着话，手里拿着剑[1]来回比画，周围的士兵都看傻[2]了。其实，诸葛亮早就算出来三天后有东南风。他故意对周瑜说自己能借东风，就是想气气周瑜。

过了一会儿，西北风真的变小了，到了夜里，果然刮起了东南风。风越刮越大，大家高兴极了。

这天晚上，黄盖带着二十条船去“投降”曹操。船上都装满了干柴[3]和油[4]，外面用黑布盖好。快到的时候，黄盖命令士兵把船

① 剑 (jiàn) *n.* sword
e.g. 这是一把宝剑，非常锋利。

② 傻 (shǎ)
adj. stunned
e.g. 诸葛亮借东风，士兵都看傻了。

③ 干柴 (gānchái)
n. dry wood
e.g. 士兵们点着干柴，烧了曹军的水寨。

④ 油 (yóu) *n.* oil
e.g. 船上的油也烧起来了。

① 映 (yìng)
v. reflect
e.g. 大火映红了山上的石头。

② 岸 (àn)
n. riverbank
e.g. 岸上的曹军也被吓得四处逃跑。

③ 石壁 (shíbì)
n. cliff
e.g. 据说石壁上的“赤壁”是周瑜刻的。

点着，二十条火船一起向曹操的船队冲了过去。曹操的船是连在一起的，一下子都烧了起来。

火越烧越大，大火映[1]红了岸[2]上的石壁[3]，也映红了天空。曹军的许多士兵

逃到了岸上，周瑜派军队冲过来，杀得曹军到处乱跑。曹操只好带着士兵逃跑了。

诸葛亮很了解周瑜。他知道打败曹操之后，周瑜肯定会因为嫉妒而杀了自己。所以在周瑜攻打曹操的时候，诸葛亮安排赵云来接他走，这时周瑜忙着攻打曹操，没有时间杀他。

周瑜打败曹操以后，用剑在石壁上刻下了“赤壁”两个字。孙权和刘备联军用很少的军队打败了曹操的数十万大军，这就是历史上著名的“赤壁之战”。

在短时间内，曹操不可能再攻打刘备和孙权了。“赤壁之战”之后，三国鼎立的局面基本形成了。

[1] 赤壁之战（Chìbì zhī zhàn）the Battle of the Red Cliffs
孙权、刘备联军在赤壁击败了曹操军队，史称"赤壁之战"。这场战役以少数战胜多数而闻名。
In the battle, the allied forces of Sun Quan and Liu Bei defeated Cao Cao's army at the Red Cliffs. This battle is famous for a smaller force defeating a larger one.

[2] 苦肉计（kǔròujì）self-injury trick
指为了赢得敌人的信任而故意伤害自己的计策。在赤壁之战中，周瑜听了老将军黄盖的计谋，通过惩罚黄盖来迷惑曹操。
This is a trick to secure the enemy's faith by intentionally injuring oneself. In the Battle of the Red Cliffs, Zhou Yu's senior general Huang Gai devised the trick. Then Zhou plotted a stratagem to confuse Cao Cao by punishing Huang Gai, a famous general of the Kingdom of Wu.

[3] 万事俱备，只欠东风（wànshì-jùbèi，zhǐqiàn-dōngfēng）everything is ready except the east wind
曹操攻打孙、刘联军，孙、刘联军决定用火攻袭击曹操的水寨。但是他们忽视了一点，就是得有东风来蔓延火势。为此，周瑜非常担忧，甚至急病了。诸葛亮来探望他的时候写下了 16 个字"欲破曹操，宜用火攻，万事俱备，只欠东风"。这 16 个字的意思是：想要打败曹操，用火攻是比较明智的选择，现在除了东风所有准备都已经完毕。"诸葛亮告诉周瑜他可以借来东风，周瑜的病就好了。现在，这个习语用来描述某人做好了所有的准备，就差最后一个最重要的因素。
Cao Cao assaulted the allied forces of Liu Bei and Sun Quan. The allied forces decided to attack Cao Cao's naval camp with fire, but neglected one point that there would be an east wind to spread the fire. Over this, Zhou Yu worried so much that he fell ill. Zhuge Liang came to see him and wrote down the 16 Chinese characters 欲破曹操，宜用火攻，万事俱备，只欠东风, meaning "To defeat Cao, we should resort to a fire attack. Now all is ready except the east wind". Zhuge told Zhou that he could borrow the east wind, and Zhou became well again. Now this phrase is used to describe when one has made all preparations except the crucial one.

[4] 借东风（jiè dōngfēng）borrow the east wind
在赤壁之战中，诸葛亮计划用东风火攻曹操的军营。在准备过程中，他通过观察天象，巧妙地预测了刮东风的时间，却说东风是自己借来的。后来这个惯用语用来比喻借助有利条件或大好时机。
In the Battle of the Red Cliffs, Zhuge Liang planned to launch a fire attack on Cao Cao's army by making use of the east wind. In making his preparations, he foresaw the east wind by observing the weather while claiming that the wind was borrowed by him. The idiom has come to be used to refer to someone taking advantage of a favorable condition or a good opportunity.

练习题 Reading exercises

一、选择填空。Choose proper words to fill in the blanks.

1. 周瑜假装要杀黄盖，将军们都为他（　　）。

A. 求情　　B. 要求

C. 感动　　D. 感情

2. 周瑜认为诸葛亮“借”东风是在（　　），因为冬天江上常常刮西北风。

A. 吹风　　B. 吹牛

C. 正确　　D. 计划

3. 黄盖船上的火把曹操的水寨全部（　　）了。

A. 烧掉　　B. 发烧

C. 着火　　D. 烧水

二、判断正误。Read the following sentences and decide whether the statements are true or false.

1. 曹操的士兵上了船就晕，于是他们把所有的船都连在一起，还铺上了木板。(　)

2. 周瑜因为黄盖要去投降曹操非常生气，就打了他。(　)

3. 诸葛亮“借”的东风帮助周瑜打败了曹操的军队，周瑜很高兴，非常感谢诸葛亮。(　　)

答案：

一、1. A　　2. B　　3. A

二、1. 正　　2. 误　　3. 误

12. 关羽义释曹操

主要人物和地点：
Main Characters and Places

华容道（Huáróng Dào）：中国古代地名，今湖北省潜江市西南。曹操在赤壁之战失败后逃跑时经过的地方。

Huarong Path: A place in ancient China that was in the southwest of present-day Qianjiang City, Hubei Province. After his defeat in the Battle of the Red Cliffs, Cao Cao fled with his troops through this path.

葫芦谷（Húlu Gǔ）：《三国演义》里的地名。这个山谷像个葫芦，被称为"葫芦谷"，入口小，进去之后不利于军队撤退。

Gourd Valley: A place mentioned in the novel *Romance of the Three Kingdoms*. The valley looked like a gourd; hence it was named Gourd Valley. With a narrow entrance, it was not convenient for troops to retreat.

① 把守 (bǎshǒu)
v. defend; guard
e.g. 为了抓住逃跑的罪犯，警察把守着路口。

周瑜和诸葛亮在赤壁烧了曹操的船，曹操想占领东吴的计划失败了。为了阻挡曹操和他的士兵逃跑，诸葛亮在几个重要的地方都安排了军队把守①。

其他的将军都领了兵马走了，只有关羽没有任务。于是，关羽问诸葛亮为什么不给他安排任务。

诸葛亮说："我本来是要派你去把守最重要的华容道，只是有些担心，还是不让你去了。"

关羽生气地问："有什么好担心的？"

诸葛亮说："我担心你受过曹操的好处，会放走曹操。"

关羽听后，马上说：

"我为他打过仗，他的恩情[1]我早就还清了，我是不会放走他的。"

诸葛亮说："要是你放走了曹操，怎么办呢？"

关羽说："你要是不相信，我可以立军令状来表示我的决心。"

关羽立刻写好了军令状，诸葛亮就派关羽带着兵马去把守华容道。

曹操的船队被烧毁了以后，跟着曹操逃出来的士兵不多。曹操在这些将士[2]的保护下，来到了山地边的树林里。这里地势非常险要。

曹操忽然大笑起来。将士们感到很奇怪，问他："打仗打输了，曹丞相怎么

① 恩情 (ēnqíng)
n. kindness
e.g. 他不会忘记父母的恩情。

② 将士 (jiàngshì)
n. generals and soldiers
e.g. 将士们努力冲杀，终于冲出了敌人的包围。

① 埋伏 (máifú)
v. ambush
e.g. 敌人在树林里埋伏了军队。

还笑得出来？”

曹操说：“我笑的是，如果诸葛亮和周瑜在这里埋伏①一支人马的话，我们就一定逃不了了。”

曹操刚说完，突然赵云带着一支人马冲了出来，将士们连忙保护着曹操逃走。

天快亮的时候下起了大雨，曹操等人又冷又饿。这时他们走到了一个叫葫芦谷的地方，曹操命令将士们停下来休息。

曹操坐在一片树林中，四下看了看，又大笑起来。将士们很奇怪，不知道曹操为什么又笑。

曹操说：“我笑的是，如果诸葛亮他们在这里埋伏一支人马，我们就算不死也得受重伤①。”

曹操刚说完，从葫芦谷又冲出一支人马，包围②了曹军。张飞是领兵的将军，曹操见了，吓得骑上马就跑。

曹操带着将士们一路逃跑，狼狈不堪③。这时他们来到一个路口④。前面的士兵报告说：“前面有两条路，一条大路，一条小路。大路比较好走，但是离荆州远；小路叫华容道，离荆州近，但是不好走。”曹操害怕诸葛亮在大路上安排埋伏，就命令将士们走小路。

因为下雨，小路非常滑，走起来很困难。突然，

① 重伤 (zhòngshāng)
v. be seriously wounded
e.g. 这个士兵受了重伤。

② 包围 (bāowéi)
v. surround; besiege
e.g. 关羽带领军队包围了曹操的军队。

③ 狼狈不堪 (lángbèi-bùkān)
in a very awkward position
e.g. 曹操一路逃跑，又渴又累，狼狈不堪。

④ 路口 (lùkǒu)
n. road junction; crossroads
e.g. 他们站在路口，观察周围的情况。

① 炮 (pào)
n. gunfire
e.g. 他们用火炮打退了敌人。

② 尿 (niào) *n.* urine
e.g. 曹军看见关羽冲过来，吓得尿都快出来了。

曹操又大笑起来。将士们问曹操为什么又笑，曹操说："如果诸葛亮和周瑜在这里埋伏一支人马，我们就只能投降了！"

曹操刚说完，突然一声炮①响，关羽带着一支人马出现在路上。曹操的士兵吓坏了，一个个尿②都快吓出来了，不知道怎么办才好。

这时，曹操的一个谋士对他说："关羽很讲义气[1]，您曾经收留过他，他一定会记住您对他的恩情。您如果劝劝他，关羽也许会被感动。"

曹操听从了谋士的建议，走上前跟关羽谈起了以前的事情。

虽然关羽知道自己签了军令状，放走曹操会受到惩罚，可是他想到曹操的恩情，还是不忍心[1]杀曹操，放曹操他们通过了华容道。

关羽带着人马回到诸葛亮的军营，诸葛亮看到关羽回来了，上前迎接。

① 忍心 (rěnxīn)
v. have the heart to
e.g. 刘备不忍心丢下百姓，就带着百姓一起撤退。

① 严肃 (yánsù)
adj. serious
e.g. 父亲的态度非常严肃。

关羽说："我是来领死罪的。"

诸葛亮问："难道曹操没有走华容道？"

关羽说："走了。是我无能，让曹操逃走了。"

诸葛亮说："恐怕是将军念及旧情，所以才放走了曹操。但是您立下了军令状，只好按军法处置了！"说完就让将士把关羽推出去杀头。刘备的将领们都吓坏了，赶紧跪下为关羽求情。

刘备也向诸葛亮求情说："请军师暂时记下关羽的死罪，这次就不杀他了，让他以后将功补过[2]吧。"

其实诸葛亮也并不想杀关羽，只是为了严肃[1]

军纪①，吓一吓关羽。诸葛亮看见大家都着急了，就说："好吧！关羽，死罪先记下。你要记得今天的事情，今后要将功补过！"

大家又高兴起来了，整个军营都在热烈庆功。实际上，让关羽把守华容道、放走曹操是诸葛亮的计谋。因为当时刘备的军队还不够强大，曹操在北方还有几十万的大军，还不到杀曹操的时候。

曹操铩羽而归[3]后，刘备与孙权又开始争夺荆州。诸葛亮和周瑜在争夺荆州的过程中各显神通②。

① 军纪 (jūnjì)
n. military discipline
e.g. 将士都必须遵守军纪。

② 各显神通
(gè xiǎn shéntōng)
each one showing his special prowess
e.g. 参加比赛的人各显神通，都想获得第一名。

[1] 讲义气（jiǎng yìqi）be loyal to one's friends
对朋友非常忠诚。在《三国演义》中，曹操非常看重关羽的才能，对关羽非常友善，并曾收留了关羽一段时间，因此关羽对曹操仍然很讲义气。
In *Romance of the Three Kingdoms*, Cao Cao values Guan Yu's talent and is kind to him. Cao even takes in Guan for a time. For this reason, Guan remains faithful to Cao.

[2] 将功补过（jiānggōng-bǔguò）making amends for one's fault through good deeds
用某人的功劳补偿错误。在《三国演义》中，关羽放曹操通过了华容道，按军令状是要杀头的。大家都为关羽求情，所以诸葛亮没有杀关羽，而是让他以后多立战功来弥补这次错误。
In *Romance of the Three Kingdoms*, Guan Yu lets Cao Cao pass through the Huarong Path without capturing him, which is a serious dereliction of duty. Guan should have been sentenced to death according to the military directive. However, because others plead for him to be treated leniently, Zhuge Liang spares his life and asks him to make amends by performing good services later.

[3] 铩羽而归（shāyǔ'érguī）coming back frustrated
这个成语最初表示某人在战斗失败后归来，现在多比喻某人在蒙受损失和遭受挫败后返回。在本故事中，曹操在赤壁之战失败后撤退到北边，他感到非常沮丧。
This idiom previously meant someone comes back after being defeated in a battle. Now, this idiom implies someone returning after serious losses. In the story, Cao Cao is defeated in the Battle of the Red Cliffs, retreating to north China and feeling frustrated.

练习题 Reading exercises

一、选词填空。Choose proper words to fill in the blanks.

恩情　　阻挡　　忍心　　吓　　义气

1. 诸葛亮说要杀关羽只是为了（　　）他，并不是真的要杀他。
2. 曹操曾经收留过关羽。诸葛亮担心这份（　　）会让关羽放走曹操。

3. 曹操的谋士觉得关羽讲（　　　），曹操以前收留过他，他一定记着曹操的恩情。

二、根据故事，给下面的句子排序。Put the following sentences in order according to the story.

1. 为了抓住曹操，诸葛亮派关羽把守华容道，关羽立下了军令状。
2. 诸葛亮是故意让关羽放走曹操的，他不是真的想杀关羽。
3. 在逃跑时，曹操故意选择了不好走的小路华容道。当遇到关羽时，曹操用旧情感动关羽，让关羽放走了他。

答案：

一、1. 吓　2. 恩情　3. 义气

二、1-3-2

13. 赔了夫人又折兵[1]

主要人物和地点：
Main Characters and Places

曹仁（Cáo Rén）(168–223)：曹军大将军，曹操的堂弟。
Cao Ren (168–223): Grand General of Cao Cao's army and Cao Cao's cousin.

孙尚香（Sūn Shàngxiāng）：孙权的妹妹。她嫁给了刘备，也被称作孙夫人。
Sun Shangxiang: Sun Quan's younger sister. She married Liu Bei, and was also known as Madam Sun.

乔国老（Qiáo guólǎo）：东吴的重要人物。他有两个非常漂亮的女儿——大乔和小乔。大乔是孙策的夫人，小乔是周瑜的夫人。
Qiao Guolao: An important figure in the Kingdom of Wu. He had two beautiful daughters—Da Qiao and Xiao Qiao. Da Qiao was Sun Ce's wife and Xiao Qiao was Zhou Yu's wife.

吴国太（Wú guótài）：孙策、孙权、孙尚香的母亲。姓吴，被尊称为"吴国太"。
Wu Guotai: Mother of Sun Ce, Sun Quan and Sun Shangxiang. Her surname was Wu.

南郡（Nánjùn）：中国古代地名，今湖北省公安北部。
South Prefecture: A place in ancient China that was located in the north of present-day Gong'an County, Hubei Province.

赤壁之战后，诸葛亮派赵云攻打南郡，占领了荆州和周围其他一些城市，使刘备终于有了自己的地盘[1]。刘备在南，孙权在东，曹操在北，基本上形成了三国鼎立的局面。

不久，刘备的夫人甘夫人去世了。周瑜知道后，就向孙权建议，可以假装把孙权的妹妹孙尚香嫁给刘备，然后利用刘备来娶亲的这个机会抓住他，占领荆州。孙权同意了。

诸葛亮早就猜出了孙权和周瑜的计谋，于是定下了三条妙计。在刘备出发之前，诸葛亮交给赵云三个锦囊，让他一定在关键时刻再打开。

① 地盘 (dìpán)
n. territory
e.g. 魏蜀吴三国，曹操占领的地盘最大。

① 礼服 (lǐfú)
n. ceremonial robe or dress
e.g. 参加婚礼的人都穿着礼服。

刘备等人来到东吴，这时赵云打开了诸葛亮的第一个锦囊。

赵云看完了锦囊里诸葛亮写的计谋之后，命令大家穿上礼服①到东吴的市场上买婚礼用的东西和各种礼物，同时跟百姓们说，刘皇叔（刘备）和孙权的妹妹要结婚了。很快，东吴的百姓都知道了这件婚事。

乔国老是东吴非常重要的人物，他的女儿大乔是孙策的夫人，小乔是周瑜的夫人。赵云让刘备去拜见乔国老，想办法得到他的帮助。

乔国老见到刘备非常高兴。送走刘备后，乔国老就去见孙权的母亲吴国太，向她表示祝贺。

吴国太很吃惊，原来她不知道这件婚事，孙权和周瑜没跟她说过。于是吴国太派人叫来孙权和周瑜，问他们这是怎么一回事。

孙权说："这是我和周瑜的一个计谋，是为了把刘备骗来，然后把刘备留在东吴，不是真的要把妹妹嫁给刘备。"

吴国太十分生气，大骂孙权和周瑜。吴国太决定先见见刘备，再决定怎么办。孙权没有办法，只好答应母亲见刘备。

没想到，吴国太看见刘备相貌堂堂[1]，非常喜欢。

[1] 相貌堂堂 (xiàngmào-tángtáng) handsome; elegant in appearance e.g. 关羽相貌堂堂，一看就是位大英雄。

她满意地对乔国老说："刘备这个人不错，我同意把女儿嫁给他！"

孙权没办法，只好同意把妹妹嫁给刘备。接着，吴国太就为刘备和自己的女儿孙尚香举行了婚礼。

孙权为了继续控制刘备，让人给刘备和妹妹修了漂亮的宫殿，还天天给

刘备提供各种美食和唱歌跳舞的美女。刘备多年来都在打仗，突然过上了富贵的生活，果然忘了自己的事业，不想回荆州了。

赵云看刘备不想回荆州，十分担心，于是他又打开了诸葛亮的第二个锦囊。

赵云看过诸葛亮的计谋后，赶紧告诉刘备说："荆州情况危急，我们得马上回去！"其实这只是诸葛亮让刘备回荆州的计谋。

刘备一听非常担心，但是又不愿意离开孙夫人，心情很不好。

孙夫人看出刘备有心事①，就问他是怎么回事。刘备告诉孙夫人，荆州情

① 心事 (xīnshì)
n. something weighing on one's mind
e.g. 刘备因为有心事，吃不好，睡不好。

① 元旦 (Yuándàn)
n. New Year's Day
e.g. 他们决定在元旦这天举行婚礼。

② 祭祖 (jìzǔ)
v. worship one's ancestors
e.g. 清明节的时候，很多人都要祭祖。

况危急，他很担心。孙夫人听后，决定陪刘备回荆州。

刘备他们害怕孙权不同意，就假装对吴国太说，元旦[1]那天要去江边祭祖[2]。吴国太立刻就答应了他们。

到了元旦这天，刘备和孙夫人在赵云的保护下，朝着江边逃跑。孙权知道后，立刻派人去追他们。

刘备正往江边走，忽然在他们的前面冲出了一支人马。这时，后面的士兵也快要追上他们了。在这个危急时刻，赵云想起了诸葛亮的第三个锦囊。

赵云打开了第三个锦囊，把诸葛亮写的计谋给了刘备。刘备一看，原来诸葛亮让他请孙夫人帮忙。

刘备告诉孙夫人，东吴的士兵不让他们走。孙夫人听后十分生气，把孙权的士兵大骂了一顿。因为孙夫人是孙权的妹妹，士兵们不敢不听她的话，只能让刘备他们离开。

可是没过一会儿，周瑜就带着士兵追来了，刘备十分紧张。正在这危急的时候，刘备突然看见诸葛亮带着人和一条船来到江边，赶紧带着夫人上船逃走了。

周瑜看刘备上了船，赶紧下令让士兵坐船去追。诸葛亮命令停船上岸，周瑜也一路追上岸来。不料岸上有诸葛亮事先埋伏的士兵，双方打了起来，东吴的士兵死了不少人。周瑜逃到船上，十分后悔，这时却听见岸上刘备的士兵一起大声喊："赔了夫人又折兵[1]。"

周瑜一听，气得一下子晕了过去。本来周瑜打算把刘备留在东吴，然后杀了刘备。可是没有想到偷鸡不成蚀把米，反而中了诸葛亮的锦囊妙计[2]。

后来，周瑜又中了好几次诸葛亮的计谋，被气得生病了。周瑜临死前叹着气说："既生瑜，何生亮[3]！"

[1] 赔了夫人又折兵（péile fūrén yòu zhé bīng）giving one's enemy a wife and losing one's soldiers as well
这个习语用来表示某人想占便宜，反而遭受了双重损失。与这个习语意思相近的一句俗语是"偷鸡不成蚀把米"。这句话表示某人偷鸡不成功，反而损失了一把米。
The idiom means suffering a double loss while attempting to gain something. A similar saying is "stealing a chicken only to end up losing the rice", which means going for wool and coming back with shorn sheep.

[2] 锦囊妙计（jǐnnáng-miàojì）wise counsel
锦囊是封藏秘密文件的织锦口袋。在旧小说里，足智多谋的人把对付敌方的计谋写在纸条上，放在锦囊里。执行计谋的人在紧急时刻打开锦囊，阅读锦囊里面的妙计，处理危急的情况。现在"锦囊妙计"借指能及时解决紧急问题的办法。
In ancient times, *Jinnang*（锦囊）was a small bag made of brocade, in which a secret document or order was put and sewed inside. In ancient novels, there are plots that involve resourceful men making brocade bags for people. When the carrier is in danger, he opens the small bag, looks at the scheme, and follows the instructions to cope with an emergency. Now the idiom usually refers to instructions for dealing with emergencies or wise counsel.

[3] 既生瑜，何生亮（jì shēng Yú，hé shēng Liàng）Since (Zhou) Yu has come to this world, why should (Zhuge) Liang have to?
这是周瑜说过的非常有意思的一句话，意思是既然有周瑜在这个世界上，为什么还会有诸葛亮呢？周瑜和诸葛亮都具有非凡的才智。在与足智多谋的诸葛亮的竞争中，周瑜非常嫉妒诸葛亮的才能，并试图陷害诸葛亮。正是这种心态，导致周瑜英年早逝。
This is a famous remark made by Zhou Yu. In fact, both Zhou Yu and Zhuge Liang are very wise and talented. Faced with the competition of the resourceful Zhuge Liang, Zhou becomes so envious that he plots several times to murder him. This obsession leads to Zhou's death at an early age.

练习题 Reading exercises

一、选词填空。Choose proper words to fill in the blanks.

嫁　　地盘　　锦囊　　心事

1. 孙权假装把自己的妹妹（　　）给刘备。
2. 刘备成亲后，过上了富贵生活，不想回荆州了。赵云根据诸葛亮的第二个（　　），骗他说荆州情况紧急，请他马上回去。
3. 刘备占领了荆州，终于有了自己的（　　）。

二、判断正误。Read the following sentences and decide whether the statements are true or false.

1. 孙权邀请刘备去吴国，诸葛亮准备了三个锦囊给刘备。（　）
2. 刘备没有娶孙权的妹妹孙尚香。（　）
3. 刘备逃走的时候，赵云用完了三个锦囊，成功地等到诸葛亮来救他们回到荆州。（　）

答案：
一、1. 嫁　2. 锦囊　3. 地盘
二、1. 误　2. 误　3. 正

14. 大意失荆州[1]

主要人物和地点：
Main Characters and Places

关平（Guān Píng）：蜀国将军，关羽的儿子。
Guan Ping: General of the Kingdom of Shu and Guan Yu's son.

曹仁（Cáo Rén）(168–223)：曹军大将军，曹操的堂弟。
Cao Ren (168–223): Grand General of Cao Cao's army and Cao Cao's cousin.

华佗（Huà Tuó）(约 145–208)：东汉末年著名医学家。
Hua Tuo (c.145–208): A renowned doctor in the late Eastern Han Dynasty.

曹丕（Cáo Pī）(187–226)：魏国的开国皇帝，曹操的儿子。
Cao Pi (187–226): The founding emperor of the Kingdom of Wei and Cao Cao's son.

蜀地（Shǔdì）：中国古代地名，主要包括今四川省、贵州、云南和陕西省部分地区。
Shu: A vast region in ancient China that covered present-day Sichuan, Guizhou, and Yunnan provinces and part of Shaanxi Province.

汉中（Hànzhōng）：中国古代地名，主要包括今陕西省汉中地区。
Hanzhong: A place in ancient China that mainly included present-day Hanzhong City in Shaanxi Province.

麦城（Màichéng）：中国古代地名，今湖北省当阳市境内。
Maicheng: A place in ancient China that was located in the present-day Dangyang City, Hubei Province.

成都（Chéngdū）：三国时蜀国都城，今四川省成都市。

Chengdu: The capital of the Kingdom of Shu during the Three Kingdoms Period. It was present-day Chengdu City, Sichuan Province.

建业（Jiànyè）：中国古代地名，吴国都城，今江苏省南京市。

Jianye: A place in ancient China, which was the capital of the Kingdom of Wu. It was present-day Nanjing City, Jiangsu Province.

魏国（Wèiguó）：曹丕建立的政权，国号为“魏”。公元220年，曹丕逼汉献帝退位，在洛阳称帝，国号为“魏”，历史上也称魏国为“曹魏”。公元265年灭亡。

The Kingdom of Wei: The kingdom established by Cao Pi. In 220, Cao Pi forced Emperor Xiandi of the Eastern Han Dynasty to abdicate, and proclaimed himself emperor in Luoyang. The kingdom founded by him was known as Cao Wei. It came to an end in 265.

蜀国（Shǔguó）：刘备建立的政权，国号为“汉”。公元221年，刘备在成都称帝，历史上称为“蜀国”或“蜀汉”。公元263年灭亡。

The Kingdom of Shu: The kingdom established by Liu Bei. Its official name was Han. In 221, Liu Bei proclaimed himself emperor in Chengdu, and his kingdom was known as Shu or Shu Han. It came to an end in 263.

吴国（Wúguó）：孙权建立的政权，国号为“吴”。历史上也把“吴”称为“孙吴”或“东吴”。公元222年，孙权接受曹魏的领导，被封为吴王。公元229年，孙权在武昌

（今中国湖北省鄂州市境内）称帝，把建业（今中国江苏省南京市）定为都城。公元 280 年灭亡。

The Kingdom of Wu: The kingdom established by Sun Quan. It was also called Sun Wu or Eastern Wu. In 222, Sun Quan acknowledged the leadership of Cao Wei and was given the title the King of Wu. In 229, Sun Quan proclaimed himself emperor in Wuchang (present-day Ezhou City, Hubei Province), and later chose Jianye (present-day Nanjing City, Jiangsu Province) as the capital. The kingdom came to an end in 280.

公元213年，刘备进入蜀地，诸葛亮与将士们一起把守荆州。第二年，刘备在平定①蜀地时非常需要支援②，就让张飞、赵云、诸葛亮来蜀地，让关羽把守荆州。

公元219年，刘备在汉中称王③，诸葛亮担任④蜀国的丞相。关羽一心想帮助刘备统一北方，于是他让儿子关平把守荆州，自己带着军队去攻打北方的樊城。

樊城是曹魏的地盘，守城的将军是曹仁。关羽攻打樊城时，不但没打败曹仁，自己右臂⑤还中了一支毒箭⑥。关羽只好撤回军营。他的右臂肿⑦得很厉

① 平定 (píngdìng)
v. pacify
e.g. 那个国家的动乱很快被军队平定了。

② 支援 (zhīyuán)
v. assist; aid
e.g. 关羽的军队被包围了，没有人支援他们。

③ 称王 (chēng wáng)
proclaim oneself king
e.g. 三国鼎立，曹丕、刘备、孙权各自称王。

④ 担任 (dānrèn)
v. hold (a post)
e.g. 刘备让诸葛亮担任蜀国的丞相。

⑤ 右臂 (yòu bì)
n. right arm
e.g. 关羽的右臂肿得很厉害，将士们很着急。

⑥ 毒箭 (dú jiàn)
n. poisoned arrow
e.g. 他中了毒箭，伤得很重。

⑦ 肿 (zhǒng)
adj. swollen
e.g. 他的腿肿了，走不了路。

害，不能活动，原来毒箭上的毒已进入骨头里了。

关羽的儿子关平和将士们去找关羽，想把关羽带回荆州治疗。

关羽问："你们来找我有什么重要的事吗？"

关平回答："您右臂受伤，恐怕不适合打仗了。我们想，您不如就先回到荆州，等您的伤好了再说。"

关羽听了非常生气，说："我们兴复汉室马上就要成功了，怎么能因为我这点小伤而耽误了大事？你们竟然敢说这样的话！退下去！"关平等将领只好退下。

大家见关羽不答应退

兵[1]，他右臂的伤又没有好，只好到处找医生来为他治病。

一天，有一个人从东吴划着小船来到关羽的军营，士兵们把他带到关平那里。这个人自我介绍说："我叫华佗。关羽大将军是天下的英雄，我听说他现在中了毒箭，所以来给他治疗。"华佗是天下闻名的神医[2]，关平和将军们一听这个人是华佗，赶紧把他带到关羽面前。

华佗检查了关羽的伤，然后对关羽说："你的病是毒箭造成的，毒已经进入到骨头里了，如果不治，这条胳膊就保不住了。"

关羽说："那用什么办

① 退兵 (tuìbīng)
v. retreat
e.g. 曹操怕中了诸葛亮的埋伏，退兵了。

② 神医 (shényī)
n. miracle-working doctor
e.g. 关羽的伤好了，华佗被看作神医。

法可以治好？”

华佗为难地说：“现在从外面用药已经没有用了。我只有一种办法，但是会非常疼，不知道将军敢不敢尝试。”

关羽笑着说：“我死都不怕，还怕治病吗？有什么办法尽管说。”

华佗说：“要先找一个安静的地方，立一根柱子[1]，在柱子上钉个铁环[2]，把将军的右臂套在铁环里，用绳子系好，再把将军的脸蒙上，我用刀割[3]开将军右臂的皮肉[4]，露出骨头，然后刮[5]掉骨头上的毒并上药，最后缝[6]好伤口。”

关羽听完，笑着说：“不就是割开右臂上的皮肉

① 柱子 (zhùzi)
n. pillar
e.g. 大门口有两根柱子，柱子上挂着军旗。

② 铁环 (tiěhuán)
n. iron hoop
e.g. 士兵们找来柱子，钉上了铁环。

③ 割 (gē) v. cut
e.g. 他做菜时，不小心割破了手。

④ 皮肉 (píròu)
n. skin and flesh
e.g. 华佗用刀割开皮肉。

⑤ 刮 (guā) v. scrape
e.g. 华佗把骨头上的毒刮下来。

⑥ 缝 (féng)
v. sew; stitch
e.g. 妈妈把他的衣服缝好了。

① 下棋 (xià qí)
play chess
e.g. 华佗给关羽做手术，而关羽却在下棋。

嘛，直接割就是了！”说完命人摆上酒宴。

关羽一边跟别人下棋[1]一边伸出右臂给华佗。华佗对关羽说：“我要开始了，请将军不要害怕。”

关羽说：“你放心治，我不怕疼。”

华佗拿刀割开关羽的皮肉，看到里面的骨头

已经发黑了。华佗开始用刀刮骨头，发出“嘎吱嘎吱[1]”的声音。旁边的人有的不敢看，有的吓得变了脸色。可是关羽有说有笑，一边喝酒一边下棋，好像一点儿也不疼。

华佗刮完了骨头上的毒，给关羽上好药，缝好伤口。关羽大笑着站了起来，动了一下胳膊，说：“这只胳膊又能活动了，一点儿都不痛，先生真是一位神医啊！”

华佗十分佩服关羽，说：“我当了这么久的医生，从来没有见过将军您这样的人啊！”这就是著名的“刮骨疗毒[2]”的故事。

后来吴国在关羽攻打

① 嘎吱嘎吱 (gāzhī gāzhī) *onom.* creak
e.g. 大风刮得门嘎吱嘎吱响。

① 陷入 (xiànrù)
v. be caught in
e.g. 关羽的军队没有粮草，陷入了困境。

② 困境 (kùnjìng)
n. plight
e.g. 公司没有钱了，得想办法借钱脱离困境。

樊城时偷偷地占领了荆州，关羽失去了荆州。这就是“大意失荆州”的故事。荆州对蜀国非常重要。关羽的失败使蜀国陷入①困境②。

曹操派人支援东吴，又将关羽包围在麦城。关羽被困在麦城，没有粮草，支援他们的兵马又没有及时到达。最后，关羽中了孙权的埋伏，被孙权的士兵抓住了。这就是关羽“兵败麦城”[3]的故事。

孙权想让关羽投降，为东吴打仗，可是关羽坚决不投降。孙权就把关羽杀了。

在公元219年到公元229年的十年里，魏、蜀、吴三国发生了很多变化：

公元219年，关羽攻打樊城失败，蜀国失去荆州，陷入困境。孙权杀死了关羽。

公元220年，曹操去世。曹操的儿子曹丕逼迫汉献帝退位，自己当了皇帝，建立了魏国。

公元221年，刘备在成都当了皇帝，建立了蜀汉，也就是蜀国。

公元229年，孙权在建业当了皇帝，建立了东吴，也就是吴国。

曹丕、刘备、孙权分别建立了魏国、蜀国、吴国，正式形成了三国鼎立的局面。

[1] 大意失荆州（dàyì shī Jīngzhōu）losing Jingzhou due to negligence
三国时期，蜀国因为关羽的粗心大意而失去了荆州。荆州是三国时期非常重要的战略基地，关羽负责把守荆州。他觉得荆州很安全，就离开荆州去攻打曹军占领的樊城，这时孙权趁机占领了荆州。现在“大意失荆州”这个典故用来表示由于粗心大意而导致失败或造成损失。
In the story, when Guan Yu is attacking Fancheng in northwestern Hubei, the Kingdom of Wu makes a sneak attack on Jingzhou, an important strategic place during the Three Kingdoms Period. In the end, Guan loses Jingzhou because of his negligence. Now this idiom is used to describe someone who suffers a major setback due to carelessness.

[2] 刮骨疗毒（guāgǔ-liáodú）scraping the poison off the bone with a scalpel
这是《三国演义》中一个著名的故事。关羽的右手手臂被一支毒箭射伤，医术高明的华佗用刀将骨头上的毒刮去。在手术过程中，营帐中的每个人都万分恐慌，而关羽却一边喝酒一边与人下棋，而且脸上一直挂着微笑。后来用“刮骨疗毒”比喻从根本上解决问题。
A famous story in *Romance of the Three Kingdoms*. It tells of Guan Yu, who is shot in his right arm with a poisoned arrow. He invites the highly skilled doctor Hua Tuo to scrape the poison off his bone with a scalpel. Everyone in the tent is panic-stricken except for Guan, who drinks liquor, plays chess, and manages a smile during the operation. This idiom is later used to indicate that one should address the root causes of a problem.

[3] 兵败麦城（bīngbài-màichéng）defeat at Maicheng
关羽在北方发动攻打曹操的战役时，遭到了孙权的突然袭击。关羽的军队被迫撤退到麦城（位于湖北东南部）。最后，关羽中了埋伏，被孙权的士兵抓住。孙权让关羽投降，但是关羽拒绝了。孙权害怕关羽会对自己造成威胁，听从了手下的意见，最终决定处死关羽。后人以“败走麦城”比喻陷入绝境，形容经常成功的人也有失败的时候。
When Guan Yu was waging a campaign in the north against Cao Cao's stronghold, he suffered a sudden attack by the Kingdom of Wu. His army was forced to retreat to Maicheng in the southeast of Hubei Province. By then, Guan was ambushed and captured by Sun Quan. Sun asked Guan Yu to surrender, but Guan refused. On the advice of his followers and for fear that Guan might pose a threat to him, Sun eventually ordered Guan to be executed. Now the idiom often refers to a situation in which an able and successful person suffers a major setback.

练习题 Reading exercises

一、选词填空。Choose proper words to fill in the blanks.

1. 关羽右臂中了毒箭，华佗说得割开他的皮肉，刮掉毒，再（　　）好刀口。

A. 上　　B. 肿　　C. 埋　　D. 缝

2. 华佗刮骨疗毒治好了关羽，关羽说华佗是（　　）。

A. 神医　　B. 谋士　　C. 军师　　D. 医生

3. 关羽只想着攻打樊城，没想到吴国偷偷地（　　）了荆州，结果荆州失守了。

A. 攻打　　B. 占领　　C. 打击　　D. 看了

二、根据故事，给下面的句子排序。Put the following sentences in order according to the story.

1. 关羽被包围，没有粮草，支援的人马没有及时赶到，丢失了荆州。
2. 华佗治好了关羽右臂上的伤。
3. 关羽攻打樊城失败，被孙权杀了。

答案：

一、1. D　2. A　3. B

二、2-1-3

15. 刘备白帝城托孤 ①

主要人物和地点：

Main Characters and Places

刘禅（Liú Shàn）(207–271)：小名"阿斗"，刘备的儿子，蜀汉的第二个皇帝。中国历史上也称他为"后主"。

Liu Shan (207–271): Liu Bei's son and the second emperor of the Kingdom of Shu Han. His pet name was "Edou".

白帝城（Báidì Chéng）：中国古代地名，今重庆市奉节东白底山上。

Baidicheng: A place in ancient China that was located on Mount Baidi, to the east of present-day Fengjie County, Chongqing Municipality.

① 托孤 (tuō gū)
v. (of an emperor) entrust his young sons to the care of his ministers
e.g. 刘备去世前，托孤给诸葛亮。

刘备和张飞听说关羽被孙权杀了，都非常悲痛①。张飞因为关羽的死性格大变，经常打骂士兵。一次张飞喝醉了，结果被两个部下杀了。他们杀了张飞之后，跑到吴国投奔了孙权。

刘备知道了更加悲痛，决心要替关羽和张飞两位兄弟报仇②。诸葛亮劝刘备不要急着报仇，可是刘备没有听诸葛亮的建议。

刘备带领几十万大军去讨伐孙权，结果中了吴国火攻的计谋，他的七百里军营都被孙权烧了。后来刘备逃到白帝城，没过多久就生了重病。

到了第二年，刘备的

① 悲痛 (bēitòng)
adj. sorrowful
e.g. 刘备去世了，诸葛亮悲痛万分。

② 报仇 (bàochóu)
v. revenge
e.g. 刘备决心为兄弟报仇，结果被孙权打败了。

① 蜡烛 (làzhú)
n. candle
e.g. 停电了，大家只好点蜡烛看书。

病更严重了。一天晚上，窗外忽然吹来冷风，把屋里的蜡烛[1]吹得摇摇晃晃。刘备在梦中看见关羽和张飞站在烛光下，听到关羽说："大哥，过不了多久，我们兄弟三人就能在一起了。"刘备非常想念关羽和张飞，心情悲痛，大哭起来。

忽然，关羽和张飞不见了。刘备醒了，发现自己在做梦。

刘备说："唉，我活不了多久了！"他赶紧让人去成都请来诸葛亮等人，安排自己死后的事情。

诸葛亮赶来了。刘备对诸葛亮说："自从有了丞相的帮助，我的军队发展得很快。可是由于我没有听丞相的话，给蜀国造成这样大的失败，我非常后悔。现在，我的病好不了了！我的儿子能力太差，我就把国家大事交给你了！”刘备说完，流下了眼泪。

诸葛亮听刘备说得这么伤心，也哭了起来。刘备低声对诸葛亮说：“在你身边做事的马谡，你要注意观察他，不能太相信他说的话。”

接着，刘备写了遗嘱[1]，交给诸葛亮。刘备对大家说：“我想和大家一起打败曹丕，兴复汉室，可是我已经不行了。麻烦丞相把这份遗嘱交给太子刘禅，希望丞相今后能继续

① 遗嘱 (yízhǔ)
n. will; testament
e.g. 刘备写了遗嘱，让儿子做善良的人。

① 知遇之恩
(zhīyùzhī'ēn)
gratitude for someone who is appreciative of one's ability
e.g. 诸葛亮感激刘备的知遇之恩。

帮助他！”

诸葛亮跪在地上，说：“请陛下放心，我们一定尽全力帮助太子刘禅，以此来报答您的知遇之恩①。”

刘备又低声对诸葛亮说：“你的才能远远超过曹丕，一定能够当个好皇

帝！太子刘禅现在还小，如果他有当皇帝的才能，你就帮助他当皇帝；如果他确实没有才能，你就替他做蜀国的皇帝吧！”

诸葛亮看到刘备这么相信自己，跪在地上，说：“我不想当皇帝，我一定尽全力去帮助太子！”

刘备又对赵云说：“兄弟啊！希望你也能多多地帮助我的儿子！”赵云流着眼泪跪在地上，说：“我也一定会尽全力帮助太子！”

最后，刘备又对其他人说：“你们大家都要做好自己的事情！”刘备说完就闭上了眼睛。那年是公元223年，刘备死的时候六十三岁。

① 葬礼 (zànglǐ)
n. funeral
e.g. 诸葛亮在成都为刘备举行了葬礼。

② 长寿 (chángshòu)
adj. long-lived
e.g. 这是一位长寿的老人。

③ 遗憾 (yíhàn)
adj. regretful
e.g. 诸葛亮对失去荆州非常遗憾。

④ 贤明 (xiánmíng)
adj. wise and able
e.g. 刘备希望自己的儿子当一个贤明的皇帝。

⑤ 美德 (měidé)
n. virtue
e.g. 忠诚是一种美德。

诸葛亮回到成都，为刘备举行了葬礼①，在刘备的儿子们面前宣读了刘备的遗嘱。

刘备在遗嘱中写着："我听说，人活到五十岁就已经是长寿②了。我现在已经六十多岁了，没有什么遗憾③了！我放心不下的，就是你们兄弟几个啊！你们要记住：勿以恶小而为之，勿以善小而不为[1]。只有你贤明④并且有美德⑤，人们才愿意服从你啊！你们要多向丞相学习做人和做事的道理，对他要像对自己的父亲一样，一定要尊重他！你们一定要努力成为优秀的人！"

读完遗嘱，诸葛亮对大

家说："国不可一日无君[2]。"于是，诸葛亮帮助太子刘禅做了蜀国的皇帝。

诸葛亮为了完成刘备兴复汉室的理想，尽全力帮助刘禅。朝廷中大大小小的事情都由诸葛亮管理，蜀国又慢慢地强盛①起来了。

① 强盛 (qiángshèng) *adj.* powerful and prosperous
e.g. 刘备想使蜀国强盛起来，但他的理想没有实现。

[1] 勿以恶小而为之，勿以善小而不为（wù yǐ è xiǎo ér wéi zhī, wù yǐ shàn xiǎo ér bù wéi）Don't engage in evil even if it's minor; don't fail to do good even if it's trivial.
不要因为坏事很小就去做，也不要因为好事很小就不做。刘备在遗嘱中给自己的儿子们写了这句话，是希望他的儿子们做一个聪明睿智、贤良正直的人。
This is an old Chinese saying which tells people they should not engage in bad actions just because they are trivial and that they should not refrain from performing a virtuous act because it is minor. In his will, Liu Bei says this to his sons, hoping they will become wise and virtuous.

[2] 国不可一日无君（guó bù kě yí rì wú jūn）a country cannot endure a day without an emperor
一个国家不可以一天没有皇帝。如果一个国家的皇帝去世，而又没有继承人，那这个国家就会陷入混乱。
This was a common saying in ancient China. If the emperor of a country died without an heir, the country would be thrown into chaos.

练习题 Reading exercises

一、选词填空。Choose proper words to fill in the blanks.

打败　　痛苦　　安排　　理想

1. 刘备因为张飞和关羽的死，决定讨伐孙权，结果中了计，被孙权（　　）了。
2. 刘备知道自己快死了，所以叫来诸葛亮（　　）自己死后的事情。
3. 诸葛亮为了完成刘备兴复汉室的（　　），尽全力帮助刘禅。

二、根据故事，给下面的句子排序。Put the following sentences in order according to the story.

1. 诸葛亮尽全力帮助新皇帝刘禅，蜀国逐渐强盛起来。
2. 刘备叫来诸葛亮，让他照顾好自己的儿子并安排好蜀国的事情，然后就去世了。
3. 刘备的兄弟关羽和张飞被杀了，他去攻打孙权失败，得了重病。

答案：

一、1. 打败　2. 安排　3. 理想

二、3-2-1

16. 诸葛亮安居[1]平五路

主要人物和地点：
Main Characters and Places

司马懿（Sīmǎ Yì）(179–251)：曹魏权臣，西晋的奠基人。他先在曹操手下担任官职，后为曹丕的大将军。他足智多谋，多次率领军队与诸葛亮对抗。

Sima Yi (179–251): As a powerful minister of the Kingdom of Wei, he laid the foundation for the Western Jin Dynasty. He first served as an official under Cao Cao, and then became the Grand General of Cao Pi. As a resourceful man, he led his army against Zhuge Liang several times.

孟获（Mèng Huò）：蜀国南方的少数民族首领。他率领军队反对蜀国，被诸葛亮抓住七次，放了七次。最后他对诸葛亮心服口服，成为蜀国的官员，管辖南方各地少数民族。

Meng Huo: An ethnic minority chief in the south of the Kingdom of Shu. He led his army against Shu, but was captured and released by Zhuge Liang seven times. In the end, he conceded his defeat and pledged his loyalty to Shu. He then served as an official of Shu and governed the ethnic minorities in the south of the Kingdom of Shu.

轲比能（Kēbǐ Néng）(?–235)：东汉末年鲜卑族的首领。

Kebi Neng (?–235): The chief of the Xianbei people in the late Eastern Han Dynasty.

① 安居 (ānjū)
v. live in peace and comfort
e.g. 诸葛亮出山之前，安居在山里。

孟达（Mèng Dá）（?–228）：三国时期名将。先为蜀将，后投奔曹魏。

Meng Da (?–228): A famous general of the Three Kingdoms Period. He first served as a general of Shu and then defected to the Kingdom of Wei.

曹真（Cáo Zhēn）（?–231）：曹魏的大将军。

Cao Zhen (?–231): The Grand General of the Kingdom of Wei.

马超（Mǎ Chāo）（176–222）：汉朝名将。曹操曾多次请他为曹军打仗，但都被拒绝。最后他投降了刘备。

Ma Chao (176–222): A famous general of the Han Dynasty. Cao Cao asked him to fight for his army several times, but Ma Chao refused. Eventually, he surrendered to Liu Bei.

魏延（Wèi Yán）（?–234）：蜀汉著名将领。

Wei Yan (?–234): A famous general of the Kingdom of Shu.

李严（Lǐ Yán）（?–234）：蜀汉重要的大臣。

Li Yan (?–234): An important minister of the Kingdom of Shu.

关兴（Guān Xīng）：蜀国将军，关羽的儿子。

Guan Xing: A general of the Kingdom of Shu, and son of Guan Yu.

张苞（Zhāng Bāo）：蜀国将军，张飞的儿子。

Zhang Bao: A general of the Kingdom of Shu, and son of Zhang Fei.

邓芝（Dèng Zhī）（178–251）：蜀国大臣。他奉命去吴国说服孙权联合蜀国共同对抗魏国。

Deng Zhi (178–251): A minister of the Kingdom of Shu. He

was ordered to go to the Kingdom of Wu where he persuaded Sun Quan to join forces with the Kingdom of Shu against the Kingdom of Wei.

西平关（Xīpíng Guān）：《三国演义》中的地名。
Xiping Pass: A place mentioned in *Romance of the Three Kingdoms*.

涪城（Fúchéng）：中国古代地名，今四川省绵阳市。
Fucheng: A place in ancient China that was located in present-day Mianyang City, Sichuan Province.

阳平关（Yángpíng Guān）：中国古代地名，今陕西勉县境内。阳平关连接着四川、甘肃、陕西等重要地方，在三国时期是重要的军事关卡。
Yangping Pass: A place in ancient China located in present-day Mianxian County, Shaanxi Province, which connects important places in Sichuan, Gansu, and Shaanxi provinces. It was a key military pass during the Three Kingdoms Period.

西川（Xīchuān）：今四川成都一带。
Xichuan: A place that was located near present-day Chengdu City, Sichuan Province.

① 路 (lù) *n.* route
e.g. 诸葛亮用计谋击退了司马懿的五路军。

魏国皇帝曹丕听说刘备死了，非常高兴，准备去攻打蜀国。

魏国大将军司马懿对曹丕说："我们应该用五路大军，从东西南北四个方向攻打蜀国。首先要联合鲜卑的国王轲比能，让他带上十万兵马去攻打西平关，这是第一路[1]军。再给南蛮王孟获一些钱财，让他带上兵马十万，攻打蜀国南部的益州等地，这是第二路军。联合东吴，让孙权带上十万兵马攻打涪城，这是第三路军。让孟达带上十万兵马从西边攻打汉中，这是第四路军。命令曹真带上十万兵马，从阳平关出去攻打西川，这是第五路军。五路大军一共五十万兵马，同时进攻蜀国，一定会让诸葛亮没有办法阻挡！”曹丕听了非常高兴，立刻下令按照司马懿的计划行动。

蜀国人听说魏国派了五路大军来攻打他们，非常害怕。诸葛亮却整天待在家

① 观赏 (guānshǎng)
v. view and enjoy
e.g. 曹操请刘备去观赏树上的青梅。

② 击退 (jītuì)
v. beat back; repel
e.g. 他们用箭击退了敌人。

③ 能言善辩 (néngyán-shànbiàn)
be eloquent
e.g. 诸葛亮能言善辩，使东吴的谋士们心服口服。

④ 谈判 (tánpàn)
v. negotiate
e.g. 蜀国派谋士去和东吴谈判。

里不出门。刘禅非常着急，决定亲自去找诸葛亮。

刘禅来到诸葛亮的相府，看见诸葛亮在花园里静静地观赏①鱼。刘禅走近诸葛亮，对他说："丞相，魏国派了五路大军攻打我们，可是您竟然在这里赏鱼！"

诸葛亮笑着说："五十万大军马上就快到蜀国了，我怎么会不知道呢？我已经把其中四路军队给击退②了。孙权这一路兵，我已经想好了击退他们的办法，不过还需要一个能言善辩③的人去跟吴国的孙权谈判④。"

刘禅听了以后非常高兴，问诸葛亮："您是怎么击退他们的？"

诸葛亮回答说："兵法[①]最奇妙[②]的地方就在于出其不意[1]。我让马超安排好埋伏，把守西平关，对付轲比能的第一路军。我派魏延等待孟获的第二路军，一会儿从大路的右边跑到左边，一会儿从大路的左边跑到右边。孟获看见路上尘土飞扬，肯定会以为我们兵马多，不敢继续往前走。对于第三路军的孟达，我知道他和我国的李严以前是好朋友，所以我以李严的名义[③]给他写了一封信，让他不要攻打蜀国。第四路军曹真要来攻打阳平关，我派赵云去把守。阳平关地势险要，很难攻打，我们不用出兵迎

① 兵法 (bīngfǎ)
n. art of war
e.g. 懂兵法的将军才会打仗。

② 奇妙 (qímiào)
adj. wonderful; marvelous
e.g. 诸葛亮总能想出奇妙的计谋。

③ 名义 (míngyì)
n. name
e.g. 曹操以皇帝的名义控制各地诸侯。

① 以防万一
(yǐfáng-wànyī)
be prepared for the emergency
e.g. 开车时要小心，以防万一。

② 慌张
(huāngzhāng)
adj. flustered; frantic
e.g. 刘禅听了诸葛亮的计谋后，就不慌张了。

战。曹真看见我们不出兵，他就会走的。另外，我还让关兴、张苞带着士兵把守在一些重要地方，互相支援，以防万一①。因为我派出去的这几路军都没有从成都经过，所以没有被任何人发现。至于吴国，因为前段时间曹丕攻打了吴国，所以孙权不会愿意听他的。现在我们需要派一个能言善辩的人去东吴，把情况跟孙权说清楚，让孙权退兵。我正在考虑派谁去呢。”

刘禅听后恍然大悟，“丞相真是知己知彼[2]，对症下药[3]啊！”

诸葛亮送刘禅出丞相府时，看见站在外面的大臣们都很慌张②，只有大臣邓芝面带微笑。诸葛亮派人把邓芝请到家里聊天。原来邓芝也认为蜀国应该与吴国联盟，共同击退魏国。于是，诸葛亮就派邓芝去吴国把情况告诉孙权。

东吴的孙权已经听说诸葛亮击退了魏国的四路大军。邓芝见到孙权，问："您是想和蜀国联合，还是想跟魏国联盟呢？"

孙权说："其实我想和蜀国联合，可是……"

邓芝对孙权说："您是一位人才，诸葛亮丞相也是一位人才。您要攻打蜀国，山路不好走；蜀国要攻打吴国，长江又不容易通过。如果两国联盟，可以互相帮助，兼并[1]天下，

[1] 兼并 (jiānbìng) v. annex; amalgamate e.g. 这家大公司兼并了很多小公司。

① 和睦 (hémù)
adj. harmonious
e.g. 这里的邻居和睦相处，关系很好

也可以和睦[1]相处，各自发展。如果您现在服从魏国，魏国一定不会让您当皇帝的。但如果您不服从魏国，魏国就一定会来攻打吴国。到时候，要是蜀国也来攻打您，那吴国可就危险了！”

孙权对邓芝说：“先生说的话和我想的一样。我决定和蜀国联合，请先生回去告诉诸葛丞相吧！”于是吴国和蜀国两国联合了。这样一来，孙权的第五路军也退了。

这就是诸葛亮运筹帷幄[4]，用才智击退魏国五路大军的故事！

[1] 出其不意（chūqíbúyì）taking someone by surprise
在对方没有想到或没有准备的时候就开始行动。在《三国演义》中，诸葛亮曾经说过：战略中的关键就是要出乎敌人的意料。
It means taking actions before others realize them or are prepared for them. In *Romance of the Three Kingdoms*, Zhuge Liang says that the key to the art of war is going against the enemy's expectations.

[2] 知己知彼（zhījǐ-zhībǐ）know yourself and the enemy
这个短语出自春秋时期军事家孙武的《孙子兵法·谋略》中的“知己知彼，百战不殆”。孙武提出，完全了解敌人与自己的情况至关重要，只有这样，打起仗来才能百战百胜。在这个故事中，诸葛亮认真研究五路军队和司马懿，然后提出了具体的战略，击败了魏国五路军队。
This phrase is from a military strategy outlined in the “Attack by Stratagem” section of Sun Tzu's work *The Art of War*, which was produced during the Spring and Autumn Period (770-476 BC). The strategist Sun Wu advocates the idea that it is vital to fully know your enemy and yourself. In this way you can win a hundred battles without suffering a single defeat. In the story, Zhuge Liang carefully studies Sima Yi and the the enemy troops on five routes first, and then implements specific strategies to defeat them.

[3] 对症下药（duìzhèng-xiàyào）prescribing the right remedy for an illness
这个成语的最初意思是指医生能针对疾病开出正确的处方，现在通常表示运用不同的方法解决不同的问题。
The idiom originally meant that a doctor prescribes the right remedy for an illness. Now it often refers to using appropriate methods to solve specific problems.

[4] 运筹帷幄（yùnchóu-wéiwò）devising strategies within a command tent
在军帐中制定作战策略。在这个故事中，司马懿计划用非常强大的五路军队从不同方向进攻蜀国，蜀国面临着巨大的危机。这时，诸葛亮却只是整天待在家中筹划反击司马懿的计策。现在这个成语表示制定策略，做出决定。
In the story, Sima Yi devises a scheme to launch an attack against the Kingdom of Shu with powerful troops on five routes. At this juncture, Zhuge Liang simply stays at home and devises a scheme to fight Sima Yi. The idiom now refers to devising strategies and making decisions.

练习题 Reading exercises

一、选择填空 Choose proper words to fill in the blanks.

1. 魏国派了五路大军来攻打蜀国，刘禅看到诸葛亮在家中（　　）鱼，非常着急。

A. 安居　　B. 观赏

C. 安静　　D. 动作

2. 刘禅听了诸葛亮的计划之后，（　　）。

A. 以防万一　　B. 运筹帷幄

C. 恍然大悟　　D. 能言善辩

3. 邓芝被派去和孙权谈判，他劝吴国和蜀国（　　）相处。

A. 交战　　B. 联合

C. 联盟　　D. 和睦

二、判断正误。Read the following sentences and decide whether the statements are true or false.

1. 魏国派了一路军队来攻打蜀国。（　）
2. 诸葛亮亲自去吴国劝孙权和蜀国联盟。（　）
3. 诸葛亮运用智慧击退了魏国进攻蜀国的五路大军。（　）

答案：

一、1. B　2. C　3. D

二、1. 误　2. 误　3. 正

17. 七擒[1]孟获

主要人物和地点：
Main Characters and Places

马谡（Mǎ Sù）（190–228）：蜀国大臣。最初跟随刘备入蜀地，担任官职。他喜欢谈论兵法，受到诸葛亮的重视。诸葛亮攻打魏国时，马谡担任将军，失守了街亭，后来被诸葛亮处以死罪。

Ma Su (190–228): A minister of the Kingdom of Shu. He followed Liu Bei into Shu, and served as an official there. He liked to talk about the art of war and was valued by Zhuge Liang. When Zhuge attacked the Kingdom of Wei, Ma served as a general. He was held responsible for the loss of Jieting, and was thus put to death by Zhuge Liang.

王平（Wáng Píng）(?–248)：蜀国后期重要的将军。

Wang Ping (?–248): An important general in the later period of the Kingdom of Shu.

关索（Guān Suǒ）：蜀国将军，关羽的儿子。

Guan Suo: A general of the Kingdom of Shu and Guan Yu's son.

马岱（Mǎ Dài）：蜀国著名将领，马超的堂弟。

Ma Dai: A famous general of the Kingdom of Shu and Ma Chao's cousin.

[1] 擒 (qín)
v. capture
e.g. 诸葛亮用计谋擒住了孟获。

孟优（Mèng Yōu）：孟获的弟弟。
Meng You: Meng Huo's younger brother.

木鹿大王（MùLù DàiWang）：孟获的朋友。
King Mu Lu: Meng Huo's friend.

杨锋（Yáng Fēng）：孟获的部下。
Yang Feng: Meng Huo's subordinate.

兀突骨（Wūtū Gǔ）：孟获的朋友。
Wutu Gu: Meng Huo's friend.

银坑山（Yínkēng Shān）：《三国演义》中的地名，孟获的老家。
Silver Pit Mountain: A place mentioned in *Romance of the Three Kingdoms*, where Meng Huo lived.

公元225年，蜀国南边的少数民族首领孟获叛乱[1]。蜀国这几年经过发展生产，粮食富足，人心安定[2]，军队也比以前强大了。诸葛亮考虑到魏国和吴国刚刚打过仗，目前不会攻打蜀国，决定亲自带领五十万大军平定南边的叛乱。

诸葛亮和马谡商量平定叛乱的事情。马谡认为，只有让南边的少数民族心服口服，才能彻底平定叛乱。诸葛亮心想：马谡很有才智，看得远，想得周到。于是诸葛亮让马谡跟着自己去平定叛乱。

孟获和诸葛亮第一次交战，孟获的将领不是被

① 叛乱 (pànluàn)
v. revolt
e.g. 朝廷腐败，军阀叛乱，百姓们生活在战乱之中。

② 安定 (āndìng)
adj. stable; settled
e.g. 很长时间没有战乱了，百姓们生活安定。

① 活捉 (huózhuō)
v. capture alive
e.g. 孟获被活捉了七次。

② 服 (fú)
v. be convinced
e.g. 孟获被活捉了六次，还是不服诸葛亮。

③ 山谷 (shāngǔ)
n. canyon; gorge
e.g. 诸葛亮在山谷里埋伏了军队。

活捉[①]，就是被杀死。诸葛亮放了两位孟获的将领，让他们回去告诉孟获，自己还会跟他打仗。

诸葛亮猜到孟获一定不服[②]，还会再来。果然，孟获带着兵又来了。诸葛亮让王平、关索先把孟获引进山谷[③]，然后抓住了孟获。

诸葛亮问孟获："以前皇帝对你那么好，你不记

得皇帝的恩情了吗？你为什么要叛乱？我现在活捉了你，你服不服我们？”

孟获说：“你们占领了我的地盘，我不服！”

诸葛亮说：“既然你不服，那我就再放你回去，可是如果我再一次活捉了你，你就心服口服了吧！”诸葛亮说完就把孟获放了。这是诸葛亮第一次活捉孟获。

将士们不理解诸葛亮为什么要放走孟获。诸葛亮解释说：“我要抓孟获很容易，但是只有让他心服口服，才能彻底平定南方。”

孟获回到军营后，又派他的将领带兵来跟蜀军交战。蜀军大将马岱对着孟获的将领大骂："诸葛丞相上次活捉了你的首领孟获，放他回去，他竟然忘恩负义[1]，还敢来，还不快走！"

孟获的将领很惭愧地回去了。孟获知道后，打了这个将领一百军棍。这个将领非常生气。他看到孟获喝醉了，就活捉了孟获，把孟获献给了诸葛亮。

诸葛亮问孟获："这次你服不服？"

孟获说："这次是我的部下背叛了我，不是你们抓住的。我还是不服。"

诸葛亮又一次放了孟获。这是诸葛亮第二次擒获孟获。

孟获回去后又想到一

个计谋。他命令他的弟弟孟优带着礼物和一群士兵去蜀军的军营，假装把礼物献给诸葛亮，实际上想打败蜀军。诸葛亮立刻就识破了他的计谋，给了他们很多好酒喝，但是在酒中放了药，结果孟优和士兵们都醉倒了。

孟获以为诸葛亮已经上当，于是带领士兵攻打蜀军军营。可是他刚进入蜀军军营，就又一次被诸葛亮活捉了。

诸葛亮笑着说："我已经第三次擒获你了，你服不服？"

孟获说："这次是因为我弟弟上了你的当，不是我没有能力。如果你愿意把我和弟弟一起放了，要是我再次被你抓住，我一定心服口服。”

诸葛亮于是放了孟获和他的弟弟孟优，这是诸葛亮第三次擒获孟获。

孟获回去后，穿上用犀牛皮①做的衣服，骑着牛，带领着士兵又来攻打蜀军。孟获的士兵光着身子，披散②着头发，像野人③一样又冲向蜀军军营。诸葛亮这次却命令蜀军不许出去迎战。孟获的士兵看见蜀军不出战，也没有了士气。

就在这时，诸葛亮突然派士兵攻打孟获，孟获的士兵没有准备，四处逃跑。孟获又一次被诸葛亮

① 犀牛皮 (xīniúpí)
n. rhino hide
e.g. 孟获的士兵穿着犀牛皮打仗，被蜀军打败了。

② 披散 (pīsǎn)
v. (of hair) hang down loosely
e.g. 孟获的士兵打仗时披散着头发。

③ 野人 (yěrén)
n. wild man; savage
e.g. 孟获让士兵打扮成野人攻击蜀军。

活捉了。

诸葛亮对孟获说："你又一次被我擒获了，你服不服？"

孟获说："如果你再次把我擒获，我一定把钱财都献给蜀国，再也不叛乱了。"于是诸葛亮又一次放了孟获。

孟获跑到他的部下杨锋那里。杨锋感谢诸葛亮以前的恩情，就抓住孟获送给了诸葛亮。

诸葛亮问孟获："这一次你该服了吧？"

孟获说："这次是我的部下背叛我，我还是不能服你！我老家在银坑山，你要是能在那里擒获我，我子子孙孙[1]都会服你的。"

① 子子孙孙 (zǐzǐsūnsūn) descendants; offspring e.g. 他希望子子孙孙都能安居乐业。

① 野兽 (yěshòu)
n. wild animal; beast
e.g. 孟获让野兽冲向蜀军，想吓退蜀军。

② 鞭炮 (biānpào)
n. firecracker
e.g. 诸葛亮让士兵点上鞭炮，把野兽吓跑了。

③ 羽扇 (yǔshàn)
n. feather fan
e.g. 诸葛亮手里的羽扇象征着智慧。

诸葛亮再次放了孟获，这是诸葛亮第五次擒获孟获。

孟获回去后，找到木鹿大王帮忙。木鹿大王有一种很特别的才能，他可以指挥老虎、狼、蛇等各种野兽①。孟获他们和蜀军交战时，木鹿大王一下命令，老虎、狼、蛇立刻开始攻击蜀军。蜀军赶紧后退，回到军营。当晚，诸葛亮命令士兵把20辆车装饰成野兽的样子，还在车内放了鞭炮②。

第二天，木鹿大王指挥老虎、狼、蛇等野兽再次冲向蜀军。诸葛亮摇着羽扇③，让士兵点燃车上的鞭炮，推车冲向木鹿大王的野兽。这些野兽吓得往回跑，踩[1]死了孟获的很多士兵。蜀军在孟获的老家银坑山又一次抓住了他。

诸葛亮说："你说我如果能在你的老家银坑山把你活捉你就心服，现在，你服不服？"

孟获说："这次是野兽不听指挥，不是我的错，我不服！"

诸葛亮又一次放了孟获。这是诸葛亮第六次活捉孟获。

孟获回去后去找兀突骨。兀突骨拥有一支藤甲兵[2]，藤甲兵穿上藤甲，刀和枪都刺不进去。但是藤甲十分怕火烧，诸葛亮就用火攻把藤甲兵都烧死了。

① 踩 (cǎi)
v. step on; trample
e.g. 请不要踩公园里的草坪。

① 智慧 (zhìhuì)
n. wisdom
e.g. 诸葛亮用智慧使孟获心服口服。

孟获又一次被活捉。

这次，诸葛亮没有问孟获服不服，反而故意放了孟获。孟获却哭着说："我服了，我永远不背叛蜀国了。"

这就是诸葛亮用智慧①七次擒获孟获的故事，也叫"七擒七纵[3]"。后来，诸葛亮让孟获做了蜀国的官，管理南方的少数民族。孟获再也没有叛乱过。

诸葛亮平定了南方以后，带领蜀军回到成都，准备攻打魏国，兴复汉室，统一天下。

[1] 忘恩负义（wàng'ēn-fùyì）forgetting the kindness of others and turning their back upon them
在这个故事中，诸葛亮释放了南方少数民族首领孟获，可是孟获又反过来袭击诸葛亮。现在，这个成语表示某人忘记别人的恩情，反而做出对不起别人的事。
In the story, Zhuge Liang releases Meng Huo, ethnic minority chief in the south, but afterward Meng returns to attack Zhuge's army. This term is now used to describe someone who has forgotten another's kindness and instead acts in a way that is unfair to them.

[2] 藤甲兵（téngjiǎbīng）vine armor troops
孟获的朋友兀突骨的军队。这支军队穿着用藤甲编成的衣服，据说刀枪不入，但缺点是怕火烧。
An army led by Meng Huo's friend Wutu Gu. It was said that the soldiers who wore helmets and armor made of vine feared neither swords nor spears. However, they did fear fire attacks.

[3] 七擒七纵（qīqín-qízòng）capture and release seven times
三国时期，诸葛亮在南方作战的时候，七次抓住孟获又七次放了他。最终，诸葛亮的足智多谋征服了孟获，使孟获归顺蜀国。现在，这个成语用来描述某人用计谋让对方心服口服。
During the Three Kingdoms Period, Zhuge Liang went to the south to suppress the rebels, where he captured their chief Meng Huo seven times. In an attempt to gain his support, Zhuge released Meng seven times. Finally, Zhuge conquered Meng with his resourcefulness, and Meng submitted to the Kingdom of Shu. Now this idiom is used to describe someone conspiring to cause their opponent to submit.

练习题 Reading exercises

一、选择填空 Choose proper words to fill in the blanks.

1. 蜀国经过几年的发展，粮食富足，人心（　　）。

A. 安全　　B. 安静

C. 平安　　D. 安定

2. 第二次擒获孟获时，他认为这是因为部下的（　　）才被诸葛亮抓住的。

A. 不服　　B. 背叛

C. 错误　　D. 失败

3. 第四次攻打蜀国时，孟获的士兵穿得像野人一样，但是蜀国一直不出兵，后来他们没有了（　　）。

A. 时间　　B. 安排

C. 士气　　D. 计划

二、根据故事，给下面的句子排序。Put the following sentences in order according to the story.

1. 孟获最终心服口服，不再背叛蜀国。
2. 诸葛亮用智慧七次活捉了孟获。
3. 孟获是南边少数民族的首领，他背叛了蜀国，同蜀军多次交战。

答案：

一、1.D　2.B　3.C

二、3-2-1

18. 失街亭

主要人物和地点：
Main Characters and Places

曹睿（Cáo Ruì）(204–239)：曹丕的儿子，魏国第二个皇帝，被称为“魏文帝”。

Cao Rui (204–239): Cao Pi's son and the second emperor of the Kingdom of Wei. He was called Emperor Wendi of Wei.

司马昭（Sīmǎ Zhāo）(211–265)：司马懿的儿子，魏国大将军。

Sima Zhao (211–265): Sima Yi's son and Grand General of the Kingdom of Wei.

高翔（Gāo Xiáng）：蜀国著名将领。

Gao Xiang: A famous general of the Kingdom of Shu.

街亭（Jiētíng）：中国古代地名，今甘肃天水秦安县境内，是重要的军事城镇。

Jieting: A place in ancient China that was located in present-day Qin'an County, Tianshui City, Gansu Province and was an important military town.

天水（Tiānshuǐ）：中国古代地名，今甘肃省天水市西北。

Tianshui: A place in ancient China that was located in the north-west of present-day Tianshui City, Gansu Province.

安定（Āndìng）：中国古代地名，今甘肃省泾川北，是通往长安的交通要道。

Anding: An important gateway to Chang'an that was located in the north of present-day Jingchuan County, Gansu Province.

金城（Jīnchéng）：中国古代地名，今中国甘肃省兰州市。

Jincheng: A place in ancient China that is present-day Lanzhou City, Gansu Province.

陇西（Lǒngxī）：中国古代地名，今甘肃省陇西县。
Longxi: A place in ancient China that is present-day Longxi County, Gansu Province.

公元226年，魏国皇帝曹丕去世，曹丕的儿子曹睿当了皇帝。曹睿让司马懿担任大将军，掌管军队。诸葛亮用"反间计[1]"让曹睿怀疑司马懿，曹睿中了诸葛亮的计谋，不让司马懿担任大将军了。

公元228年，诸葛亮借这个机会，准备讨伐魏国。这个时期，诸葛亮写了著名的《出师表》[2]。在诸葛亮的安排下，蜀军占领了很多地方，打了很多胜仗①。魏国皇帝曹睿赶紧又找来司马懿，让他担任大将军，命令他带领魏军迎战蜀军。

街亭位于一条很窄②的山地上，是通向关中、天

① 胜仗 (shèngzhàng)
n. victorious battle
e.g. 魏国军队在街亭打了胜仗。

② 窄 (zhǎi)
adj. narrow
e.g. 山谷的地势险要，入口很窄。

水、安定、金城的路口，地势险要。街亭南边靠着山，北面是一条河，是一个非常重要的地方。蜀军只要把守住街亭，就可以阻挡魏军进入陇西；如果失去街亭，蜀军运输粮草的路就断了，也就不能继续攻打魏国了。

司马懿出发前对部下说：“我们首先要占领街亭这个地方。如果我们占领了街亭，蜀军就没有办法运输粮草了。如果诸葛亮不撤退，不出一个月蜀军就会被饿死；如果诸葛亮撤退，我们就从小路埋伏，也一定会打个大胜仗。”大家都十分佩服司马懿的才智。

诸葛亮知道司马懿一定会去攻打街亭，决定增加把守街亭的军队。青年将领马谡要求承担这项重要的任务。

诸葛亮对马谡说：“街亭地方虽小，关系却十分重大。如果我们蜀军失去了街亭，就会失败。街亭这个地方没有城墙，没有好的地势，把守是很难的。”

马谡认为自己熟悉兵法，坚持要去，还立下了军令状，说他如果丢失了街亭，愿意接受军法处置。

诸葛亮说：“司马懿非常有才智，你一定要小心。”诸葛亮想到在平定南方的时候马谡表现得很有

① 副手 (fùshǒu)
n. assistant
e.g. 马谡非常骄傲，不听副手的劝告。

② 扎营 (zhāyíng)
v. encamp
e.g. 马谡没有在路口扎营，结果被打败了。

能力，心想，马谡也算是足智多谋，这次就给马谡一次锻炼的机会吧！就这样，诸葛亮将把守街亭的重要任务交给了马谡。

但是，诸葛亮还是很担心马谡，怕他把守不住街亭，就派了大将王平做马谡的副手[1]。在出发之前，诸葛亮还对他们说，要在重要的路口扎营[2]，千万不要在山上扎营。说完，马谡和王平就离开了。诸葛亮又派高翔和魏延各带领一万人在街亭附近扎营，随时准备支援街亭。安排完后，诸葛亮认为街亭已经十分安全了，就准备攻打魏国的都城长安。

马谡、王平二人到街

亭后，马谡认为街亭这个小地方司马懿是不会来的，于是命令士兵在山上扎营。王平却认为应当在路口扎营。

马谡说："兵书上说，'凭高视下，势如劈竹'[3]。我们应该在山上扎营。魏军来的时候，我们从山上冲下去，可以打败魏军。"

王平劝马谡说："如果我们在山上扎营，一旦被魏军包围，山上没有水，士兵喝不上水，不用魏军进攻，自己就先乱了。"

马谡却说："孙子说过，'置之死地而后生'[4]。如果我们的将士喝不到水，难道不会拼命抵抗吗？"

马谡不听王平的建议，

① 大惊失色
(dàjīng-shīsè)
be fluttered
e.g. 曹操看到关羽从山上冲下来，大惊失色。

王平没有办法，只好自己带领兵马在山下扎营，如果魏军来了，两边可以互相支援。王平连夜派人把马谡在山上扎营的消息告诉了诸葛亮，诸葛亮听了大惊失色[1]。

司马懿带领魏军人马赶到街亭，发现街亭有士兵把守。司马懿叹气说："诸葛亮神机妙算，想到我前边去了。"

司马懿的儿子司马昭却笑着说："马谡在山上扎营，山上没有水，只要不让蜀军得到水，蜀军就得投降。"

司马懿听了之后，非常高兴，笑着说："马谡只会纸上谈兵[5]，诸葛亮也有失误[1]的时候啊！”他马上召集将领，派一路魏军跟王平的军队交战，又派另一路兵马阻挡山上的蜀军下山找水找粮食，自己带领魏军包围了山的四面。

山上的蜀军没有粮食，也没有水。蜀军看见山下魏军很多，十分害怕，开始逃跑。这时，魏军又攻上山来，马谡也只好赶紧逃跑。本来王平还想联合高翔与魏延救马谡，但他们却被魏军阻挡在半路上，根本赶不过来。

诸葛亮听说街亭已经失守了，叹气说："我不应该派马谡去把守街亭，这是我的失误啊！”诸葛亮命令关兴和张苞带领三千

① 失误 (shīwù)
v. make a mistake (out of negligence)
e.g. 司马懿高兴地发现诸葛亮失误了。

人阻挡司马懿，自己亲自带领五千兵马到西城搬运粮草，准备撤回汉中。

马谡丢失了街亭，迫使诸葛亮放弃攻打魏国的计划，退回了汉中。

[1] 反间计（fǎnjiànjì）discord-sowing stratagem
原指利用敌人的间谍使敌人获得虚假的情报，后来指用计谋使敌人的内部不团结。
This stratagem originally refers to using enemy spies to provide them with false information. It later evolved into a stratagem to sow distrust among the enemies.

[2]《出师表》（Chūshībiǎo）*Northern Expedition Memorial*
《出师表》是 227 年蜀汉丞相诸葛亮在北上伐魏之前写给后主刘禅的奏章。这篇著名的奏章劝勉刘禅做一个明智的君主，并表达了自己对蜀国的忠心。
This passage was the first memorial written by Zhuge Liang in 227. It was presented to Emperor Liu Shan before his northern expedition against the Kingdom of Wei. In this famous passage, Zhuge Liang advises Liu Shan to be a wise ruler and expresses his loyalty to the Kingdom of Shu.

[3] 凭高视下，势如劈竹（píng gāo shì xià，shì rú pī zhú）Attacking the enemy from above is like splitting bamboo with crushing force
这是军事上的一种指挥方法，指从高处攻击在低处的敌人，就像用锋利的刀把竹子从上往下一口气劈开那么顺利，容易获得胜利。
A military tactic which explains that attacking enemy troops from high ground is like splitting bamboo with crushing force. It implies that use of such a strategy ensures victory.

[4] 置之死地而后生（zhì zhī sǐ dì ér hòu shēng）Confronted with death, a person will fight for his life
这句话出自孙武的《孙子兵法》，指作战时把军队布置在无法退却、只有战死的境地，兵士就会奋勇前进，杀敌取胜，后比喻事先断绝退路，就能下决心取得成功。
This is a phrase from Sun Tzu's *The Art of War*. It implies that deploying troops in such a manner that there is no room for escape will force soldiers to fight out of necessity, in turn leading to victory. Later, the term comes to refer to leaving a person with no leeway, so he will be more determined to succeed.

[5] 纸上谈兵（zhǐshàng-tánbīng）fighting only on paper
指在文字上谈论用兵策略，比喻只会空谈理论，不能解决实际问题。在这个故事中，马谡认为他自己精通《孙子兵法》，但他没有实战经验，最终导致了街亭之战的失败。
This idiom is used to describe an armchair strategist who only engages in idle theorizing. In the story, Ma Su is proficient in the art of war, but he lacks practical fighting experience and eventually is defeated in the Battle of Jieting.

练习题 Reading exercises

一、选择填空。Choose proper words to fill in the blanks.

阻挡　　安排　　包围　　扎营　　失误

1. 在诸葛亮的（　　）下，魏军打了很多败仗。
2. 马谡在山上（　　），一旦蜀军没有水，就会十分危险。
3. 由于马谡只会纸上谈兵，诸葛亮这次也（　　）了，丢失了街亭。

二、判断正误。Decide whether the following statements are true or false.

1. 诸葛亮派马谡把守街亭。（　）
2. 马谡用兵书上的知识，合理地安排好了扎营的地点。（　）
3. 蜀军最后失去了街亭，诸葛亮只好安排蜀军退回汉中。（　）

答案：

一、1. 安排　2. 扎营　3. 失误

二、1. 正　2. 误　3. 正

19. 空城计

主要人物和地点：
Main Characters and Places

蒋琬（Jiǎng Wǎn）(?–246)：蜀国大臣，在诸葛亮死后成为蜀汉的宰相。
Jiang Wan (?–246): A minister of the Kingdom of Shu. He succeeded Zhuge Liang as the Prime Minister after the latter's death.

西城（Xīchéng）：中国古代县名，今甘肃省天水市附近。
Xicheng: A county in ancient China that was located near present-day Tianshui City, Gansu Province.

① 文官 (wénguān)
n. civil official
e.g. 听说魏军来了，文官们十分慌张。

② 城楼 (chénglóu)
*n.*gate tower
e.g. 这座城楼历史悠久。

③ 旗帜 (qízhì)
n. flag; banner
e.g. 山上突然出现了关羽军队的旗帜。

④ 城门 (chéngmén)
n. city gate
e.g. 古老的城市四面都有城门。

失去街亭之后，诸葛亮赶紧带领五千兵马到了西城，让一半士兵去搬运粮草，城中只剩下了两千五百名士兵。突然，有士兵报告说司马懿正带领十五万魏军朝西城赶来。这时候，诸葛亮身边没有一个能打仗的将军，只有一些文官[1]，情况十分危急，文官们都大惊失色。

诸葛亮走上城楼[2]向远处望去。果然，魏军兵分两路朝西城赶来。诸葛亮命令:"拿掉城中旗帜[3]，禁止士兵们大声说话，把四面的城门[4]都打开，每个城门安排二十个士兵穿上百姓的衣服，打扮成百姓打扫街道。等魏军到时，我会有计谋的，不要害怕。”说完，诸葛亮让两个小孩儿拿来香炉[1]和古琴[2]，点上香[3]，坐在城楼上开始慢慢地弹琴[4]。

司马懿前面的魏军到了西城，见到城里这么安静，就在城外停了下来，不敢进城。这时司马懿也赶到了。司马懿看见诸葛

① 香炉 (xiānglú)
n. censer; incense burner
e.g. 诸葛亮让人把香炉搬到了城楼上。

② 古琴 (gǔqín)
n. *guqin*, a seven-stringed plucked instrument in ancient China
e.g. 他从小就开始学习古琴。

③ 香 (xiāng)
n. incense
e.g. 香炉里点上了香。

④ 弹琴 (tánqín)
v. play stringed musical instrument
e.g. 诸葛亮坐在城楼上平静地弹琴。

亮坐在城楼上弹琴，脸上还带着微笑，身边有两个小孩儿，城内有二十多个百姓在打扫街道，觉得很奇怪，心想，城里一定有埋伏，立刻命令撤退。司马懿的小儿子司马昭劝父亲，诸葛亮是故意假装平静，不要撤退。司马懿却坚持认为诸葛亮有计谋，不能中了他的计谋，赶紧退兵。

诸葛亮见司马懿退兵后，拍手大笑。文官们不知道司马懿为什么会退兵。诸葛亮对众文官解释说："我假装平静，司马懿以为我有埋伏，所以不敢进城。"然后，诸葛亮赶紧安排士兵们带领百姓退回汉中。

司马懿撤退到北山，对众将说："这回诸葛亮白费心机了，我们没有中他的计谋。"刚说完，只听见一声炮响，北山后面响起一片喊杀声，张苞带着一群人马冲了出来。司马懿大惊失色，"又中了诸葛亮的埋伏了！"慌忙逃跑。跑了一阵，又听见山谷里一片喊杀声音，关兴带着一群人马追了过来。魏军丢下兵器和粮草，逃回街亭去了。

司马懿跑回街亭，一个密探来报告说，西城其实是一座空城，没有埋伏，北山里也只有五六千名蜀军，只是装样子，不敢攻打魏军。司马懿听了，气得目瞪口呆[1]，连连叹气说："我不如诸葛亮，我不如诸葛亮啊！"

诸葛亮带着蜀军退回汉中，心中非常难过。马谡把自己捆了起来，跪在诸葛亮面前。

诸葛亮说："你怎么会闯下这样的大祸[2]？你要是听了王平的意见，也不会输得这么惨[3]呀！你立下军令状，现在失去了街亭，如果我不用军法处置你，我用什么来管理军队？你不要怨[4]我。你死以后，我会替你照看你的家人。"

马谡跪倒在诸葛亮面前，哭着说："我有罪，是死罪。谢谢丞相以后照顾我的家人。"诸葛亮忍不住

① 目瞪口呆 (mùdèng-kǒudāi) be struck dumb with astonishment
e.g. 这个问题让大家目瞪口呆，不知道怎么回答。

② 祸 (huò) *n.* disaster; great misfortune
e.g. 这个男孩儿又闯祸了。

③ 惨 (cǎn) *adj.* disastrous; severe
e.g. 叛军到处杀人，百姓死得很惨。

④ 怨 (yuàn) *v.* blame; resent
e.g. 他总是怨别人不给他机会。

流下了眼泪。

在马谡被士兵推到门外正要砍头的时候，大将蒋琬从成都来了。蒋琬看见士兵要杀马谡，忙说："刀下留人！"他走进大帐[1]，劝诸葛亮不要杀马谡。诸葛亮说，他要管理好军队，就要严格遵守军法。诸葛亮还是按照军法杀了马谡。马谡死的时候只有三十九岁。

不一会儿，士兵把马谡的头拿了上来。诸葛亮忍不住大哭起来，一边哭一边后悔没有听刘备去世前告诉他的话——不能太相信马谡。蜀军的大小将士们也都哭了。

诸葛亮擦干眼泪，又

① 大帐 (dàzhàng) *n.* central military camp
e.g. 诸葛亮坐在大帐中指挥千军万马。

① 嘉奖 (jiājiǎng)
v. commend
e.g. 王平因为劝阻马谡，受到了嘉奖。

宣布了一个命令，嘉奖[1]劝阻马谡的王平。诸葛亮因为自己的过错，辞去了丞相一职，只担任将军，但是他仍然尽全力帮助皇帝刘禅。

练习题 Reading exercises

一、选择填空。Choose proper words to fill in the blanks.

1. 诸葛亮假装（　　），司马懿以为他有埋伏，所以不敢进军。

A. 平静　　B. 安静

C. 安定　　D. 肯定

2. 司马懿逃回街亭，却发现他被诸葛亮骗了，又中了诸葛亮的（　　）。

A. 庆祝　　B. 计谋

C. 幸福　　D. 欢庆

3. 诸葛亮因为没有听刘备去世前告诉他的话，非常（　　）。

A. 吃惊　　B. 害怕

C. 后悔　　D. 平静

二、根据故事，给下面的句子排序。Put the following sentences in order according to the story.

1. 诸葛亮在西城的城门上弹琴，假装有埋伏，司马懿果然上当了。
2. 司马懿逃回街亭，却发现诸葛亮用"空城计"骗了他，连连叹气。

3. 街亭失守之后，诸葛亮带领五千士兵到西城搬运粮草。司马懿带领十五万士兵来到西城。

答案：

一、1.A 2.B 3.C

二、3-1-2

20. 蜀国廉相[1] 诸葛亮

主要人物和地点：
Main Characters and Places

杨仪（Yáng Yí）（约 189–235）：蜀国大臣。
Yang Yi (c.189–235): A minister of the Kingdom of Shu.

姜维（Jiāng Wéi）（202–264）：蜀国著名将领。他足智多谋，英勇善战，是诸葛亮非常信任的将军。诸葛亮死后，姜维带领蜀军继续与魏国对抗，最后被魏国杀害。
Jiang Wei (202–264): A famous general of the Kingdom of Shu. Resourceful and intrepid as a general, he won the trust of Zhuge Liang. After Zhuge's death, Jiang continued to lead the Shu army in their fight against the Kingdom of Wei. In the end, he was killed by Wei soldiers.

秦岭（Qínlǐng）：横贯中国中部东西走向的山脉，指今陕西省南部、渭河、汉江之间的山地。
Qinling Mountains: A mountain range that runs from east to west in central China. It also refers to the mountainous regions between southern Shaanxi Province, the Weihe River and the Hanjiang River.

五丈原（Wǔzhàng Yuán）：中国古代地名，今陕西省岐山县。诸葛亮在五丈原病逝。
Wuzhangyuan：A place in ancient China that was located in

① 廉相 (lián xiàng) *n.* upright and incorruptible prime minister e.g. 诸葛亮一生为蜀国劳累，生活节俭，被称为“廉相”。

present-day Qishan County, Shaanxi Province, where Zhuge Liang passed away.

蜀中（Shǔzhōng）：中国古代地名，今四川省中部地区。
Shuzhong: A place name in ancient China for what is today called the central part of Sichuan Province.

阴平（Yīnpíng）：中国古代地名，今四川省广元市剑门关以北。
Yinping: A place in ancient China that was located to the north of present-day Jianmen Pass, Guangyuan City, Sichuan Province.

刘备去世后，诸葛亮一直尽全力帮助皇帝刘禅，无论大小事情都要亲自去处理，非常辛苦。由于诸葛亮长年劳累①，他的身体越来越差。但是为了兴复汉室，统一天下，诸葛亮仍然带病讨伐魏国。

公元234年，诸葛亮开始了第五次北伐②。诸葛亮带着蜀军从汉中出发，穿越秦岭，一路向北前进，在五丈原受到了司马懿的阻挡。五丈原地势险要，蜀军和魏军在五丈原对峙了一百多天，但司马懿一直不出来迎战。诸葛亮心里十分着急，想把魏军引出来。

有一个地方叫葫芦沟，

① 劳累 (láolèi)
adj. tired
e.g. 他每天工作十多个小时，非常劳累。

② 北伐 (běifá)
n. northern expedition
e.g. 为了打败北方的曹魏，诸葛亮组织了五次北伐。

四面都是山，只有一个出口。诸葛亮用计谋把司马懿引进了葫芦沟。司马懿进了葫芦沟之后，诸葛亮命令士兵放火烧断葫芦沟的出口，想烧死司马懿和魏军。但是没想到，突然下起了大雨，救了司马懿和魏军。司马懿和魏军没有被大火烧死，逃出了葫芦沟。

到了秋天，诸葛亮的身体越来越差。有一天忽然传来消息，吴国兵分三路讨伐魏国，想和蜀军相互配合攻打魏军。可是没想到，吴国被魏国打败了。诸葛亮听了，心里一着急就病倒了。过了两天，诸葛亮开始吐血，可他还是不休息，仍然带病处理各种事情。

一天，诸葛亮坐上小车，让士兵推着他去看看各处的军营。诸葛亮说："我再也不能讨伐魏国了！苍天[1]啊，为什么不给我时间，为什么会这样！"说完，他不停地叹气。

诸葛亮回到军营的大帐之后，病得更重了。他派人叫来大臣杨仪，对杨仪说："我活不了多长时间了。我死以后，不要发丧[2]，军营中要像以前一样平静。你们撤退时要慢慢撤退，让后面的军营先撤退。如果司马懿追上来，就把我以前的木雕像[3]放在车上，叫士兵们推出来。

① 苍天 (cāngtiān)
n. Heaven
e.g. 人们祭拜苍天，希望天下太平。

② 发丧 (fāsāng)
v. release an obituary and mourn the dead
e.g. 诸葛亮担心魏军进攻，死后不让蜀国发丧。

③ 雕像 (diāoxiàng)
n. effigy; statue
e.g. 司马懿被诸葛亮的雕像吓跑了。

① 奏折 (zòuzhé) *n.* memorial to the emperor
e.g. 诸葛亮告诉刘禅要继续兴复汉室。

司马懿见了，会以为我还没死，就不敢追了。姜维是一位有才能的将军，让他保护全军撤退。”杨仪流着眼泪，一一答应了。

诸葛亮又叫来姜维，把自己写的兵书交给了姜维。诸葛亮希望姜维能用这些兵法继续为国家尽力，兴复汉室。姜维哭着收下了这些兵书。

诸葛亮接着说：“蜀中的各个地方都不用担心。但是阴平这个地方一定要注意。这个地方虽然地势险要，但是时间长了也会出问题。”姜维哭着一一记下了。

诸葛亮又给皇帝刘禅写了一封奏折[1]。他写道：

"我听说生死是一件平常的事情，我活不了多久了，但是我要表示我对蜀国的忠诚。在兴复汉室的过程中，我担任丞相，指挥各路人马出兵北伐，但是没有成功。我现在不能再为皇上效劳[1]了，真是遗憾啊！我死后，请皇上一定清心寡欲[2]，爱人民，爱国家。请皇上记住您父亲兴复汉室的理想，要用贤明和忠诚的人，不要用小人和奸臣，要形成良好的社会风气。我自己的家人都在成都，他们靠种地生活，不用担心他们。我在外面只有随身的几件衣服，没有别的钱财。皇上信任我这么多年，我死后也不想

① 效劳 (xiàoláo)
v. serve; work for
e.g. 诸葛亮让大臣们效劳蜀国。

② 清心寡欲
(qīngxīn-guǎyù)
have a pure heart and few desires
e.g. 僧人应该清心寡欲，不爱钱财。

有什么不义之财[1]。”诸葛亮写完奏折就晕了过去。

众将领们一看诸葛亮晕过去了，十分慌乱。这时，皇帝刘禅派来的人到了。他一见到诸葛亮就大哭起来。诸葛亮慢慢睁开眼睛，对他说：“很遗憾，我得了重病，不能北伐了。我耽误了国家大事，没有实现兴复汉室、统一国家的理想。我死后，你们要继续帮助皇上。国家原有的制度不能轻易改变。我把兵法都交给了姜维，他会继续为国家效劳。我这个奏折，请帮我交给皇上。”说完诸葛亮又闭上了眼睛。

公元234年，诸葛亮

① 不义之财 (búyìzhīcái) ill-gotten wealth e.g. 官员不应该接受不义之财。

在五丈原军营中去世，死时才54岁。

诸葛亮去世以后，杨仪、姜维按照诸葛亮的安排，没有发丧，而是秘密地命令各处军营撤退。

司马懿得到消息说蜀军在撤退，猜想诸葛亮可能死了，就命令魏军追赶蜀军。可是，魏军刚出军营大门，司马懿忽然怀疑是诸葛亮用的计谋，又命令停止追赶。司马懿让密探去探听情况，密探看见蜀军撤退，急忙回来报告司马懿说："听说诸葛亮死了，蜀军正在撤退。"司马懿高兴得一下子从座位上跳了起来，立刻派兵追赶。

司马懿带领魏军来到

一座山下，马上就要追上蜀军了。这时魏军忽然听见一声炮响，树林中飘出一面大旗，蜀军冲杀过来了。司马懿见了大吃一惊。几十名蜀国大将推出一辆四轮车，司马懿一看，车上坐着的正是诸葛亮。他吓得变了脸色，对身边众

将说:“诸葛亮还活着，我又中他的计了!”说完他骑上马就往回跑。

姜维带领蜀军一边追杀一边擂鼓大喊:“司马懿，你又中了诸葛丞相的计啦!”魏军吓得跑出了五十多里。司马懿摸摸头，对身边的人说:“我的头还在吗?”他的大将告诉他:“蜀军已经撤退了。”司马懿这才安下心来。

过了两天，司马懿听说诸葛亮真的死了，那天车上见的其实是诸葛亮的木雕像。蜀军到处说:“死诸葛吓走了活司马。”司马懿听到这些，真是又气又恨。

从公元228年到公元

234年，诸葛亮一共发动了五次北伐讨伐魏国。在北伐期间，诸葛亮发明了运输工具木牛流马[1]，为蜀国十万大军运输粮草。当司马懿带领魏军来到五丈原时，看到蜀军把守的险要地点，惊叹道："诸葛亮真是天下奇才啊！"

后人为了纪念蜀国丞相诸葛亮，在五丈原修建了诸葛亮庙。

[1] 木牛流马（mùniúliúmǎ）Wooden Oxen and Gliding Horses
三国时期蜀相诸葛亮发明的运输工具，载重大约四百斤以上，一天可以走好几十里，为蜀汉十万大军提供粮食，但是具体的制作方法和运输方式现已失传。
This is a type of vehicles invented by Zhuge Liang to transport military provisions over difficult terrain. Each vehicle could carry a load of over 200 kg and travel scores of miles per day. They offered food to the Shu troops during their northern expeditions. Unfortunately, the manufacturing process and operating method of this type of vehicles has since been lost.

练习题 Reading exercises

一、选择填空。Choose proper words to fill in the blanks.

引　　活着　　效劳　　不幸　　遗憾

1. 诸葛亮临死时吩咐大臣们，他死后军营里要像他（　　）时一样平静。
2. 诸葛亮说："我不能再为皇上（　　）了，非常遗憾。"
3. 诸葛亮对刘禅派来的使者说："我（　　）在北伐中途死亡，没有完成兴复汉室的愿望。"

二、判断正误。Decide whether the following statements are true or false.

1. 诸葛亮由于长年劳累，在北伐途中去世了。（　）
2. 司马懿见到了诸葛亮的木雕像，知道是计谋，没有上当。（　）
3. 诸葛亮活着的时候发明了很多有用的生产、生活工具和运输工具。（　）

答案：

一、1. 活着　2. 效劳　3. 不幸

二、1. 正　2. 误　3. 正

尾声：三国归晋

主要人物和地点：
Main Characters and Places

邓艾（Dèng Ài）（约 197–264）：魏国著名将领。他带领魏军入蜀，蜀国灭亡。

Deng Ai (c.197–264): A famous general of the Kingdom of Wei who led his army into Shu territory, thereby causing an end of the Kingdom of Shu.

钟会（Zhōng Huì）（225–264）：魏国谋士。他制定了攻打蜀国的计划，并带领魏军参加灭蜀战争。

Zhong Hui (225–264): A counselor of the Kingdom of Wei who formulated a plan to attack the Kingdom of Shu and led Wei troops in the campaign, which caused an end of the Kingdom of Shu.

曹髦（Cáo Máo）（241–260）：曹丕的孙子，魏国的第四位皇帝。

Cao Mao (241–260): Cao Pi's grandson, and the fourth emperor of the Kingdom of Wei.

曹奂（Cáo Huàn）（246–302）：曹操的孙子，魏国的最后一位皇帝。

Cao Huan (246–302): Cao Cao's grandson, and the last emperor of the Kingdom of Wei.

司马炎（Sīmǎ Yán）（236–290）：司马懿的孙子。公元 265 年，他逼迫曹奂让位，建立了晋朝，成为晋朝的开国皇帝。

Sima Yan (236–290): Sima Yi's grandson. In 265, he forced Cao Huan to abdicate the throne to him and thereafter established the

Jin Dynasty (265–420). He was the first emperor of the Jin Dynasty.

孙皓（Sūn Hào）(242–284)：孙权的孙子，东吴的最后一位皇帝。
Sun Hao (242–284): Sun Quan's grandson, and the last emperor of Eastern Wu.

杜预（Dù Yù）(222–285)：西晋著名将领、学者。
Du Yu (222–285): A famous general and scholar of the Western Jin Dynasty (265–317).

王浚（Wáng Jùn）(252–314)：西晋的著名将领。
Wang Jun (252–314): A famous general of the Western Jin Dynasty.

晋国（Jìnguó）：公元 265 年，魏国宰相司马炎建立的皇朝，国号为"晋"。
Jin Dynasty: An imperial dynasty founded in 265 by Sima Yan, who was once the prime minister of the Kingdom of Wei.

① 遗志 (yízhì)
n. deathbed behest
e.g. 刘禅投降了魏军，没有继承诸葛亮的遗志。

蜀国

公元234年，诸葛亮因为长年劳累，病死在五丈原。诸葛亮去世后，姜维继承了诸葛亮的遗志[①]，带领蜀军北上继续讨伐曹魏，与曹魏名将邓艾等人多次交战。

公元263年，司马昭命令钟会、邓艾讨伐蜀国。钟会和邓艾很快打到了成都，刘禅带领文武百官投降了魏军。这一年冬天，蜀国灭亡。

刘禅投降后离开蜀国，住在洛阳。蜀国将领看到刘禅投降魏国，都很伤心，只有刘禅十分高兴。

在一次酒宴上，司马昭问刘禅："你想念蜀国吗？”刘禅说：“我在这里很快乐，不想回蜀国了。”这就是“乐不思蜀[1]”的故事。

姜维希望蜀国再次强大起来。可是由于种种原因，姜维没能带领蜀国统一天下。

魏国

魏国早已被司马懿、司马昭控制，众人都知道司马懿和司马昭的野心①，这就是人们常常说的“司马昭之心，路人皆知[2]”。

蜀国灭亡后，魏国的皇帝曹髦封司马昭为晋王。司马昭看不起皇帝曹髦，他经常带着剑去见曹髦，还要皇帝来迎接他。

司马昭被封为晋王的

① 野心 (yěxīn)
n. ambition
e.g. 司马懿家族一直有统一天下的野心。

时候，大臣们都站起来祝贺司马昭，而皇帝曹髦却低着头没有说话。

司马昭大声喊道：“我们司马家族父子立了大功，封为晋王，有什么不合适的吗？”

曹髦慌忙说：“我怎么敢不听从您的命令，说不合适呢？”

司马昭离开之后，皇帝曹髦非常生气，想杀死司马昭。他说：“我已经不能再忍了，我决定杀死司马昭。”可是，他的部下把他的计划偷偷告诉了司马昭。结果司马昭杀死了曹髦，让曹奂当了皇帝。

公元265年，司马昭病死，他的儿子司马炎当了晋王。几个月以后，司马炎逼迫皇帝曹奂退位，自己当了皇帝，把国号改为晋，建立了晋国。魏国就这样灭亡了。

吴国

公元252年，孙权病死，那年他71岁。公元264年，孙权的孙子孙皓当了吴国的皇帝，掌握了吴国的大权。孙皓不愿意听别人的意见，杀了四十多名对吴国忠诚的大臣，还修建大宫殿，百姓们都十分不满。吴国开始走向衰落①。

司马炎了解了吴国这些情况，就派杜预将军带领军队攻打吴国。最后晋国的王浚将军带领军队冲

① 衰落 (shuāiluò)
v. decline
e.g. 吴国的衰落使司马炎顺利地统一了全国。

进了吴国的都城建业，孙皓向晋国投降。公元280年，吴国也灭亡了。

最后，三国归晋，司马炎统一了天下，魏、蜀、吴三国鼎立的局面结束了。这正是：天下大势，合久必分，分久必合[3]。

[1] 乐不思蜀（lèbùsīshǔ）be so happy as to forget one's home and duties
刘禅是蜀国最后一位皇帝。蜀国灭亡后，他非常享受被俘之后的生活，忘记了先帝刘备告诉他的兴复汉室的遗嘱。现在，这个成语用来表示某人沉浸在快乐安逸中，忘记了自己的责任。
Liu Shan, the last emperor of the Kingdom of Shu, enjoyed his life as a captive and did not think about the restoration of the Han Dynasty that Liu Bei had entrusted to him. Now, this idiom is used to describe someone indulging in pleasure and forgetting his or her home and duties.

[2] 司马昭之心，路人皆知（Sīmǎ Zhāo zhī xīn，lùrén jiē zhī）Sima Zhao's ill intent is known to all
司马昭是司马懿的儿子，在三国时期，他是一个非常有野心的将军。他计划要掌控魏国。魏国每一个人都知道他的野心。现在，这个俗语用来指某人野心非常明显，人所共知。
Sima Zhao, Sima Yi's son, was an ambitious general during the Three Kingdoms Period. He schemed to control the Kingdom of Wei. Everyone in the kingdom knew of his unbounded ambition. Now, this phrase is used to describe someone whose ambition is obvious.

[3] 天下大势，合久必分，分久必合（tiānxià dàshì，hé jiǔ bì fēn，fēn jiǔ bì hé）division leads to unity, and unity to division
天下的大体趋势就是：国家经过长时间的分裂后，会再形成一个统一的国家；而国家长期统一后，又会分裂。在中国历史上，周朝的统治衰弱后，涌现出了七个小国，这七个小国相互交战，直到秦国统一整个国家。秦国完成了统一的使命后，国家不久又分裂成了两个相互对立、为争夺统治权而斗争的势力，就是楚和汉。汉朝最终获得了胜利。而此后魏蜀吴三国在经过七十多年的战争后，最终又被晋朝统一了。
The nation, after a long period of division, tends to unite; after a long period of union, it tends to divide. This has been a general trend since ancient times. Looking back on Chinese history, when the rule of the Eastern Zhou Dynasty (770-256 BC) weakened, seven contending kingdoms sprang up, fighting against one another until the State of Qin prevailed and united the whole country. When the Qin empire collapsed, there arose two opposing powers, Chu and Han, to fight for supremacy. Han then became the ultimate winner. Subsequently, the Three Kingdoms of Wei, Shu, and Wu were finally united under Jin after more than 70 years of war.

练习题 Reading exercises

一、选择填空。Choose proper words to fill in the blanks.

1. 由于蜀汉国力弱小等多种（　　），蜀国的姜维没有能带领蜀国成功统一天下。

A. 理由　　B. 原因

C. 因为　　D. 结果

2. 魏国的大臣司马昭很（　　）皇帝曹髦，经常带着剑见皇帝，还要皇帝来迎接他。

A. 尊敬　　B. 害怕

C. 看不起　　D. 欢迎

3. 司马炎最后统一了天下，三国统一归晋。吴、蜀、魏三国鼎立的局面（　　）了。

A. 胜利　　B. 失败

C. 结束　　D. 开始

二、判断正误。Decide whether the following statements are true or false.

1. 魏国大权早已被司马懿、司马昭控制。
2. 诸葛亮攻打魏国时受伤，最后死了。
3. 孙权去世后，吴国越来越衰落。

答案：

一、1.B　2.C　3.C

二、1. 正　2. 误　3. 正

English Version

1. Oath of the Peach Orchard

During the late Eastern Han Dynasty, the emperor was young and unable to run the country. The imperial court was corrupt, and many young people had to leave their homes to perform military service. One year, there was a very long drought. Due to lack of rain, peasants had a poor harvest and didn't have enough food to eat. They led such a hard life that many of them rose up against the royal court.

A peasant called Zhang Jiao formed a peasant insurrectionary Yellow Turban Army, which won popular support. In the span of one month, the revolt spread to various parts of the country. Battles raged nationwide, and people lived in the turmoil of war.

Liu Yan, the magistrate of Youzhou, became extremely frightened as he watched the rapid growth of the rebel forces, so he put up the conscription notice to fight the Yellow Turban Army and protect the city.

A hero stopped in front of a notice to read it. He was tall and handsome. His ears were so long that he could see them with his own eyes, and he also had long arms and hands. He was Liu Bei, a descendant of the Han royal family.

Liu Bei came from a poor family and lived with his mother. As a dutiful son, he loved his mother dearly. He liked reading books, and he had cherished lofty aspirations since childhood. He was fond of making friends with countrywide heroes.

Seeing the draft notice, Liu Bei thought of people's suffering, yet he could do nothing to help bring about any change to the situation. Feeling sad, he heaved a sigh.

Suddenly, Liu Bei heard a man shout, "The nation is in deep crisis and you do nothing but sigh here. How can you be a true hero?" Liu Bei turned his head, only to see the tall and strong man with round eyes and a pitch-black beard. He spoke with a sonorous voice and looked just like a hero.

The man said, "My family name is Zhang. I'm called Zhang Fei, and Yide is my courtesy name. I like to make friends with all the nationwide heroes. I saw you sigh while reading the notice, and that's why I ask you this question."

Liu Bei then told Zhang Fei the truth: He was unable to help the people, so he felt very sad. Learning this, Zhang replied, "I have some money to recruit some soldiers. I want to join you and fight for our goal, how does that sound?" Liu Bei was very glad to hear this. The two went to a pub for a drink while discussing what to do next.

Just then, a man came in. Liu took a close look at the man: He was even taller than Zhang Fei and himself. He had a long beard and a red face, and looked quite handsome. Liu stood up at once, invited him to have a drink and asked for his name.

The man said, "My family name is Guan. I'm called Guan Yu, and Yunchang is my courtesy name. I heard that there was a draft notice here, so I came to have a look." The three became acquainted with each other and started drinking wine. Liu and Zhang told Guan Yu about their plan to save the country and bring peace to the people. Guan rejoiced to learn about it and decided to join them.

Zhang Fei said, "There's a peach orchard in my backyard. Tomorrow we can become sworn brothers there and fight together for our aim!" The other two readily agreed.

The next day, Liu, Guan and Zhang headed for the peach orchard to hold an oath-taking ceremony. They swore together, "We have different family names, we were born on different days, but today, we swear to become brothers. We will fight shoulder to shoulder to achieve our common goal: to bring peace to the country and the people." The three henceforth became sworn brothers.

As the oldest among them, Liu Bei was called the eldest brother; Guan Yu was younger than Liu but older than Zhang Fei, and was called the second elder brother by Zhang; Zhang Fei was the youngest, and was called the younger brother by the other two. This is the famous story of the "Oath of the Peach Orchard" from *Romance of the Three Kingdoms.*

After the oath-taking ceremony, they held a banquet which drew over 300 warriors. They received a lot of weapons, but didn't get any horses, which were indispensable for fighting battles. At that juncture, two horse traders heard that they were going to do something big, so they sent them many horses and a lot of money. They also provided them with 500 kg of iron to make more weapons. The three brothers had their own weapons made and then gathered many more warriors. Afterwards, they led more than 500 warriors and headed for Youzhou to meet with the magistrate Liu Yan.

As they arrived there, Liu Yan took them in because Liu Bei was the offspring of the royal family. From then on, Liu, Guan and Zhang began their undertaking to save the country, which was already in a severe crisis when the royal court was corrupt.

2. Cao Cao Presents a Sword

Around 189, Emperor Lingdi of the Han Dynasty was leading an extravagant and idle life that caused him to neglect state affairs. After his death, his son succeeded to the throne and was called Emperor Shaodi. As a 14-year-old child, he was too young and inexperienced to run the country, and as a result the nation was in chaos.

At that time, a warlord called Dong Zhuo emerged. He led his troops into the capital, Luoyang, and then replaced the emperor with his younger brother, who later became Emperor Xiandi. But Xiandi was no more than a puppet, as the whole royal court was actually under Dong Zhuo's control. Gradually, he seized state power.

After that, he began deceiving the emperor and oppressing the common people, living a dissipated life. His wrongdoings were detested by all ministers and the ordinary people.

Some ministers wanted to kill him, but none of them got the chance because he was constantly protected by guards. Wang Yun, one of those ministers, racked his brains to figure out a plan.

One day, Wang held a banquet at his residence, inviting some ministers to celebrate his birthday. After several rounds of toasting, Wang Yun wept and said, "Actually, today is not my birthday. I invited you over to discuss a matter, but I was worried this would raise Dong Zhuo's suspicions. This is why I told you today is my birthday." Hearing this, all the guests became silent.

Wang continued saying, "With Dong Zhuo in control of state power, the fate of our dynasty hangs by a thread. Whenever

I think of this, I can't hold back my tears." Everyone present began wailing upon hearing Wang's words. They cursed Dong Zhuo, but none could come up with a solution to wipe out the scourge.

At that moment, Cao Cao clapped his hands and laughed, "Look at us, we are weeping like women. But will that end Dong Zhuo's life? I would like to kill Dong Zhuo and repay the people."

Wang Yun asked him immediately, "What's your plan?"

Cao Cao replied, "Lately I've been working for Dong Zhuo. He trusts me. I heard that you have a 'seven-star precious sword' that is very sharp. Can I borrow it to kill Dong Zhuo?"

Wang became overjoyed to see Cao was so brave and resourceful. He immediately handed the precious sword to Cao Cao.

The next day, Cao Cao took the sword with him to visit Dong Zhuo at the prime minister's residence. Dong was sitting on his bed as if he would soon go to sleep. Standing behind him was Lü Bu, his adopted son.

Cao explained that he was late because his horse was a bit slow. Dong was aware that Cao was a very capable person and wanted to have him work as his aide, so he was thinking about doing Cao a favor. Thus he promised Cao a fine horse. He asked Lü to select a horse for Cao, and Lü left. Dong was too fat to sit very long, so he lay on the bed.

Cao thought that, with the absence of Dong's adopted son, it was a good chance to kill Dong. He immediately took out the precious sword. Quite unexpectedly, Dong spotted Cao's move through a mirror on the bed. Dong was shocked and jumped up at once. He shouted, “Cao Cao, what are you doing?” At that moment, Lü came to the doorstep with the horse he had led.

Seeing that Lü had returned, Cao realized he had already missed the opportunity to kill Dong as Cao was no match for Dong’s adopted son at all. At that critical juncture, Cao hit upon an idea. He kneeled down and said to Dong, “Your Highness, I would like to present this ‘seven-star precious sword’ to you.” Dong took the sword from him and found that was a sharp weapon with seven precious gems inlaid on it—it was indeed a precious sword. Dong was pleased and accepted the gift. Cao was afraid that Dong might kill him once he discovered the truth. So he said to Dong, “I want to go and try riding the horse.” As Dong agreed, he mounted the horse and fled the prime minister’s residence.

3. Three Heroes Battle Lü Bu

After his failed attempt to assassinate Dong Zhuo, Cao Cao began rallying warlords and heroes from across the country to fight the tyrant. Before long, many warlords assembled near Luoyang and elected Yuan Shao, who enjoyed the highest prestige, as their head. Yuan then formed an allied army. Liu Bei, Guan Yu and Zhang Fei also joined the army to fight Dong Zhuo.

The allied forces headed by Yuan Shao marched to Hulao Pass in Henan Province and prepared to launch an attack on Dong’s army. Dong led Lü Bu and an army of 500,000 soldiers to Hulao Pass. Yuan Shao then dispatched Gongsun Zan to command his army and take on the enemy.

Dong Zhuo dispatched Lü Bu to spearhead the attack. The

handsome general was riding a red horse (called the Red Hare), carrying a bow and arrows and holding a special halberd. This was the manifestation of the common saying "Lü Bu stands out among men; the Red Hare stands out among horses". With 3,000 cavalrymen, Lü Bu charged to the frontline to battle the allied forces.

A general from the allied forces rode his horse to battle Lü Bu. In less than five rounds of fighting, Lü struck the general with his halberd and the general fell off his horse. The allied forces suffered great casualties as Lü Bu seemed invincible. Yuan Shao became anxious and discussed with the other warlords who should fight Lü Bu.

As they were racking their brains to find a way, a soldier rushed over and reported, "Lü Bu is clamoring about outside again!" Hearing this, two generals from the allied forces, Mu Shun and Wu Anguo, immediately mounted their horses and dashed out. Unfortunately, they were defeated very quickly. Then the allied forces all charged out together.

Seeing the enemy all dashing toward him, Lü Bu realized he wouldn't stand a chance as his soldiers were far outnumbered. So he immediately ordered a retreat. Yuan Shao and his allies didn't ask their troops to chase the enemy. Instead, they consulted with each other again to come up with a better way to defeat Lü.

In a short while, Lü Bu led his soldiers to challenge the allied forces again. Gongsun Zan commanded his troops to meet the enemy head-on. Within only a few rounds of fighting, he was also defeated. At that juncture, a general dashed out from Gongsun's side. He was none other than Zhang Fei. He yelled out at Lü Bu, "Don't go, you shameless traitor (domestic servant with three surnames)! Zhang Fei is here!" Hearing this curse, Lü was outraged and turned his horse back at Zhang Fei. Neither of the two gained an upper hand after more than 50 rounds.

Watching Zhang Fei hardly beat Lü Bu on his own, Guan Yu rode his horse to help his younger brother—the three horses became entangled with each other. The three fought for 30 rounds. Seeing that his two brothers were still not winning, Liu Bei also pitched in.

Lü Bu realized that he was no match for Liu, Guan and Zhang, so he thrust at Liu Bei and turned around to flee. The three brothers chased him all the way to the foot of a hill. Zhang Fei looked up and saw a carriage. He shouted, "The man sitting in the carriage must be Dong Zhuo. There's no point chasing Lü Bu. It's much better to catch Dong, the head of the enemy." So he rode his horse, trying to dash up the hill to capture Dong Zhuo. To his surprise, a lot of stones and arrows began flying from the hill toward him like rain. Zhang Fei found it impossible to move forward, so he retreated on horse. Lü Bu seized the chance to return to Dong's side.

Although Liu Bei, Guan Yu and Zhang Fei did not capture Dong Zhuo and Lü Bu, they displayed their bravery and capability. This is the famous story "Three Heroes Battle Lü Bu" in *Romance of the Three Kingdoms*. The three brothers gradually became known among the allied forces.

As Dong Zhuo continued to deceive the emperor and bully the common people, the heroes still sought a way to launch the punitive expedition against him.

4. A Beauty Trap

Having seized state power, Dong Zhuo decided to move the capital of the Eastern Han Dynasty from Luoyang to Chang'an. Upon leaving Luoyang, he killed many rich people and grabbed a lot of wealth from them. After arriving in Chang'an, the new capital, he continued living his dissipated life and dreamed of becoming the emperor. The people's lives were miserable.

Given Dong's great power and his adopted son's valor, no one could do anything to defeat them. The minister, Wang Yun, was worried about the imperial court, but he couldn't get an opportunity to kill Dong Zhuo.

After a long period of observation, he discovered Dong Zhuo and his adopted son had one thing in common: both of them were fond of beautiful women. Wang thought: Dong Zhuo is the foe of the imperial court. Things would be much easier if his adopted son could be used to kill him.

There was a beautiful young lady who lived in Wang Yun's residence. The girl was called Diao Chan. She was very good at singing and dancing. Wang hit upon an idea: Why not take the girl as my adopted daughter first and present her to Lü Bu as his concubine. Afterward, I can send her to Dong Zhuo to sow hatred between the two. Lastly, I can use Lü to kill Dong.

So Wang decided to end Dong Zhuo's life with the "beauty trap" and protect the imperial court.

He then told Diao Chan about his plan. The girl, who also harbored hatred toward Dong Zhuo, was willing to become Wang's adopted daughter and help him in killing Dong Zhuo.

Wang Yun began by tricking Lü Bu into coming to his residence and presented Diao Chan to him as a concubine. A few days later, he treated Dong Zhuo to a feast at his residence. He told Dong the beautiful girl was his adopted daughter and that he would like to present her to him. Overjoyed, Dong Zhuo brought Diao Chan back to his residence. Wang Yun then found Lü Bu and said to him, "Your adoptive father came to my residence today and took Diao Chan away."

The next day, Lü Bu learned that Dong Zhuo and Diao Chan had stayed together. He went over to Dong's residence, only to find the two hadn't got up yet. Outraged, he sneaked near their room. Diao Chan was at the window. Seeing Lü Bu, she pretended to wipe away tears. Lü stood still for a long time and then left. He entered the room after Dong Zhuo got up. Diao Chan stood beside Dong, casting loving glances at Lü. Discovering what the two were doing, Dong became very angry and began to believe they were having an affair.

On one occasion, Lü Bu visited Dong Zhuo because he had an ailment. Dong was asleep at the time. He saw Diao Chan standing behind the bed. Missing his lover so much, Lü Bu was filled with rage and the hatred toward his adoptive father grew.

One day, Dong Zhuo left his residence for the court. Taking advantage of his absence, Lü Bu had a secret date with Diao Chan. By the side of the lotus pool at Dong's residence, the girl told Lü she didn't want to be with Dong Zhuo. She wanted to die. After saying this, she tried to jump into the pool. Lü Bu immediately held her in his arms—they hugged together and started crying.

At that moment, a shout was heard and the lovers jumped with fear. Dong Zhuo had noticed his adopted son wasn't at court when he went there, so he had become suspicious. He had decided to return to the residence, where he saw the two holding each other in their arms. Lü Bu was taken aback by his father's sudden return and quickly left. Dong was too clumsy to catch up with his fast pace, so he had to stop. He asked Diao Chan why they had been hugging. The girl shed sad tears, explaining that it was Lü Bu who asked for a secret date with her. Dong Zhuo wanted to prove Diao Chan's loyalty to him by saying he would like to send her to Lü Bu. Diao Chan appeared stunned and took up a knife, telling Dong she loved him so much that she would kill herself if he decided to give her to his adopted son. Dong Zhuo was quite pleased to find Diao Chan love him so much, which dispelled his doubts.

Subsequently, Dong Zhuo was to leave Chang'an with Diao Chan and move into the newly built palace at Meiwu. Officials at various levels were present to bid them farewell. Sitting in the carriage, Diao Chan pretended to weep. Lü Bu, who observed what was going on from afar, felt heartbroken. Wang Yun then walked over to talk with him. Lü told him about what happened to him and Diao Chan. Wang immediately led Lü Bu to his house, saying, "Dong Zhuo raped my adopted daughter and seized your lover, what a scoundrel he is!" Lü Bu told Wang he had made up his mind to kill Dong Zhuo.

Wang Yun lost no time in calling up other ministers to devise a plan to kill Dong Zhuo. They decided to dispatch a general to Meiwu along with a cavalry unit. The general deceived Dong Zhuo by telling him that the emperor was about to abdicate the throne to him and that he should return to Chang'an as soon as possible. Dong was elated by the good news, so he left Meiwu right away and reached Chang'an on the same day.

The next morning, he returned to the court and was welcomed

by all ministers. When his carriage reached the gate, all his soldiers were told to wait outside. As he arrived at the palace gate, Wang Yun called out: "The scoundrel has come!" All of a sudden, more than 100 soldiers appeared, wielding their weapons against Dong Zhuo.

Dong Zhuo cried out, "Where's my adopted son?"

Lü Bu dashed out from behind the carriage, saying, "I'm here to kill you on the emperor's edict!" Then he used his halberd to stab Dong Zhuo and killed him. His corpse was thrown on the street and beaten over and over again by the resentful crowd.

Upon learning of Dong Zhuo's death, his two subordinates Li Jue and Guo Si led troops to launch an attack on Chang'an. They broke into the city and killed Wang Yun. Lü Bu fled along with Diao Chan. Afterward, he was defeated by Cao Cao and executed at the Baimenlou Gate Tower. Emperor Xiandi also escaped out of Chang'an and was found by Cao in a battle. Cao hence began controlling the emperor and became the Prime Minister. Having seized state power, he started commanding the warlords in the name of the emperor.

5. Discussing Heroes While Drinking Green Plum Wine

After putting Lü Bu to death, Cao Cao introduced Liu Bei, Guan Yu and Zhang Fei to Emperor Xiandi. Upon learning that Liu was a descendant of the imperial family, the emperor wanted to control Cao Cao by making use of Liu Bei. With this in mind, he began calling Liu Bei "uncle". Henceforth people addressed Liu Bei as "uncle of the emperor".

After becoming the Prime Minister, Cao Cao started belittling the emperor, so all court ministers saw him as a wicked minister.

One minister was called Dong Cheng. Unable to bear Cao's behavior, he called up Liu Bei and others to discuss a plan to deal with the wicked Cao. Liu Bei promised to aid him in his efforts.

It was known to all that Liu Bei, as an upright and amiable hero, had been backed by such brave generals as Guan Yu and Zhang Fei. People working for Cao Cao were worried that Liu Bei might gradually control the court, thus they tried to persuade him to kill Liu. Cao, who also harbored suspicions toward Liu Bei, decided to test his abilities.

Though he had promised Dong Cheng he would deal with Cao Cao, Liu Bei was still afraid that Cao might kill him beforehand. So he learned how to grow vegetables at his residence, pretending not to care about anything else. Guan Yu and Zhang Fei thought their elder brother was quite queer, but he didn't tell them why he did this.

One day, as Liu was growing vegetables, unexpectedly a minister came to his residence and invited him to meet with Cao Cao. At the time, Guan Yu and Zhang Fei were not there. Liu Bei had no choice but to visit Cao on his own.

Upon seeing Liu, Cao said with a laugh, "You are doing big things in your residence!" Hearing this, Liu was taken aback. He thought Cao had discovered the plan against him, and he believed this visit would be disastrous for him.

Much to his surprise, Cao took his hand and said, "You have been working so hard, learning how to grow vegetables!" This relieved Liu's worries. He replied, "I study this in my residence only to kill time."

Cao said, "Just now I saw green plums on the trees, which reminded me of something in the past: One day, my troops were marching for a long time on the road. We were running out of water, and the soldiers were too thirsty to carry on. So I told them, 'There are lots of trees ahead with many green plums on them.' Hearing what I said, all the soldiers were not thirsty and were able to march on. Seeing the green plums today, I can't help inviting you to enjoy green plum wine and have a chat." Liu was much more relieved after hearing Cao's story.

Cao put a plate of green plums along with a pot of wine and two drinking cups on the table. He invited Liu to take a seat, and the two began savoring the plum wine. They sat in the courtyard and chatted while drinking wine.

But suddenly, a strong wind blew up. They saw a tornado whirling in the distance. Cao asked Liu, "Do you know the changes of a dragon?" Liu replied, "Your Highness, I would like to hear your thoughts on the dragon."

Cao said, "The dragon can change into many forms. When large, it can blot out the sun and the sky; when small, you can hardly find its trace. Since you have visited many places and have seen quite a lot, if we compare today's heroes to dragons, you must have some idea about those heroes who are dragons."

Liu replied, "I only work at the royal court and have no idea about who the world's heroes are."

Cao said, "You may not be acquainted with the heroes, but must have heard their names!"

Given Cao's insistence, Liu had to reply, "Yuan Shu, who occupies the Huainan region, commands many generals and soldiers. He also has plentiful provisions for his army. Can he be called a hero?"

Cao laughed and said, "Yuan Shu's days have already passed!"

Liu then said, "Hebei's Yuan Shao enjoys high prestige, is he a hero?"

Cao burst into laughter and said, "Yuan Shao is too cowardly to be regarded as a hero!"

Liu went on mentioning such warlords as Liu Biao, Sun Ce and Liu Zhang, but none of them was a hero in Cao's eyes.

Liu was at his wits' end and asked, "Apart from those mentioned above, I really don't know who else could be considered heroes."

Cao said, "Only those with lofty aspirations can become heroes."

Liu replied, "So in your view, who are the ones with lofty aspirations who can be considered heroes?"

Cao pointed at Liu, then turned the finger to himself and said, "In this country, only you and I deserve to be called heroes."

Stunned at Cao's word, Liu dropped his chopsticks onto the ground. Just then, there was a clap of thunder followed by a heavy downpour. Liu Bei feigned calm and picked up the chopsticks. He apologized to Cao, "I'm sorry. I'm afraid of thunder, so I was frightened just now."

Cao laughed and asked him, "Does a great hero like you fear thunder?"

Liu replied, "All sages stand in awe of thunder, how could I be any different?"

In fact, Liu was well aware that Cao had harbored suspicions toward him. The discussions about the dragon and heroes were meant to test him. Therefore, he pretended to be fearful of thunder to give Cao the false impression that he was timid. Cao, who was taken in, became much less suspicious.

With Cao in power, Liu was on pins and needles. When he got the chance to launch an attack on Xuzhou, he fled together with Guan Yu and Zhang Fei.

6. Riding on a Solitary Journey

Liu Bei had always aspired to "revitalize the Han Dynasty". However, he was keenly aware that Cao Cao would kill him if his intention was revealed. Therefore, he seized the chance to attack Xuzhou and left Cao accompanied by Guan Yu and Zhang Fei.

Unfortunately, during the battle, the three brothers lost contact with each other. Guan Yu couldn't find his elder brother, but he got the message that his two wives, Lady Gan and Lady Mi, were still in Cao's camp. So he returned to Cao's camp to take care of his two sisters-in-law.

Cao, who adored talented people, gave Guan a lot of money and a fine horse, and then conferred on him a high position in the hope of bringing the great general under his command. But Guan, as a man who valued brotherhood above everything else, was extremely loyal to Liu. He awaited Liu's message and prepared to leave Cao's camp as soon as any new information about his elder brother came in.

One day, Guan Yu learned Liu's whereabouts and was about

to depart with his sisters-in-law, but Cao refused to issue the needed handwritten directive to him. In Cao's territory, it would be impossible for Guan to leave without the directive, because he couldn't get through the strategic passes without it. But he made up his mind to go and look for his elder brother.

As he arrived at the first pass (Dongling Pass), Kong Xiu, one of Cao's generals, asked him to present the directive.

Guan Yu cheated him by saying, "We were in such a rush that I didn't have time to ask for it."

Kong soon found out Guan was lying to him and thus refused to let them go through the pass.

Guan became furious and asked, "Do you insist on not letting us go? Don't waste our time!"

Kong was irritated because he thought Guan was behaving rudely. He told Guan, "You can go, but leave Liu Bei's two wives here."

Guan flew into a rage and rode his horse toward Kong with his big knife drawn. He slashed the knife and killed Kong immediately. They went through the first pass.

They arrived at the second pass, Luoyang. Han Fu, one of Cao's generals, heard the news that Guan Yu had killed Kong Xiu. He discussed this with his military officer Meng Tan and the two decided to kill Guan.

Han asked Guan, "Do you have Prime Minister Cao's handwritten directive?"

Guan replied, "No."

Han said, “You can’t go through the pass without it.”

Guan said, “Kong Xiu tried to stop us, but he’s been beheaded by me. Don’t you fear death?” Then the battle began.

Meng met Guan head-on. Guan was so powerful that Meng was killed at once. At that moment, an arrow struck Guan’s left arm. He endured the pain, rode his horse, caught up with and killed Han.

Hence Guan led his two sisters-in-law through the second pass.

They arrived at the third pass (Sishui Pass). Bian Xi, another general under Cao Cao, heard that Guan Yu had killed three generals. He decided to cheat Guan Yu by putting him up in a temple first and then trying to find the right moment to end his life.

Bian greeted Guan with a smile and invited them into the temple. However, he and other military officers hadn’t expected that Guan was greatly admired by the monks who subsequently tipped him off about the scheme. Upon learning the truth, Guan flew into a rage and killed Bian. They went through the pass.

The fourth pass was Xingyang. The general there was named Wang Zhi. He was keenly aware that he was no match for Guan Yu and thus planned to burn him to death.

He received Guan Yu and the others with a warm welcome and invited them to rest for a few days before setting off again. Having been travelling for so long, Guan was quite tired and accepted Wang’s offer.

There was a soldier named Hu Ban in Wang’s troops. He had long been an admirer of Guan’s fame, but had yet to meet him in person. This day he saw the hero for the first time. Upon learning that Wang would set fire to burn Guan to death, he tipped him off about Wang's plot. Guan lost no time in fleeing with his sisters-in-law.

Soon Wang found out that Guan had escaped with the others, so he immediately sent his troops in pursuit. But as he caught up with Guan, he was killed in one round. Thus Guan went through the fourth pass.

They marched on and reached the fifth pass, the Yellow River Crossing. The general there was called Qin Qi, who was a hot-tempered person. When seeing Guan Yu, he yelled, "Who are you? Where are you going? Do you have Prime Minister Cao's written directive?"

Guan replied, "I'm Guan Yu, and I'm going to look for my elder brother, Liu Bei. I don't have the directive."

Qin said, "You won't be allowed to pass without it!" He dashed toward Guan and tried to attack him with his broadsword.

Guan wasn't afraid at all—he took up his weapon and killed Qin at once. Then Guan Yu and the others boarded a boat and crossed the Yellow River.

By passing the five passes and killing the six generals, Guan Yu managed to leave Cao Cao's camp. En route to look for Liu Bei, he chanced upon Zhang Fei, his younger brother on Mount Mangdang. Afterwards, the two found Liu in Yuan Shao's troops. Guan Yu handed back his two sisters-in-law to his elder brother.

Liu Bei then left Yuan Shao. The three brothers arrived at Jingzhou to seek temporary shelter, biding their time to revitalize the Han Dynasty.

7. Liu Bei's Three Calls at the Thatched Cottage

After defeating Yuan Shao, Cao Cao conquered Northern China. Liu Bei was unwilling to return to Cao's camp, so he went to look for Liu Biao, who was also a descendent of the Han royal family.

Liu Bei had a talented military advisor named Xu Shu. To bring Xu to his side, Cao had someone send him a message telling him that his mother had a serious illness and that he should not waste any time returning home. As a dutiful son, Xu had no choice but to leave Liu's camp.

He was aware that Cao would never let him come back to Liu's camp. Ahead of his departure, Xu told Liu, "In Longzhong there is an amazingly talented man named Zhuge Liang. People address him respectfully as Mr. Crouching Dragon. Should you obtain his assistance, you can surely revitalize the Han Dynasty and reunify the whole nation." Liu was very much delighted to learn about this.

After Xu left, Liu Bei, Guan Yu and Zhang Fei collected a lot of gifts and headed for Longzhong to visit Zhuge Liang. The three met a peasant along the way who told Liu Bei where the talented man lived—a thatched cottage in the mountains.

They eventually arrived at the front door of Zhuge's house. Liu Bei dismounted his horse and knocked at the door. A servant boy opened the door and told him his master was on a faraway trip and that he had no idea when he would return. Liu Bei had to return home.

After returning to Xinye, Liu Bei often sent people to Longzhong to inquire about Zhuge Liang. One day, he was told that Zhuge Liang had returned home. He immediately decided to visit the talented man once again. The three brothers mounted their horses and went to Longzhong.

Unfortunately, they reached the cottage only to find the person there was not Zhuge Liang, but his younger brother. Liu left a letter to Zhuge Liang and returned to Xinye along with Guan Yu and Zhang Fei.

The next spring, Liu Bei was ready to make a third visit to Zhuge Liang. This time, Zhang Fei and Guan Yu expressed strong resentment and tried to stop their brother. Liu, however, insisted on his decision.

Liu said, "Without sincerity, how can we find talented people? You two don't need to go this time; I will go on my own." Given Liu's persistence, Guan and Zhang had to follow their brother. They embarked on their third trip to visit Zhuge Liang.

They traveled on their horses and arrived at Zhuge's thatched cottage. Seeing that Zhuge Liang was sleeping, Liu Bei stood outside and waited. After a long while, Zhuge still hadn't woken up. Zhang Fei became angry and threatened to set the cottage on fire. Liu urged him to calm down and not to do anything rude.

The three brothers stood outside Zhuge's room, waiting for Zhuge to wake up. After two hours, Zhuge Liang woke up. He invited them into his room.

Upon seeing Zhuge Liang, Liu Bei said, "I've long heard about your great name and finally have the chance to meet you today! It is my aspiration to revitalize the Han Dynasty, but I'm not that capable of achieving my goal. Please enlighten me with your advice."

Zhuge replied, "You brothers visited my cottage three times, which touched me very much. But instead of becoming an official, I prefer the tranquil life in the mountains."

Liu Bei began weeping and said, "Please think of the suffering of the common people and offer your help for their sake!"

Moved by Liu's sincerity, Zhuge Liang agreed to assist him.

Liu asked him, "Given the current situation, what do you think I should do?"

Zhuge sized up the situation and offered the following conclusions:

"First, Cao Cao seizes northern China with one million troops. The emperor is also under his control, so it is not the right time for you to compete with him for northern China.

"Second, Sun Quan occupies the Jiangdong region on the middle and lower reaches of the Yangtze River where access is difficult. He cherishes able bodies and has won the support of his people. But his troops are outnumbered by Cao Cao's. You should ally with him to fight against Cao.

"Third, Jingzhou is of great strategic importance. There are two rivers to its north that are key channels for transporting army provisions. It also borders Wujun to the east, which is Sun Quan's territory, so it should be easy to form an alliance with him. To the west of Jingzhou, Shujun is also of strategic importance. But its owner is unable to govern it. You can replace him and take the region.

"Fourth, Yizhou is another region of strategic importance. The difficult terrain makes it easy to defend but hard to conquer. The region is endowed with fertile land and many other natural resources. Unfortunately, its ruler, Liu Zhang, is too ignorant and weak to run the region well. As a descendant of the Han royal family, you enjoy high prestige and have brought together many heroes, why not try to conquer Yizhou?

"You should also bring the ethnic minority groups in southwest China under control and then form an alliance against Cao Cao. By doing so, you will win the support of all people and be able to revitalize the Han Dynasty."

From the perspectives of timing, geography and human conditions, Zhuge Liang formulated a comprehensive plan for Liu Bei's revitalizing the Han Dynasty. This was the famous *Longzhong Plan*. After listening to him, Liu Bei greatly admired his wisdom and decided to carry out the plan.

After Liu Bei's three visits to his cottage, Zhuge Liang became his military counselor. With his help, Liu Bei formed his own army and the triangular balance of power among Cao Cao, Liu Bei and Sun Quan began to take shape.

8. Zhao Yun Rescues the Child Lord by Himself, and Zhang Fei Repels the Enemy

In 208, Cao Cao, who controlled northern China, led his troops southward to conquer Jingzhou. In August, Liu Biao contracted a serious disease and passed away soon. Liu Cong, Liu Biao's younger son, became the new prefect. Deterred by the might of Cao's army, he surrendered. Liu Bei, who was in Fancheng at the time, didn't get the message.

When Cao's army was approaching Fancheng, Liu Bei prepared to meet the enemy head-on. At that juncture, he learned that Liu Cong had surrendered. Liu was shocked and indignant. But given that his troops were far outnumbered, he realized he would be no match for Cao without Liu Cong's support. Since Liu Cong had surrendered, he had no choice but to flee Fancheng with his army and the local people together.

Liu Bei's soldiers, along with the local people, totaled over 100,000 people. Together with so many carts and horses, they moved rather slowly. Cao Cao's army caught up with them at the Long Slope. Liu ordered Zhang Fei to call up over 20 soldiers and asked them to obstruct the enemy at the Long Slope Bridge. He led the troops and local people to retreat.

Zhang Fei arrived at the Long Slope Bridge. He ordered his soldiers to tie branches to their horse tails and ride horses around in the woods. Soon, clouds of dust flew up. Seen from afar, it appeared as though soldiers and horses were marching together in large numbers. Zhang Fei was sitting on his horse on the bridge. The scene duped Cao Cao and his soldiers into believing that all of Liu Bei's troops were stationed at the Long Slope.

As Liu Bei retreated, his family members and one of his generals Zhao Yun strayed from his troops. After being split from the main forces, Zhao Yun began battling Cao Cao's army in the early morning. He searched hard for Liu Bei's wives, and finally found Lady Gan among many local people. At that moment, he heard the crowd screaming that Cao's army was coming. Lady Mi's elder brother was bound on a horse followed by more than 1,000 soldiers.

Zhao Yun yelled and rode his horse to battle the general with his spear. With one thrust, Zhao fell Cao's general off his horse and freed Lady Mi's brother. He then fought onward and sent Lady Gan to the Long Slope Bridge. Afterwards, he returned to fight the enemy again.

Xiahou En, a major general in Cao's troops, was leading his soldiers and robbing the local people of their wealth. Upon seeing Zhao Yun, Xiahou dashed over along with a dozen cavalrymen. Zhao met the enemy head-on. He stabbed Xiahou with his spear. In only one round of fighting, Xiahou fell off his horse and died. Zhao continued fighting Cao's soldiers.

Suddenly he saw Lady Mi in a courtyard. She was sitting by a well with Edou, Liu Bei's son in her arms. The lady was weeping.

Zhao Yun dismounted his horse and tried to take Lady Mi and the baby out of the encirclement. Mi refused to go, fearing that she might burden Zhao Yun. She handed Edou over to Zhao and asked him to take the baby to his father. After that, she jumped into the well.

Zhao Yun was very sad, seeing that the lady master had drowned herself. Fearing Mi's corpse would be defiled by Cao's army, he pushed down a nearby wall to cover the well.

Having bound Edou inside his armor, Zhao Yun mounted his horse and set out to look for Liu Bei.

At that moment, Cao Cao's soldiers approached. Zhao Yun dashed towards them. Then there appeared more enemy soldiers led by General Zhang He. Zhao Yun began battling Zhang.

After about ten rounds of fighting, he managed to break the siege. Having carried Edou with him, Zhao Yun was eager to flee Zhang and find Liu Bei. He rode his horse fast with Zhang chasing close behind.

All of a sudden, Zhao's horse stumbled and fell into a pit. Zhang thrust at him with his spear. At that critical moment, a red flash of light shot out of the pit—it turned out that Zhao Yun's red horse leapt out! Zhang was taken aback and turned his horse to escape.

As Zhao was about to set out again, two of Cao Cao's generals dashed over to him. They were the brothers Zhong Jin and Zhong Shen. Zhao Yun began battling the Zhong brothers. His robe was soaked in blood. After many rounds of fighting, he managed to gallop away. But soon the two generals dashed toward him again along with many of their soldiers. Zhao used his spear to thrust at the enemies. After several rounds of fighting, Zhong Jin and Zhong Shen were both killed. Zhao immediately galloped to the Long Slope Bridge.

Cao Cao's troops were chasing closely behind. Zhao finally arrived at the bridge and saw Zhang Fei. He shouted, "Help me, Yide!" Seeing that Zhao Yun was approaching, Zhang rushed over to protect him.

Zhao Yun rode through the bridge and met Liu Bei. He told Liu about what had happened to Lady Mi. Then he brought Edou out from his clothes. Surprisingly, the baby was asleep. He handed Edou over to his father. Liu Bei took the baby, but threw him to the ground angrily, saying, "To save you, I nearly lost my great general!"

Zhao Yun picked Edou up from the ground. He kneeled down in front of Liu Bei while weeping, saying, "Were I ground to powder, I couldn't repay your kindness!"

Cao Cao's army arrived at the Long Slope Bridge, only to see great clouds of dust in the woods. They suspected that many of Liu Bei's troops could be lurking. Seeing Zhang Fei sitting on his battle steed, glaring afar and guarding the bridge, none of the soldiers dared to move forward as they were afraid of falling into the trap set by Zhuge Liang.

Cao Cao then came to the frontline. Upon seeing Cao, Zhang Fei yelled, "This is Zhang Fei, Zhang Yide. Who dares to fight with me?" Cao was also fearful.

Cao Cao said to the others, "I heard that Zhang Fei was the sort of man to breeze through an army of a million soldiers and take the head of its general with ease. We must be careful!"

As Cao finished speaking, Zhang Fei shouted again with his fierce eyes staring at the enemy, "Zhang Yide is here, who dares to fight with me?" Cao was so frightened that he turned his horse to retreat.

Zhang yelled, "Why don't you come forward? Why are you still standing there?"

At that moment, a general beside Cao named Xiahou Jie was so scared by the roar that he fell from his horse. Cao was also frightened. He led his troops to gallop away. Many of his soldiers dropped their spears and broadswords and began fleeing. No one would have expected that Zhang Fei could hold back Cao and his army with his roar!

Seeing that Cao Cao had fled along with his troops, Zhang Fei called back his soldiers and ordered them to dismantle the Long Slope Bridge.

Then he returned to Liu Bei and reported this to him. Liu said, "When Cao Cao learns you have pulled down the bridge, he will soon figure out that we don't have enough troops and chase us again." Thus, Liu Bei led his soldiers and the local people to retreat via a small path.

Upon learning that Zhang Fei had dismantled the bridge, Cao Cao realized he had been tricked. He immediately led his troops in pursuit of Liu Bei. Soon Liu Bei was within their reach. Liu looked ahead, only to see there was a river in front which blocked his way. The enemy was approaching! Suddenly, an army dashed out from behind the mountain—it was Guan Yu who came to his elder brother's rescue. In fact, he received the order from Zhuge Liang and had waited there for Liu Bei. Seeing Guan Yu, Cao Cao realized that he was taken in by Zhuge and thus ordered an immediate retreat.

During the battle, Zhao Yun killed more than 50 generals under Cao Cao and saved the life of Edou, Liu Bei's son. From that time onward, Zhao Yun's fame began spreading far and wide.

Despite the loss of many of his soldiers, Liu Bei still had Guan Yu, Zhang Fei and Zhao Yun around him. He decided to seek shelter from Liu Qi, Liu Biao's elder son.

Although Cao Cao failed to catch Liu Bei this time, he seized many places of strategic importance, including Jiangling and Jingzhou.

9. Disputing with the Southern Scholars

After occupying Jingzhou, Cao Cao's troops increased to one million. He then led his army southward to the Yangtze River and wanted to seize Eastern Wu. He wrote a letter to Sun Quan urging him to surrender. If Sun didn't comply, he would launch an attack on him.

Given the might of Cao's army, many of the Eastern Wu ministers and counselors were in awe of him. They tried to persuade Sun Quan to surrender. Zhou Yu, a young, handsome and wise major general, however, was strongly against this common view. Lu Su, Sun Quan's military advisor, also opposed surrender.

Sun Quan found himself in a dilemma. Lu suggested that Sun Quan form an alliance with Liu Bei against Cao Cao. Then Sun Quan dispatched him to discuss the matter with Liu Bei. After their meeting, Liu Bei agreed to fight Cao along with Sun Quan. He sent Zhuge Liang to visit Sun Quan in an effort to come up with a ruse to deal with Cao Cao.

Before receiving Zhuge in person, Sun Quan arranged a meeting between him and the Eastern Wu counselors. All the counselors were in favor of surrender, so they raised a lot of questions to debate with Zhuge Liang.

Zhang Zhao was the first to ask: "I heard when you once lived at Longzhong, you likened yourself to Guan Zhong and Yue Yi, who were among the great ministers in history. I also heard Liu Bei visited your home three times to seek your assistance, and now he's in his heyday! You want to capture Jingzhou, but after Liu Cong's surrender, it is now in Cao Cao's hands. I'd like to hear your opinion on this."

Zhuge Liang replied, "Jingzhou belongs to Liu Biao, who is the descendant of the Han royal family. Liu Bei didn't want to seize his territory. Unfortunately, Liu Cong, Liu Biao's younger son, surrendered to Cao and offered it to him. Now our troops are stationed at Jiangxia and bide our time. All of you lack vision, so you cannot understand our scheme."

Zhang Zhao went on asking, "What you said sounds contradictory. You claim to be the equal of the two great ministers Guan Zhong and Yue Yi, but before you helped Liu

Bei, he could battle Cao Cao; while after you joined his camp, he could only flee in the face of Cao's attack. It's clear that Liu is on the wane. Are you really the great minister like Guan Zhong and Yue Yi?"

Zhuge Liang responded with a smile, "When a patient contracts a serious illness, the physician should first treat him with a milder medicine. As the patient's condition gets better, strong medicine can be used. If the physician seeks an instant cure by using strong medicine at the very beginning, the patient might die. Liu Bei was recently defeated with less than 1,000 soldiers left under his command. Now he has only three generals: Guan Yu, Zhang Fei and Zhao Yun. Plus, we also lack weapons and provisions. If we try to fight Cao Cao's troops now, it would be just like treating the patient with strong medicine, which would be very risky. Liu Biao's son surrendered to Cao Cao and presented Jingzhou to him. But 100,000 Jingzhou people all wanted to follow Liu Bei. Feeling reluctant to leave them behind, he ordered his soldiers to take care of them en route. That is why our troops marched so slowly. Therefore, this defeat means nothing in our whole campaign." Hearing this, Zhang Zhao was speechless.

Yu Fan, another counselor went on asking, "What's your take on Cao Cao's mighty army?"

Zhuge Liang laughed and said, "Although Cao has one million troops, there is nothing to fear."

Yu Fan sneered and said, "Liu Bei suffered a big defeat and wants us to save him, how dare you say you don't fear Cao?"

Zhuge Liang replied, "We are just biding our time now! You have plenty of troops and many outstanding generals, and the

Yangtze River can serve as a great defense. In spite of all this, all of you choose to kneel before the enemy. This is laughable. Indeed, Liu Bei is not the sort of man to fear Cao Cao!" Yu was also speechless.

Another counselor, Xue Zong, asked, "What do you think of Cao Cao?"

Zhuge Liang replied, "Cao Cao's father Cao Song once served as the prime minister of the Han Dynasty, but now Cao Cao controls the emperor and orders the other warlords about in his name. He's no doubt a scoundrel against the court."

Xue Zong continued asking, "The Han Dynasty is near its end, and yet Liu Bei is trying to fight the powerful Cao Cao—failure is doomed."

Zhuge Liang retorted, "All people in the country are indignant about Cao's rebellion, how can you raise such a question? I decline to argue with you anymore!" Xue became speechless with embarrassment.

Another counselor, Lu Ji, asked, "Cao Cao's grandfather was once the prime minister of the Han Dynasty, whereas Liu Bei is no more than a straw sandals seller. How can he be a match for Cao Cao?"

Zhuge Liang laughed and said, "Although Cao Cao is a descendant of a prime minister from the Han Dynasty, he conspires against the court and thus has become a treacherous minister; as for Liu Bei, our emperor addresses him as 'emperor's uncle'. Also bear in mind that Liu Bang, founding emperor of the Han Dynasty, was just a low-ranking official in his early days, but later he became the ruler of the whole country. As such, where is the shame in selling straw sandals?" Lu became silent, too.

At that moment, senior general Huang Gai rushed into the hall and said with anger, "Cao Cao's troops are stationed on the opposite bank of the Yangtze River. Instead of discussing how to vanquish the enemy, you are just debating endlessly here!" The argument then stopped.

Zhuge Liang utterly convinced the Wu scholars of his argument with his superior wisdom.

10. Borrowing Arrows from the Enemy

After having debated with the Eastern Wu counselors, Zhuge Liang met with Sun Quan, the ruler of the Kingdom of Wu. Zhuge tried to persuade Sun to resist Cao Cao's troops. The latter eventually agreed. Zhou Yu learned about Zhuge's great wisdom and became very jealous of him. He believed Zhuge's wit would pose a serious threat to Eastern Wu and thus intended to kill him.

One day, Zhou invited Zhuge over to discuss the matter of making arrows. He told Zhuge, "As we are going to battle on the Yangtze River, bows and arrows are the ideal weapons. But now we are short of arrows, so I would like you to help us make 100,000 arrows within ten days."

Zhuge, who was keenly aware that by doing so Zhou wanted to kill him, responded by saying, "The enemy is approaching and ten days will be too long. Three days are enough for me! I am willing to write a pledge. I will be subject to punishment if I can't make 100,000 arrows in three days."

Zhou was overjoyed to hear this promise. He believed Zhuge

would surely receive capital punishment for it was impossible for him to make those arrows in only three days.

Zhou ordered his subordinates not to offer Zhuge the materials needed for making arrows so that Zhuge had to look for them by himself. He also asked his soldiers to purposely delay their work. Then Lu Su was dispatched to inquire about Zhuge's work.

Upon seeing Lu, Zhuge said, "Please lend me 20 small boats and 600 soldiers. Each boat should have scarecrows tied on both sides. Do not let Zhou Yu know about this plan, or I will be put to death." Lu agreed.

Zhou Yu asked Lu Su about Zhuge's plan. Lu only told him that Zhuge hadn't used anything to make arrows. Zhou was perplexed to hear this. He would have to wait and see how Zhuge planned to do so.

Two days passed and Zhuge Liang still did nothing. On the third night, Zhuge invited Lu to fetch arrows with him. Lu felt puzzled as he didn't believe Zhuge had fulfilled the task.

That evening, thick fog enveloped the Yangtze River. The 20 boats approached Cao Cao's naval camp. As the fleet had nearly reached the naval camp, Zhuge ordered all the boats to stop and form a single-line formation, with the bow facing east. He then asked the soldiers to beat their drums and make a battle cry. Lu Su was worried that they would be in great danger if Cao's fleet dashed out of the naval camp. Zhuge said with a smile, "The fog is so thick that Cao does not dare to come out! Let's drink wine and we shall return after the fog disperses."

Cao Cao was shocked to hear the drumbeat and battle cry.

However, the fog on the river was so thick that he couldn't see anything. He thought the Eastern Wu fleet might have arrived. Fearing that it was a trap set by Zhuge, he ordered over 10,000 soldiers to shoot arrows toward the river, most of which hit the scarecrows.

In just a short while, all the scarecrows on the 20 boats were loaded with arrows. Zhuge then ordered the sailors to turn the boats toward the west and continue beating the drums while making a battle cry—the scarecrows on the other side became loaded with arrows, too.

Day broke and the fog on the river gradually dispersed. Zhuge Liang ordered the sailors to turn the boats around and head back to their camp. He told them to shout, "Thank you, Prime Minister Cao, for the arrows!" Only then did Cao Cao realize that he had been tricked by Zhuge Liang and lost 100,000 arrows.

Zhuge told Lu Su, "We got more than 100,000 arrows while drinking wine and chatting. The arrows can be used to fight Cao Cao."

Lu replied, "You are a real genius!"

Zhuge told him, "Zhou Yu asked me to make so many arrows within ten days, but he gave neither hands nor materials to me. It's clear that he wants to kill me. Three days ago, I predicted that there would be a heavy fog today and thus hit upon the plan."

Upon returning to their camp, Zhuge ordered the soldiers to remove the arrows from the scarecrows and count. The arrows totaled 150,000 to 160,000. He then asked them to hand all the arrows to Zhou Yu. Lu Su met Zhou and told the whole story to him. Zhou was stunned and said, "Zhuge is brilliant. I am no match for him!"

Afterwards, Cao Cao had his 800,000 troops stationed on the northern bank of the Yangtze River and was ready to attack Eastern Wu. On the southern bank of the river, Sun Quan and Liu Bei's allied forces numbered merely 50,000. Both sides were locked in a face-off and prepared for the battle.

11. The Battle of the Red Cliffs

Cao Cao led his one million strong army southward to attack the Kingdom of Wu. They were stationed at Chibi on the bank of the Yangtze River. Under the threat of Cao's dreadful army, Liu Bei and Sun Quan formed an alliance to resist it.

One night, old general Huang Gai went to meet Zhou Yu. "Since we are outnumbered by the enemy, it is no good for us to have a prolonged battle," Huang said. "How about attacking Cao's army with fire?"

"This is a brilliant idea," Zhou replied. "I agree with you. I am considering sending someone to feignedly surrender to Cao, but I have no idea who is suitable for this task."

Huang volunteered, "I'd like to fulfill it."

Zhou was so grateful that he kneeled down in front of Huang, saying, "You are such a great help to me, General Huang. It seems that we have to play a ruse of self-injury."

The next day, Zhou called together his generals and said, "Cao's army is powerful indeed. Huang Gai, go and secure provisions for three months so that we are prepared for a long battle."

Huang shouted, "Now that Cao has such a powerful army, we'd

better surrender to him."

Hearing this, Zhou pretended to be angry and roared, "How dare you undermine our morale. Soldiers, put him to death!"

Huang then yelled at Zhou, "When I fought battles together with your father, you weren't even born yet! You dare to have me killed!"

Hearing this, Zhou seemed even angrier. He ordered soldiers to kill Huang right away. The other generals begged for leniency for Huang. Zhou turned to Huang, saying, "The generals have pleaded for me to show you mercy, I will spare your life! But I must punish you with 100 lashes."

Even before half his penalty had been doled out to him, Huang was bloodied all over. The generals, unable to watch Huang being beaten so hard at such an old age, asked for him to be spared. Zhou turned to the soldiers. "Stop!" he said. "The remaining lashes will be given later."

Kan Ze, a close friend of Huang, realized that Huang and Zhou were playing a trick of self-injury and that they were doing so to fool Cao's spy. Later, Kan went to see Zhou and offered to take Huang's letter of feigned surrender to Cao. Zhou agreed. That night, Kan sneaked to Cao's camp by boat.

Kan told Cao that Huang hated Zhou so much that he wanted to surrender to Cao and help him attack the Kingdom of Wu. However, Cao was somewhat suspicious while reading Huang's letter. At that moment, a letter came in from Cao's spy in the Kingdom of Wu, telling in detail the story of Huang's suffering from corporal punishment. Reading this, Cao no longer doubted Huang. He was delighted and waited for Huang's arrival.

Pang Tong, a military advisor, told Lu Su that Cao had many ships that were difficult to burn in a single attempt. Pang said that he could disguise himself as a spy, go to meet Cao and persuade him to link all his ships together, which could be burned in a fire attack. Lu forwarded Pang's plan to Zhou. Zhou was very happy and approved it.

Pretending to surrender to Cao, Pang went to Cao's barracks. Cao's troops were mostly from north China. They seldom went on the water and were prone to seasickness and consequent illnesses. Cao was deeply worried about this. Hence Pang gave him a piece of advice: link all the ships together and place planks over their decks so that his soldiers could walk on them like on the ground to avoid nausea. Hearing this, Cao immediately ordered his soldiers to do so. He was so relieved that his troops could fight as if they were on the ground.

Zhou Yu finished making all the preparations for the fire attack. However, to ensure the fire attack was a success, they still needed one thing—an east wind. Zhou waited for a couple of days, but there was no east wind at all. He was so worried that he fell ill.

Zhuge Liang went to visit Zhou Yu and wrote him a note, which read, "To defeat Cao, we should resort to a fire attack. Now all is ready except the east wind."

Reading the note, Zhou said to Zhuge, "You're so wise. This is what is on my mind. What should we do?"

Zhuge reassured him, "Don't worry. I'll help you bring an east wind in three days."

Zhou thought that Zhuge must be bragging in making this

promise.

Three days later, a strong northwest wind blew over the river. This made Zhou even more upset. If such a wind continued into the night, it would be impossible to carry out a fire attack against Cao. Therefore, he hoped Zhuge would bring an east wind with which they could defeat Cao. Meanwhile, he was worried if Zhuge succeeded, he would prove himself more clever than Zhou. But Zhuge was carefree.

As night fell, Zhuge began his performance. He ascended a high platform, from the top of which he murmured some words and wielded a sword. The soldiers around him were totally at a loss as to what he was doing. In fact, Zhuge had anticipated three days earlier that there would be a southeast wind that day. He was intending to make Zhou jealous in saying that he could bring an east wind.

After a while, the northwest wind died away. Into the night, a southeast wind started to blow. The wind grew stronger, so everyone rejoiced at this.

Then, Huang Gai led a score of ships to "surrender" to Cao. Covered with black cloth, these ships were loaded with firewood and oil. As they drew near to their targets, Huang ordered his soldiers to set fire to the ships, which then rushed toward Cao's fleet. As Cao's ships were linked together, they all burst into flames.

As the fire blazed fiercely, the flare lit up the sky as well as the cliffs on the bank. Many of Cao's soldiers fled to the land. Zhou Yu sent his troops toward them and crushed Cao's army. Cao had to flee with his remaining soldiers.

Knowing Zhou's personality, Zhuge was afraid that Zhou would have him killed out of jealousy after winning the battle, so he had Zhao Yun escort him away. They left Zhou's barracks together. At that time, Zhou was busy attacking Cao and had no time to kill Zhuge.

After defeating Cao, Zhou inscribed two Chinese characters meaning "red cliffs" on the cliff face with his sword. In this historic battle known as the Battle of the Red Cliffs, the weak allied forces of Sun Quan and Liu Bei triumphed over Cao's strong army with hundreds of thousands of soldiers.

After losing the battle, it was impossible for Cao to launch another attack against Liu and Sun in the near future. The Battle of the Red Cliffs marked the formation of the triangular balance of power among the three kingdoms of Wei, Shu and Wu.

12. Guan Yu Lets Cao Cao Go

Cao Cao's plan to seize the Kingdom of Wu fell through after his ships were burned by Zhou Yu and Zhuge Liang at Chibi. To intercept Cao and his fleeing soldiers, Zhuge Liang sent his troops to guard several key spots.

He assigned tasks to all generals except Guan Yu, so Guan asked why he had nothing to do.

Zhuge said, "I had been considering sending you to guard the Huarong Path of paramount importance, but I am a bit worried, so I didn't let you do this."

Guan asked angrily, "What are you worried about?"

Zhuge replied, "I am afraid that you may let Cao Cao go because you owe him a favor."

Guan responded at once, "I fought battles for him, but I repaid his kindness long ago. I won't let him go."

Zhuge continued, "But what if you do let him go?"

Guan promised, "If you don't trust me, I can make a pledge."

Guan Yu wrote a pledge immediately. Then Zhuge sent him to defend the Huarong Path with his soldiers.

After Cao's fleet was destroyed in the fire attack, only a small number of troops managed to escape with him. Escorted by his generals and soldiers, Cao came to the woods at the foot of a mountain. The terrain there was difficult.

Seeing this, Cao suddenly burst into laughter, which perplexed his men. They asked, "Your Excellency, since we have lost the battle, why are you laughing?"

Cao replied, "Suppose Zhuge Liang and Zhou Yu had troops lie in wait here, we would have no way to escape. That's why I'm laughing."

The moment Cao finished speaking, Zhao Yun burst into view with a contingent of troops. Seeing this, Cao's soldiers hurriedly escorted him in flight.

Shortly before dawn, there was a heavy rainfall. Cao and his men were cold and hungry. At a place called the Gourd Valley, Cao ordered his generals and soldiers to take a rest.

Sitting in the woods, Cao looked around and burst into laughter again. His men were bewildered again, having no idea why he was laughing again.

Cao explained, "If Zhuge Liang and Zhou Yu had troops lying

in ambush here, we would either die or be seriously wounded. That's why I'm laughing."

As soon as Cao finished speaking, a detachment rushed out from the valley and surrounded his army. It was headed by Zhang Fei. At the sight of this, Cao was so frightened that he mounted a horse and fled.

Cao and his men were all in a fluster as they fled. Later, they came to a junction. A vanguard soldier reported, "There are two roads ahead of us, a main road and a trail. The main road is smooth, but it will take us longer to arrive in Jingzhou by that road. The trail, called the Huarong Path, is rough, but it is a shortcut to Jingzhou." Cao feared that Zhuge's soldiers might be lying in wait along the main road, so he ordered his men to take the trail.

The trail was slippery because of the rain. As his generals and soldiers treaded the rough path, Cao laughed for a third time. Baffled, his men asked why he was laughing. Cao explained, "If Zhuge and Zhou had troops lie low here, we would have to surrender."

Just then, there came a cannon shot. It was Guan Yu heading a contingent in front of them. Cao's soldiers were terrified. Overcome by fear, they were at a loss what to do.

At this critical juncture, a military advisor reminded Cao, "Guan Yu is loyal to his friends. Since you took him in, he must still be mindful of your favor. If you try to persuade him, he might be moved and let us go."

Cao adopted the man's advice and went to meet Guan to talk of their past.

Although Guan knew that he had signed the written pledge and would be punished if he let Cao go, he was still grateful to Cao and it was against his conscience to kill Cao, so he let Cao and his men go.

Guan then led his soldiers back to Zhuge's barracks. Seeing Guan's return, Zhuge went forward to welcome him back.

Guan said, "I am here to take my capital punishment."

Zhuge asked, "Didn't Cao take the Huarong Path?"

Guan replied, "He did this. But due to my incompetence, he escaped."

Zhuge said, "I fear that you let Cao go because of his past favor to you. Nevertheless, you signed a written pledge, so I must punish you in accordance with military law." He then ordered his soldiers to execute Guan. Seeing this, Liu Bei's generals all hurriedly kneeled to beg mercy for Guan.

Liu Bei also asked for leniency for Guan, "Could you spare his life this time? How about putting his guilt on record and letting him make amends for it by good services in the future?"

In fact, Zhuge did not want to put Guan to death. He just intended to scare Guan and warn others to observe military discipline. Having seen that they were scared, he relented, "All right! Guan, your guilt will be recorded. But you must bear it in mind and make amends for it later."

Everyone was joyful again and the entire army was celebrating the victory of the battle. In fact, it was Zhuge's strategy to have Guan guard the Huarong Path and let Cao go. It was not an opportune time to kill Cao because he had hundreds of thousands of troops in north China while Liu Bei's army was still weak at the time.

After defeating Cao, Liu Bei and Sun Quan began to scramble for Jingzhou. In this process, Zhuge Liang and Zhou Yu showed their prowess respectively.

13. Sun Quan and Zhou Yu Suffer a Double Loss

After the Battle of the Red Cliffs, Zhuge Liang sent Zhao Yun to attack the South Prefecture. Zhao seized Jingzhou and some cities around it, which eventually enabled Liu Bei to have his own territory. Occupying south, east, and north China respectively, Liu Bei, Sun Quan, and Cao Cao basically formed a triangular balance of power.

Before long, Liu's wife, Lady Gan, passed away. Learning about this, Zhou Yu advised Sun Quan on a scheme: Pretend to marry off Sun's sister, Sun Shangxiang, to Liu, and catch Liu when he comes to meet his bride, so as to seize Jingzhou. Sun Quan agreed.

Zhuge Liang saw through Sun and Zhou's scheme, and made three plans in response. On Liu's departure, Zhuge gave Zhao Yun three small bags made of brocade, and told him to open them only in emergencies.

As Liu and his entourage arrived in the Kingdom of Wu, Zhao opened the first small bag.

Having read Zhuge's instructions, Zhao ordered his men to put on formal attire, purchase items for a wedding ceremony and gifts for the bride and her family, and most importantly, tell the people in the Kingdom of Wu that Liu Bei and Sun Quan's younger sister were going to get married. Soon people all over the Kingdom of Wu knew of the engagement.

Then Zhao Yun asked Liu Bei to visit Qiao Guolao, an influential figure in the Kingdom of Wu, and try to get help from him. Qiao had two daughters: one was married to Sun Ce, and the other to Zhou Yu.

Qiao Guolao was glad to meet Liu Bei. After seeing Liu off, he went to visit Sun Quan's mother, Wu Guotai, to congratulate her.

Wu Guotai was astonished. It turned out that she had been kept in the dark about the marriage. So Wu Guotai sent people to summon Sun and Zhou and asked them what was going on.

Sun said, "This is a scheme devised by Zhou Yu and me, and it aims at enticing Liu Bei to come and to detain him in the Kingdom of Wu. We won't marry off my younger sister to him."

Wu Guotai was very angry, and scolded Sun and Zhou for what they were doing. She decided to see Liu Bei first before determining what to do next. Sun had no choice but to let his mother meet Liu.

Unexpectedly, Wu Guotai was very satisfied with Liu Bei, as she found Liu had an impressive presence. Greatly pleased, she told Qiao Guolao, "Liu Bei is so imposing. I agree to marry my daughter to him!"

Thus, Sun Quan had no choice but to agree to marry his sister to Liu Bei. Then, Wu Guotai held a wedding for Liu and her daughter.

To control Liu Bei, Sun Quan had a splendid palace built for Liu Bei and his younger sister. He also provided Liu with delicious food and women entertainers. Living a comfortable life suddenly after many years of fighting, Liu Bei, as expected by Sun Quan, forgot his goals and didn't want to return to Jingzhou.

Seeing this, Zhao Yun was very worried, so he opened the second small bag given to him by Zhuge Liang.

After reading Zhuge's instructions, Zhao Yun immediately told Liu Bei, "We have to go back to Jingzhou immediately because the situation there is critical!" In fact, this was nothing but a plot.

Hearing this, Liu Bei was very concerned, but he was reluctant to leave Lady Sun. This put him in a bad mood.

Realizing that Liu Bei had something weighing on his mind, Lady Sun asked him what it was. Liu told her that the situation in Jingzhou was critical and he was deeply concerned. Hearing this, Sun decided to go to Jingzhou with her husband.

Being afraid that Sun Quan would disagree, Liu Bei told a lie to Wu Guotai that he would lead his men to go to the riverside on New Year's Day to worship his ancestors. Wu Guotai agreed right away to let him go.

On New Year's Day, Liu Bei and Lady Sun fled toward the riverside under the protection of Zhao Yun. After learning of their escape, Sun Quan immediately sent his soldiers to chase them.

As Liu Bei was rushing toward the riverside, a contingent of troops suddenly appeared in his way. In no time Sun Quan's soldiers were on his heels. At this critical moment, Zhao Yun thought of the third small bag given to him by Zhuge Liang.

Zhao Yun opened it and gave Zhuge's note to Liu Bei. The note told him to seek help from Lady Sun.

Liu Bei told Sun that the soldiers of the Kingdom of Wu were there to obstruct them. Hearing this, Lady Sun was very angry and railed at Sun Quan's soldiers. Since she was Sun Quan's younger sister, the soldiers did not dare to disobey her. They had to let Liu Bei and his entourage go.

Shortly thereafter, however, Zhou Yu appeared with his soldiers. Liu Bei got very anxious. At the crucial moment, Liu suddenly saw Zhuge Liang approaching the riverside with his men and a boat. Liu lost no time in boarding the boat with his wife and escaped.

Witnessing Liu getting on the boat, Zhou Yu ordered his soldiers to pursue them by boats. As they reached the other side of the river, Zhuge Liang ordered his men to stop the boats and go ashore, with Zhou Yu and his troops in hot pursuit. Zhou did not realize that Zhuge's soldiers had been lying in ambush on the bank. Both sides engaged in fierce fighting, and Zhou's soldiers suffered heavy casualties. Zhou Yu fled to his boat and was extremely regretful. At this time, he heard Liu Bei's soldiers shouting on the bank: "Zhou, you have given your enemy a wife and lost your soldiers as well!"

Hearing this, Zhou Yu was so angry that he fainted. According to the original scheme, he planned to detain Liu Bei in the Kingdom of Wu first and then kill him. He did not expect that he would be taken in by Zhuge and suffer losses.

Later on, Zhou was again outwitted by Zhuge Liang a few times. He was so angry that he fell fatally ill. On his deathbed, he sighed, "Why have I had to share life with Zhuge Liang?"

14. Guan Yu Loses Jingzhou Owing to Negligence

In 213, Liu Bei led his forces into Shu, and entrusted Zhuge Liang and part of his soldiers with the defense of Jingzhou. The next year, as Liu was in dire need of reinforcements in pacifying Shu, he called in Zhang Fei, Zhao Yun and Zhuge Liang to assist him, and had Guan Yu guard Jingzhou.

In 219, Liu Bei proclaimed himself a king in Hanzhong, and Zhuge Liang was appointed as the prime minister of the Kingdom of Shu. Eager to help Liu conquer north China, Guan Yu led an army to attack Fancheng in the north, leaving his son Guan Ping to defend Jingzhou.

Fancheng was on Cao Wei's territory, and the general defending it was Cao Ren. While attacking Fancheng, Guan Yu, instead of defeating Cao Ren as he expected, was shot with a poisoned arrow in the right arm. He had to retreat to his barracks. Soon his right arm was swollen and he was unable to move it. It turned out that the poison on the arrow had penetrated his bone.

Guan Ping and his generals and soldiers went to visit Guan Yu. They wanted to take him back to Jingzhou for treatment.

Guan Yu asked, "Is there anything seriously wrong back in Jingzhou?"

Guan Ping replied, "Since your right arm has been injured, I am afraid it is no longer suitable for you to continue to fight battles. We think that you should return to Jingzhou first and wait until you recover."

Hearing this, Guan Yu got very angry, and said, "We are about to succeed in restoring the Han Dynasty. How can I put such a grand mission on hold simply because of such a minor injury?

How dare you say this! Get out!" Guan Ping and the other generals had no choice but to obey.

Guan Yu refused to retreat, but had not recovered from his injury, so his men had to find a doctor to treat him.

One day, a man came to Guan Yu's barracks, and his soldiers took the man to Guan Ping. The man introduced himself, "My name is Hua Tuo," he said. "I know that General Guan Yu is a hero. I heard that he was injured by a poisoned arrow. I am here to cure him." Hua Tuo was a well-known doctor, so Guan Ping and the generals lost no time in leading him to Guan Yu.

After checking Guan Yu's injury, Hua Tuo told him, "The poison has already entered your bone. If there is a delay in treatment, your arm will have to be amputated."

Guan Yu asked, "Is there an effective therapy?"

Hua Tuo said, "It is too late to apply medicine from outside. I have only one therapy, but it is very painful. Do you dare to try it?"

Guan Yu laughed, "I don't fear death. Do you think I fear pain? Please go ahead!"

Hua said, "This is my treatment plan: First, find a quiet place, erect a pole, and nail an iron hoop onto it. Then put your right arm into the hoop and fasten it with a rope. Then you'll be blindfolded. Next, I'll cut open the flesh of your right arm and expose the bone. Then I'll scrape the poison off the bone, apply medicine, and finally sew up the wound."

Guan Yu laughed, "No problem! Just go ahead!" He had a soldier serve him liquor.

He began to play chess with someone while extending his right arm to Hua Tuo. Hua said, "I am starting now. Please don't be afraid."

Guan Yu said, "Be at ease. I am not afraid of pain."

Hua Tuo cut open the flesh of Guan Yu's right arm and found that the bone inside had turned black. Hua then scraped the bone with a scalpel. People did not dare to watch, and some were pale in their faces because of fear. However, Guan Yu was relaxed. While drinking liquor, he played chess and talked to people, as if he felt no pain at all.

After scraping the poison off the bone, Hua Tuo applied some medicine, and stitched up the wound. Guan Yu stood up, moved his arm and laughed, "Look, I can move this arm again. It doesn't hurt at all. Mr. Hua, you are really a legendary doctor!"

Hua Tuo also admired Guan Yu very much and said, "I have been a doctor for so long, but I have never seen a person as brave as you!"

Later, the Kingdom of Wu seized Jingzhou when Guan Yu was busy attacking Fancheng. As Jingzhou was strategically important to the Kingdom of Shu, Guan Yu's loss of the city rendered Shu at a disadvantage.

Later on, Cao Cao sent troops to support the Kingdom of Wu and besieged Guan Yu in Maicheng. Trapped in Maicheng, Guan Yu ran out of provisions, and his reinforcements did not arrive in time. In the end, Guan Yu was ambushed and captured by Sun Quan's soldiers.

Sun Quan wanted Guan Yu to surrender and fight for the Kingdom of Wu, but Guan refused to do so resolutely, so Sun had him executed.

The decade from 219 to 229 saw many changes in the Three Kingdoms of Wei, Sui and Wu.

In 219, Guan Yu failed in capturing Fancheng, and the Kingdom of Shu lost Jingzhou and fell into a plight. Guan Yu was killed by Sun Quan.

In 220, Cao Cao passed away. Cao Cao's son Cao Pi coerced Emperor Xiandi of the Eastern Han Dynasty to abdicate. Cao Pi then became an emperor and established the Kingdom of Wei.

In 221, Liu Bei proclaimed himself an emperor in Chengdu and established Shu Han, also known as the Kingdom of Shu.

In 229, Sun Quan became an emperor in Jianye and established the Kingdom of Wu.

By then, Cao Pi, Liu Bei, and Sun Quan had established the Three Kingdoms of Wei, Shu, and Wu respectively, and formally entered a triangle balance of power.

15. Liu Bei Entrusts His Young Sons

After hearing that Sun Quan had killed Guan Yu, Liu Bei and Zhang Fei were in great agony. In particular, Guan's death led to a significant change in Zhang Fei's temper, and he often abused his soldiers. One day, when he was drunk, he was murdered by two of his subordinates. The two fled to the Kingdom of Wu after having killed Zhang Fei and defected to Sun Quan.

This made Liu Bei even sadder, and he resolved to avenge the death of Guan and Zhang. Zhuge Liang tried talking him out of too hasty revenge, but Liu did not heed his advice.

Liu Bei led hundreds of thousands of troops to attack Sun Quan, but they fell into a trap—a fire attack. His barracks were burned by Sun's troops. Later, Liu fled to Baidicheng, and before long, he became seriously ill.

The next year, Liu Bei's illness had gotten even worse. One night, a cold wind suddenly blew into his bedroom through the window, and a candle on his table flickered. Liu Bei dreamed that Guan Yu and Zhang Fei were standing in the candlelight, hearing Guan saying, "Elder brother, it won't be long before the three of us are reunited." Deeply missing Guan Yu and Zhang Fei, Liu Bei was agonized and began to wail.

Suddenly, Guan Yu and Zhang Fei disappeared. Liu Bei woke up and realized that he had just been dreaming.

He sighed, "Alas, my death is imminent." So Liu immediately sent people to Chengdu for Zhuge Liang and others to make arrangements after his death.

After Zhuge Liang's arrival, Liu Bei said to him, "Thanks for your help, Prime Minister, my army has grown rapidly. However, I did not follow your advice, and thus I caused a great failure to our kingdom. I feel bitter remorse over this. Now that I am deadly ill and my sons don't have the capacity to govern our kingdom, I entrust you to oversee state affairs!" After saying these words, Liu Bei shed tears.

Zhuge Liang also wept upon hearing Liu's words. Liu Bei whispered to Zhuge, "You need to keep an eye on Ma Su, who is working at your side, do not readily place your trust in him."

After that, Liu Bei wrote a will, handed it to Zhuge Liang, and said to everyone in attendance, "I want to defeat Cao Pi together with all of you; I want to restore the imperial family of Han, but I am already at death's door. Prime Minister, please hand over this will to Crown Prince Liu Shan. I hope you will continue to help him in the future."

Kneeling on the ground, Zhuge Liang replied, "Rest assured, Your Majesty, we will do our utmost to help Crown Prince Liu Shan, so that we can repay our debt of gratitude for your appreciation and trust."

Liu Bei whispered again to Zhuge Liang, "Since you are far more capable than Cao Pi, you can be a good emperor. Crown Prince Liu Shan is still young. If he is competent enough to be an emperor, please help him become a good one. If he is truly unfit for the emperor, you can take his place."

Deeply touched by Liu Bei's trust in him, Zhuge Liang kneeled on the ground and reassured him, "I am not interested in becoming an emperor. I will do all I can to assist the Crown Prince."

Liu Bei turned to Zhao Yun, "Brother, I hope you can help my son, too!" Kneeling on the ground, Zhao Yun shed tears and promised, "I will definitely do my best to help the Crown Prince."

Finally, Liu Bei said to the others, "I hope each and every one of you will perform your duties well." Having finished speaking, Liu Bei passed away. Liu died in 223 at the age of 63.

Returning to Chengdu, Zhuge Liang held a funeral for Liu Bei, and read Liu's will to his sons.

In the will, Liu Bei had written, "I heard that people are considered to have lived a long life beyond the age of 50. Now that I am over 60 years old, I have no regrets. But I am only worried about you, my sons! You must remember: don't engage in evil even if it's minor, and don't fail to do good even if it's trivial. Only if you are wise and virtuous will people obey you. You must learn from the Prime Minister how to behave and do things. You must respect and treat him as if he were your father. You must strive for excellence."

After reading the will, Zhuge Liang said to everyone present, "A country cannot endure a day without an emperor." So he helped Crown Prince Liu Shan to ascend to the throne.

To fulfill Liu Bei's dream of reviving the imperial family of Han, Zhuge Liang did his best to assist Liu Shan. All affairs in the imperial court, big or small, were handled by Zhuge Liang, and thanks to his great efforts, the Kingdom of Shu gradually became strong and prosperous again.

16. Zhuge Liang Calmly Foils the Enemy Attacks on Five Routes

Cao Pi, the emperor of the Kingdom of Wei, was excited when he heard that Liu Bei had died. So he planned to attack the Kingdom of Shu.

Sima Yi of Wei made a proposal to Cao Pi: "We should mobilize our troops to attack the Kingdom of Shu on five routes from the east, west, south, and north at the same time. First, we should unite with Kebi Neng, the king of the Xianbei people, and ask him to lead his 100,000 soldiers to attack Xiping Pass. This is our army on the first route. Second, let's give Meng Huo, the king of ethnic minority groups in the south, some money and ask him to mobilize his 100,000 soldiers to attack Yizhou and other places in southern Shu. This is our army on the second route.

Third, we should ally with Eastern Wu and urge Sun Quan to lead his 100,000 men to attack Fucheng. This is our army on the third route. Fourth, we can have Meng Da command his 100,000 soldiers to attack Hanzhong from the west. This is our army on the fourth route. Fifth, we should order Grand General Cao Zhen to bring his 100,000 soldiers to attack Xichuan from the Yangping Pass. This is our army on the fifth route. With a total of 500,000 soldiers on five routes, our army will attack Shu at the same time. This will certainly make it impossible for Zhuge Liang to block them!" Hearing this, Cao Pi was very happy and immediately issued an order to have Sima Yi's plan carried out.

Knowing that Wei had sent its army to attack them on five routes, the people of Shu were extremely scared. Zhuge Liang, however, stayed at home all day long. Liu Shan was so anxious that he went to consult Zhuge in person.

Arriving at Zhuge's residence, Liu found that he was quietly watching the fish in his garden. Liu Shan approached Zhuge and said, "Prime Minister, Wei has sent its army to attack us on five routes, but you are idly watching fish!"

Zhuge Liang smiled, "I already know that a 500,000 strong army is marching toward us, but I have repulsed the enemy troops on four routes. As for the enemy troops on the fifth route, Sun Quan's troops, I have an idea about how to repel them. But I still need an eloquent person to negotiate with the ruler of Wu, Sun Quan."

Hearing this, Liu Shan was very happy. He asked Zhuge Liang, "How did you repel the enemy troops on four routes?"

Zhuge Liang replied, "The essence of the art of war is making maneuvers that outwit the enemy troops. I ordered Ma Chao to guard the Xiping Pass and fight the army of Kebi Neng on the first route. I sent Wei Yan to wait for Meng Huo's army on the second route and ordered his cavalrymen to run from side to side and back and forth on the road to fill the air with dust. When Meng Huo saw the dust ahead, undoubtedly he believed that we had a strong army ahead, so he didn't move forward. As for Meng Da on the third route, I knew that he used to be a close friend of our fellow countryman Li Yan. So I wrote a letter to him in the name of Li and asked him not to attack Shu. I sent Zhao Yun to guard the Yangping Pass, which was the target of Cao Zhen's army on the fourth route. Given the difficulty of the terrain, it is a difficult place for Cao to attack, so we didn't need to send our troops out to battle. Once Cao Zhen saw that our troops were remaining put, he retreated. In addition, I also ordered Guan Xing and Zhang Bao to guard some important places and provide support to each other, just in case any emergencies were to arise. Since our troops I sent out did not pass through Chengdu, the people in the capital had no knowledge of my maneuvers. As for the Kingdom of Wu, since Cao Pi attacked it some time ago, Sun Quan will not help him. Now I need to send an eloquent person to Wu to persuade Sun to withdraw. I've been pondering over who fulfils the task."

Hearing Zhuge's words, Liu Shan suddenly saw the light and said, "Prime Minister, you truly understand yourself and the enemy, and you've responded properly!"

When Zhuge Liang saw Liu Shan out, he found that the ministers waiting outside were panicked. Only one of them, Deng Zhi, smiled. Later, Zhuge sent people to invite Deng to his house for a chat. It turned out that Deng also believed that Shu should form an alliance with Wu and jointly fight Wei. Therefore, Zhuge sent Deng to the Kingdom of Wu to persuade

Sun Quan.

Wu's ruler Sun Quan had heard that Zhuge Liang had repelled Wei's troops on four routes. When Deng Zhi met with him, he asked, "Do you want to ally yourself with Shu or with Wei?"

Sun Quan replied, "In fact, I want to ally myself with Shu, but ...."

Deng said to Sun, "You are a wise man, so is Prime Minister Zhuge Liang. If you attack Shu, you have to conquer the rough mountain roads first; if Shu wants to attack Wu, its troops have to face the natural barrier of the Yangtze River. If the two kingdoms join forces, we can help each other and rule the whole nation. We can also coexist peacefully and both develop in our own way. If you yield to Wei now, its ruler will definitely not allow you to become an emperor. But if you do not obey Wei, they will surely attack you. If that is the case and Shu also attacks you, your kingdom will be in dire straits."

Sun Quan said to Deng Zhi, "Such are my thoughts exactly. I've decided that I will ally myself with your kingdom. Please go back and tell Prime Minister Zhuge Liang." So Wu and Shu became allies. As a result, Sun Quan's army on the fifth route also withdrew.

17. Zhuge Liang Captures Meng Huo Seven Times

In 225, Meng Huo, the ethnic minority chief in the south of the Kingdom of Shu, led his people in rebellion. Thanks to the development over the past few years, Shu enjoyed sufficient food, peace among the general public, and a stronger army. Knowing that Wei and Wu had just battled and for the moment were unable to attack Shu, Zhuge Liang decided to personally lead a 500,000 strong army to the south to quell the revolt there.

Zhuge Liang consulted Ma Su about the rebellion, who believed that the insurrection could be completely quelled only if the ethnic minorities were subdued in their hearts. Zhuge Liang appreciated Ma Su's perspective, and had Ma accompany him to suppress Meng Huo's revolt.

In the first battle, Meng's generals were either captured alive or killed. Zhuge Liang released two generals and told them to go back and tell Meng that he would like to fight them again.

Zhuge Liang predicted that Meng would not accept the defeat as final and return. Sure enough, Meng came back with his soldiers in tow. Zhuge had Wang Ping and Guan Suo lure Meng into a valley where they captured him.

Zhuge Liang asked Meng, "The emperor treated you so well in the past. Have you forgotten the emperor's kindness? Why do you rebel against us? Now that I've captured you, do you concede your defeat?"

Meng replied, "No! You occupied my territory!"

Zhuge Liang said, "Since you remain defiant, I'll let you go, but if I catch you again, I'm certain you will concede!" With these words, Zhuge Liang released Meng. This was the first time Zhuge captured Meng.

Zhuge's generals and soldiers did not understand why he had let Meng go. He explained, "It's easy for me to catch Meng, but only if he submits to us sincerely can we completely pacify the south."

After Meng returned to his barracks, he again sent his troops to fight the Shu army. Ma Dai, a general of Shu, yelled at Meng's general, "Prime Minister Zhuge caught your chief and let him go. How bold and ungrateful he is to launch another attack on us! Please leave soon."

Meng's general felt embarrassed and withdrew. After Meng learned about this, he punished the general with 100 lashings. The general was very angry. He arrested Meng while he was drunk and turned him over to Zhuge.

Zhuge Liang asked Meng, "Will you submit this time?"

Meng replied, "This time I wasn't caught by you. I was captured because my subordinate betrayed me. I still cannot admit defeat."

Zhuge once again set Meng free. This was the second time that Zhuge captured Meng.

After he returned, Meng Huo devised a scheme. He ordered his younger brother, Meng You, to take gifts with him and lead a group of soldiers to the barracks of the Shu army. He would pretend to present gifts to Zhuge Liang with a view to defeating the Shu army. Zhuge Liang immediately saw through the scheme and treated Meng's men to a lot of liquor. He had the liquor drugged, so Meng You and his soldiers passed out.

Meng Huo thought that he had fooled Zhuge Liang, so he led his soldiers to attack the Shu barracks. However, as soon as he entered the Shu barracks, he was captured once again by Zhuge Liang.

Zhuge Liang smiled, "I've captured you three times. Do you admit defeat?"

Meng said, "This time I was captured because my brother was taken in by you, not because I'm incapable. If you let my brother and me go, and I'm caught by you again, I'll acknowledge my defeat."

Thus Zhuge released Meng and his younger brother. This was the third time Zhuge Liang captured Meng.

After returning, Meng put on clothes made of rhino skin. Riding a bull, he led his soldiers to attack the Shu army yet again. Naked and with their hair disheveled, Meng's soldiers rushed toward the Shu barracks like barbarians. Zhuge Liang ordered his army not to go out and fight. Seeing this, Meng's soldiers were deflated.

All of a sudden, Zhuge Liang sent his soldiers to attack Meng Huo. Unprepared for such a surprise attack, Meng's soldiers fled in every direction. Meng was caught by Zhuge Liang once again.

Zhuge Liang asked Meng, "You have been captured by me again. Are you convinced?"

Meng replied, "If you catch me another time, I'll give all my belongings to Shu, and I will never rebel again." And Zhuge Liang let Meng leave once again.

Meng then went to his subordinate Yang Feng's barracks. Yang had been well-treated by Zhuge Liang in early days. So he seized Meng and handed him over to Zhuge Liang.

Zhuge Liang asked Meng, "I suppose you should submit this time."

Meng replied, "This time I was betrayed by my subordinate. I still can't submit myself to you. My home is in the Silver Pit Mountain. If you can capture me there, I will be obedient to you, so will my posterity."

Zhuge Liang released Meng once again. This was the fifth time Meng was captured.

After Meng went back, he sought help from King Mu Lu, who possessed the magic ability to command tigers, wolves, snakes, and other beasts. When Meng fought the Shu army, King Mu Lu sent tigers, wolves, and snakes to attack the Shu army. Seeing this, the Shu soldiers quickly retreated to their barracks. That night, Zhuge Liang ordered his men to decorate 20 chariots like beasts and put firecrackers in them.

The next day, King Mu Lu again commanded tigers, wolves, snakes, and other beasts to rush toward the Shu army. Calmly waving his feather fan, Zhuge Liang ordered his soldiers to light the firecrackers in the chariots and drive the vehicles to the beasts of King Mu Lu. The beasts were terrified and fled, trampling many of Meng's soldiers to death, and then the Shu army caught Meng Huo in the Silver Pit Mountain.

Zhuge Liang said, "You said that if I captured you in your hometown, you would submit. Will you concede now?"

"This time the beasts did not fight as commanded," Meng said. "It was not my fault. I still refuse to submit to you."

Zhuge Liang set Meng free once again. This was the sixth time Zhuge Liang had captured Meng.

After he returned, Meng went to Wutu Gu to ask for help. Wutu Gu had an army that wore vine armor. The armor was so hard that it could withstand swords and spears, but it was no match to fire. So Zhuge Liang launched a fire attack and burned Meng's soldiers to death. Meng was once again caught alive.

This time, Zhuge Liang did not even ask Meng whether he would submit or not; instead, he directly let him go. Meng was moved to tears by this and pledged, "I submit! I will never rebel against Shu again."

This is the story of how Zhuge Liang wisely captured Meng Huo seven times. It is also called "Seven Captures and Seven Releases". Later, Zhuge Liang appointed Meng an official of the Kingdom of Shu and let him govern the ethnic minorities in the south. Meng remained loyal to Shu from that point on.

After pacifying the south, Zhuge Liang led the Shu army back to Chengdu and began to prepare an expeditionary attack on the Kingdom of Wei. He hoped to revive the imperial family of Han and unify the country.

18. Losing the Battle of Jieting

In 226, Cao Pi, the emperor of Wei, passed away. His son Cao Rui ascended to the throne and appointed Sima Yi Grand General in command of the entire army. Zhuge Liang, however, sowed discord between the two, causing Cao Rui to become suspicious of Sima. Cao Rui fell for Zhuge's "discord-sowing stratagem" and eventually removed Sima from his position.

In 228, taking advantage of Sima's removal, Zhuge Liang prepared to make another expeditionary attack on the Kingdom of Wei. It was during this period that he wrote the famous "Northern Expedition Memorial". Under his command, the Shu army seized many places and won a number of battles. Under these circumstances, the Wei emperor Cao Rui had to reappoint Sima Yi Grand General and order him to battle the Shu troops.

Jieting was situated in a narrow mountainous area. It was

a strategic gateway to Guanzhong, Tianshui, Anding, and Jincheng. To its south, there was a mountain; to its north, there was a river. As long as the Shu army could defend it, they would be able to block the Wei army from entering Longxi; if they lost it, the route for transporting provisions of the Shu army would be cut off, resulting in their abortive expeditionary attack on the Kingdom of Wei.

Before setting off, Sima Yi told his subordinates, "We first need to seize Jieting. If we succeed in doing so, the Shu troops won't be able to transport their provisions. If Zhuge refuses to retreat, his soldiers will die of hunger within a month; if he retreats, we can ambush the enemy from a small path and win a great victory!"Everyone present was impressed by his wisdom.

Expecting Sima to launch an attack on Jieting, Zhuge decided to increase his soldiers defending it. The young general Ma Su volunteered himself to assume this important task.

Zhuge told him, "Small as Jieting is, it is of vital importance. If we lose it, our failure is certain. Jieting is very hard to defend because there is no city wall surrounding it and its terrain is not good."

In spite of Zhuge's warning, Ma insisted on going because he thought he was adept at military tactics. He even wrote a pledge, promising that he would accept punishment by military law if Jieting was lost.

"Sima Yi is resourceful," Zhuge reminded Ma. "You must be careful!" After thinking the matter over more, Zhuge decided that Ma had displayed great talent in the battle to quell rebellion in the south and proved himself a wise and resourceful general, so Zhuge figured, why not give him a chance to further get tempered himself? With such reasoning, Zhuge entrusted Ma with the responsibility of guarding Jieting.

But Zhuge remained worried that Ma would not be able to fulfil the task by himself, so he appointed Major General Wang Ping to serve as Ma's assistant. Prior to their departure, Zhuge reminded the two that they should pitch camp at main road junctions and avoid camping on the mountains. With this advice, Ma and Wang set off. After their departure, Zhuge dispatched another two generals, Gao Xiang and Wei Yan, who each had 10,000 strong troops under their command, to camp near Jieting. These generals were ready to offer Ma Su and Wang Ping assistance if necessary. After ordering these deployments, Zhuge believed that Jieting would be safe, so he began preparing an attack on Chang'an, the capital of the Kingdom of Wei.

After Ma Su and Wang Ping arrived at Jieting, Ma thought Sima Yi would not come to such a small place, so he ordered the troops to camp on the mountains. Wang Ping disagreed and said they should pitch camp at the road junctions.

Ma said to Wang, "Books on the art of war tell us that 'attacking the enemy from above is like splitting bamboo with crushing force.' Thus, we should camp on the mountains and barrel down and defeat them when the Wei troops arrive."

Wang tried to persuade him, saying, "If we pitch camp on the mountains, once the Wei army lays siege on us, our water supply will be cut off. Without water, our soldiers will be disorderly even before the enemy attacks us!"

Ma refuted him, saying, "Master Sun once said, 'When a man is confronted with death, he will fight for his life.' If our army is devoid of water, they will fight desperately to the end!"

Seeing that Ma Su refused to heed his advice, Wang Ping had no choice but to lead his own troops to camp at the foot of the mountains. The two army units could help each other when the Wei army launched its attack on them. Wang sent a messenger to Zhuge that very night, telling him Ma had camped atop the mountains. The message left Zhuge filled with great shock.

Meanwhile, Sima Yi was hurriedly leading the Wei troops to Jieting. Upon arrival, he discovered it was already guarded by the Shu soldiers. He sighed, "Zhuge is so brilliant that he acted before I could!"

His son Sima Zhao, however, just laughed and said, "Ma Su pitched camp on the mountains where there is no water to speak of. We just need to cut off the water supply, and the Shu troops will have to lay down their weapons!"

Hearing his son's advice, a smile beamed across Sima's face as he gleefully declared, "Ma Su is a general who fights only on paper. Even Zhuge is not devoid of error!" He immediately summoned his generals and dispatched one army unit to fight Wang Ping, another to stop the Shu soldiers from coming down the mountains to seek food and water, and then led the rest of his army to lay siege over the mountains.

The Shu soldiers on the mountains were running out of food and water. Seeing swarms of Wei troops down the mountains, they became filled with panic and began to flee. At that moment, the Wei soldiers began their assault up the mountains, and Ma Su had to flee for his life. Wang Ping, along with Gao Xiang and Wei Yan, tried to rescue Ma, but they failed as they were blocked halfway by Wei troops.

Upon learning that Jieting had been captured, Zhuge Liang

sighed, "Dispatching Ma Su to guard Jieting was my mistake!" He then ordered Guan Xing and Zhang Bao to command 3,000 strong soldiers and asked them to obstruct Sima Yi, and then he personally led 5,000 strong soldiers to Xicheng to transport provisions, preparing for a retreat to Hanzhong.

Ma Su's defeat at Jieting forced Zhuge Liang to abandon his plan of attacking the Kingdom of Wei. As a result, all of the Shu troops retreated to Hanzhong.

19. Empty Fort Strategy

After losing the battle of Jieting, Zhuge Liang rushed to Xicheng with 5,000 strong troops in tow. He ordered half of the soldiers to go out of town to fetch provisions, leaving only 2,500 soldiers positioned in the county. Suddenly, a soldier came to report to Zhuge that Sima Yi was leading 150,000 Wei soldiers toward Xicheng. At that time, there was no general at Zhuge's side except only a few civil officials. The civil officials were thrown into a state of panic as their lives seemed to be hanging by a thread.

Zhuge went to the top of the gate tower to look out into the distance, only to see Wei troops approaching Xicheng on two routes. He then said to his troops, "Remove the banner, keep from talking loudly, open all four gates, and dispatch 20 soldiers to each gate. Have the soldiers at the gates dress like common people and pretend to clean the streets. I will have a scheme to repel the Wei troops once they arrive. Don't be afraid." After that, he asked two boys to fetch an incense burner and his *guqin*, and then he lit the incense and sat down to play it at the gate tower.

When the vanguard of Sima's army reached Xicheng and saw

such a quiet county, they stopped in their tracks, not daring to march into the county. Sima Yi then arrived, only to find Zhuge Liang sitting at the gate tower and playing the *guqin* with a smile beaming across his face. He also saw two young boys standing beside Zhuge and roughly 20 people cleaning the streets of the county. He sensed something wasn't right with the sight before him, and decided that there must be an ambush awaiting him in the county. So Sima ordered his soldiers to retreat immediately. Sima Zhao, his younger son, advised his father not to retreat, arguing that Zhuge was just pretending to be calm. But Sima Yi did not heed his son's words and insisted that it was a trap and they should immediately withdraw.

Seeing that Sima had retreated, Zhuge Liang clapped his hands and laughed. All the civil officials wondered why Sima Yi had withdrawn. "I pretended to be calm to make Sima think there was an ambush in the county," Zhuge explained. "As a result, he didn't dare to continue marching into the county." He then ordered his soldiers to lead the common people back to Hanzhong.

Sima Yi retreated to the North Hill and said to his other generals, "Zhuge schemed in vain this time—we saw right through his scheme!" No sooner had he finished speaking than the sound of a cannon firing followed by a war cry came to their ears. Zhang Bao was leading his men toward them. Shocked, Sima Yi said, "We fell into Zhuge's ambush again!" The Wei troops ran for their lives, and as they were fleeing, another war cry emanated from the mountain valley. Guan Xing and his men chased them as well. The Wei soldiers dropped their weapons and provisions and fled back to Jieting.

Soon after Sima Yi returned to Jieting, a Wei spy rushed over and told him that Xicheng had actually been empty and there had been no ambush planned. In addition, there were only 5,000 to 6,000 Shu soldiers on the North Hill, They had simply made a false show of strength and did not dare to battle the Wei army. Sima was astonished and angry over this information. He sighed, "Zhuge is smarter than me, smarter than me!"

With a heavy heart, Zhuge Liang led the Shu troops back to Hanzhong. Ma Su tied himself up and kneeled before Zhuge.

Zhuge asked him, "How could you make such a grave mistake? Had you accepted Wang Ping's advice, you wouldn't have suffered such a great loss! You wrote the pledge and Jieting was lost. If I don't punish you according to military law, how can I run the army? Don't blame me for this. After you die, I will be sure to take good care of your family."

Ma kneeled down before Zhuge and wailed, "I'm guilty of the death penalty. Thank you, Prime Minister, for looking after my family!" Zhuge Liang couldn't help shedding his tears.

Ma Su was then carried outside the camp to be beheaded. Just then Grand General Jiang Wan arrived from Chengdu, the capital of the Kingdom of Shu. Seeing that Ma Su was set to be executed, he shouted, "Stop! Please!"Jiang Wan rushed into the camp and tried to persuade Zhuge to spare Ma's life, but Zhuge insisted that if he were to run the army well, he needed to strictly enforce military law. As a result, Ma Su was put to death at the age of 39.

A short while later, a soldier returned to the camp carrying Ma's head. Zhuge couldn't help wailing upon seeing it. He said that he regretted not following the instructions Liu Bei had given to him on his deathbed and instead placed too much trust in Ma Su.

The other generals and soldiers also wept upon hearing this.

Zhuge Liang dried his tears and issued another decree to award Wang Ping, who had tried hard to correct Ma Su's mistake. Moreover, on account of his own fault, Zhuge Liang resigned from his position as Prime Minister and only served as a general. Nevertheless, he continued to do all he could to assist the young emperor Liu Shan.

20. Zhuge Liang—The Upright Prime Minister of the Kingdom of Shu

After Liu Bei's death, Zhuge Liang did his utmost to assist Liu Shan, the young emperor of the Kingdom of Shu. He personally attended to all affairs no matter how big or how small, so much so that his health progressively deteriorated. Despite his illness, Zhuge still led his troops on several expeditions against the Kingdom of Wei with the intent of reviving the imperial family of Han and unifying the country.

In 234, Zhuge Liang began his fifth northern expedition. With the Shu army under his command, he set off from Hanzhong. They traveled through the Qinling Mountains, marching northward. His troops were blocked by Sima Yi's army at Wuzhangyuan, a strategic location of difficult access. The two sides were locked in a face-off for over 100 days, but Sima Yi refused to accept the Shu army's challenge and Zhuge Liang could only anxiously hope that the Wei army would be lured out.

The Gourd Valley, which was surrounded by the mountains, had only one exit. Zhuge tricked Sima into the valley and ordered his soldiers to set fire to the exit, hoping to burn Sima and his soldiers to death. However, an unexpected heavy rain fell at that moment, saving the Wei army. Having escaped the fire, Sima and his soldiers fled from the valley.

Autumn arrived, and Zhuge's health continued to grow worse. One day, a message arrived, saying that the Kingdom of Wu had sent its army out on three different routes to attack the Kingdom of Wei and intended to join forces with the Shu army to attack the Wei army. Unfortunately, Wu was defeated in the campaign. Hearing the news, Zhuge became extremely anxious and fell ill. Two days later, he began spitting up blood. Despite this, he refused to rest and continued handling all affairs.

One day, Zhuge took to his wheelchair and asked his soldiers to push him out, so he could look over the barracks. He said, "I won't be able to fight against the Kingdom of Wei again! Vast heavens, why won't you allow me more time? Why must things be like this?" After saying this, he sighed incessantly.

Zhuge then returned to the barracks, and his illness deteriorated even further. He sent someone to call up a minister by the name of Yang Yi, and said to him, "After I die, do not release an obituary and keep the barracks as calmly as they usually are. Then order a gradual retreat starting with the rear barracks. If Sima Yi and his soldiers catch up, place my wooden statue on the wheelchair and ask the soldiers to push it out to make Sima believe that I'm still alive. If he sees this, he won't dare to chase you any longer. Jiang Wei is a capable general, you can ask him to cover the retreat of the army." Yang wept and nodded his head.

Zhuge then called Jiang Wei in and handed him the books regarding the art of war, which he had written entirely by himself. He hoped that Jiang could use the art of war to serve the country and revive the imperial family of Han. Jiang accepted the books with tears in his eyes.

Zhuge added, "You don't need to worry about the Shuzhong region, just pay special attention to Yinping. Although it is rather easy to defend given its difficult terrain, over a longer period of time problems might arise there." Weeping, Jiang Wei committed these words to his memory.

Zhuge then wrote a memorial to Emperor Liu Shan, which said, "I heard that life and death are common occurrences among the people. Though I haven't much time left, I would still like to express my loyalty to the Kingdom of Shu. During our quest to revive the imperial family of Han, I served as the Prime Minister and led the Shu army on several northern expeditions. Unfortunately, I haven't accomplished my task. It is pitiful that I can no longer serve Your Majesty! After I die, you should have a pure heart and few worldly desires. Love your people and your country. Please bear firmly in mind the dream of your father to revive the imperial family of Han. Appoint those that are wise and loyal to important positions and steer clear of those that are mean and evil, this will foster positive conduct throughout the society. My family members live in Chengdu. They sustain themselves by farming and there's no need to worry about them. Apart from a few articles of clothes I brought with me, I haven't any fortune to my name. It was an honor to have had the trust of Your Majesty for so many years, and I've no desire to keep any ill-gotten wealth in the afterlife." After Zhuge finished writing the memorial, he fainted.

The generals were alarmed and bewildered to see him faint. At that moment, Emperor Liu Shan's envoy had just arrived. He burst into tears at the sight of Zhuge Liang, who then slowly opened his eyes, saying, "It's a great pity that I'm seriously ill and can't continue the northern expedition. I'm guilty of delaying the Shu's goal of reviving the imperial family of Han and unifying the country. After I die, continue to assist the emperor. Do not make rash changes to the established system. I've given all my military books to Jiang Wei, and he will carry on my unfinished task. Please hand over this memorial to His Majesty." After that, he closed his eyes again.

In 234, Zhuge Liang passed away in the barracks at Wuzhangyuan. He died at the age of 54.

After Zhuge's death, Yang Yi and Jiang Wei followed his arrangements. They didn't announce his death, but issued a secret order to the barracks, telling them to retreat in quick succession.

Upon knowing the information that the Shu troops were retreating, Sima Yi assumed that Zhuge Liang might have died, so he sent his army in pursuit. But just as his troops were leaving the barracks, Sima realized it might be a trap designed by Zhuge. Subsequently, he called back his troops and dispatched a spy to gather more information. The spy saw that the Shu troops were indeed retreating and hurried back to report this to Sima, "I've received word that Zhuge Liang has died and the Shu troops are retreating." Sima jumped up from his seat out of excitement and sent his troops back out in pursuit.

Sima led his army to the foot of a mountain, from where the Shu troops were in sight. Just then, he heard a cannon firing and a large banner appeared from the woods as Shu soldiers poured out from them. Sima was taken aback. Then he saw a cart being pushed out by dozens of Shu generals. Sitting on the cart was none other than Zhuge Liang. Sima's face grew pale with shock, and he said to the other generals, "Zhuge is still alive. I've been fooled by him again!" He turned his horse back and fled.

Jiang Wei led the Shu army in pursuit. They beat their drums and shouted, "Sima Yi, you've been fooled again by Prime Minister Zhuge!" The Wei troops were so frightened that they ran for dozens of miles. Sima Yi touched his head and asked the person beside him, "Is my head still with me?" One of his generals responded, "The Shu army has already gone." Only then did Sima let out a sigh of relief.

Two days later, Sima Yi learned that Zhuge Liang had indeed passed away, and what he had seen two days before was actually a wooden statue of Zhuge. A saying then spread among the Shu soldiers, "A dead Zhuge can frighten away a living Sima." Hearing this saying, Sima Yi was furious and resentful.

From 228 to 234, Zhuge Liang launched five northern expeditions against the Kingdom of Wei. During that period, he invented a tool called the "Wooden Oxen and Gliding Horses" to help his 100,000 strong troops transport provisions. When Sima Yi led his army to Wuzhangyuan to take on the Shu army, he saw the fortress and sighed deeply, "Zhuge Liang is indeed a rare genius!"

Later on, a temple was built at Wuzhangyuan to commemorate Zhuge Liang, the outstanding Prime Minister of the Kingdom of Shu.

The End: Three Kingdoms Unified Under the Jin Dynasty

The Kingdom of Shu

In 234, Zhuge Liang passed away at Wuzhangyuan due to constant overwork. Jiang Wei, who carried out the unfinished tasks left by Zhuge, led the Shu expeditionary army to attack the Kingdom of Wei, during which period several battles took place between him and the famous Wei general Deng Ai.

In 263, Sima Zhao ordered Zhong Hui and Deng Ai to launch an attack on the Kingdom of Shu. The two generals led their troops, and before long they reached Chengdu, capital of the Kingdom of Shu. The incapable Shu emperor, Liu Shan, had to surrender to the Wei army along with all the ministers and generals. The Kingdom of Shu came to an end in winter that year.

Subsequently, Liu Shan was ordered to leave the Kingdom of Shu and live in Luoyang. Seeing that their emperor had surrendered to his enemy, the Shu generals all felt heartbroken. However, Liu Shan seemed not to care at all.

One day at a banquet, Sima Zhao asked him, "Do you miss your hometown Shu?" Liu replied, "I'm having a good time here, and I don't want to return to Shu now."

Jiang Wei had been longing to revitalize the Kingdom of Shu. But, for a variety of reasons, he failed to bring about a unified country.

The Kingdom of Wei

Wei had long been under the control of Sima Yi and Sima Zhao, and the father and his son's ambition was abundantly clear, hence the idiom "Sima Zhao's ill intent is known to all".

After the Kingdom of Shu was wiped out, the emperor of the Kingdom of Wei, Cao Mao, conferred the title "Duke of Jin" on Sima Zhao. However, Sima was rather scornful of the emperor, so much so that he often went to court with his sword and even asked the emperor to receive him in person.

When Sima Zhao was conferred the title of "Duke of Jin", all the ministers at court stood up to offer him congratulations, whereas Cao Mao lowered his head and didn't utter a word.

Sima yelled at the emperor, "We, the Sima family, have rendered great services for the Kingdom of Wei. Is there any problem with me becoming the 'Duke of Jin'?"

Cao Mao said in fear, "How can I disobey your order and say there's a problem?"

After Sima had left the court, the emperor was so angry that he wanted to kill him. He said, "I can't bear it anymore, I've made up my mind to kill Sima Zhao!" However, one of his subordinates tipped Sima off about the plan. Sima then killed Cao Mao and designated Cao Huan as the new emperor.

In 265, Sima Zhao died of an illness. His son Sima Yan succeeded him and became the new Duke of Jin. Several months later, Sima Yan forced Cao Huan to abdicate the throne to him, hence the Kingdom of Wei came to an end. Sima Yan then founded the Jin Dynasty.

The Kingdom of Wu

In 252, Sun Quan died of an illness at the age of 71. In 264, Sun Hao became the emperor of the Kingdom of Wu and began controlling the whole kingdom. He never listened to the advice offered to him and even killed more than 40 loyal ministers. He also ordered a grand palace to be built which triggered strong dissatisfaction among the common people. The kingdom was on the wane.

After learning about the situation in the Kingdom of Wu, Sima Yan dispatched General Du Yu to lead an army to attack the kingdom. Eventually, another Jin general named Wang Jun led his troops into Jianye, capital of the Kingdom of Wu. Sun Hao had to surrender to the Jin Dynasty. In 280, the Kingdom of Wu came to an end.

With the three kingdoms unified under the Jin Dynasty, Sima Yan managed to unify the whole nation. Hence the tripartite confrontation among the Three Kingdoms of Wei, Shu and Wu that had lasted many decades finally came to an end. Just as the saying goes, "The nation, after a long period of division, tends to unite; after a long period of union, it tends to divide. This has been a general trend since ancient times."

词汇表
Vocabulary List

安定	*adj.*	āndìng	stable; settled
安居	*v.*	ānjū	live in peace and comfort
岸	*n.*	àn	riverbank
把守	*v.*	bǎshǒu	defend; guard
百姓	*n.*	bǎixìng	common people; ordinary people
败仗	*n.*	bàizhàng	lost battle
拜见	*v.*	bàijiàn	pay a formal visit
包围	*v.*	bāowéi	surround; besiege
宝石	*n.*	bǎoshí	gem
保卫	*v.*	bǎowèi	protect; defend
报仇	*v.*	bàochóu	revenge
悲痛	*adj.*	bēitòng	sorrowful
北伐	*n.*	běifá	northern expedition
背叛	*v.*	bèipàn	betray
比作		bǐzuò	compare to
鞭炮	*n.*	biānpào	firecracker
辩论	*v.*	biànlùn	debate
兵法	*n.*	bīngfǎ	art of war
兵器	*n.*	bīngqì	arms；weaponry
不义之财		búyìzhīcái	ill-gotten wealth
部下	*n.*	bùxià	subordinate
才智	*n.*	cáizhì	intelligence; wisdom
踩	*v.*	cǎi	step on; trample
惭愧	*adj.*	cánkuì	ashamed
惨	*adj.*	cǎn	disastrous; severe
苍天	*n.*	cāngtiān	Heaven
草人	*n.*	cǎorén	scarecrow
草鞋	*n.*	cǎoxié	straw sandals
拆	*v.*	chāi	dismantle; pull down
长寿	*adj.*	chángshòu	long-lived
朝廷	*n.*	cháotíng	royal court

撤退	*v.*	chètuì	retreat
尘土	*n.*	chéntǔ	dust
称王		chēng wáng	proclaim oneself king
丞相	*n.*	chéngxiàng	prime minister
诚意	*n.*	chéngyì	sincerity
城楼	*n.*	chénglóu	gate tower
城门	*n.*	chéngmén	city gate
惩罚	*v.*	chéngfá	punish
吃喝玩乐		chīhē-wánlè	indulge in eating, drinking, and pleasure-seeking
耻辱	*n.*	chǐrǔ	disgrace; humiliation
仇恨	*v.*	chóuhèn	feel great hatred toward
船头	*n.*	chuántóu	bow (of a boat)
船尾	*n.*	chuánwěi	stern
吹牛	*v.*	chuīniú	boast; brag
打败	*v.*	dǎbài	defeat
打雷	*v.*	dǎléi	thunder
打天下		dǎ tiānxià	seize state power by armed force; 天下 land under heaven; the country
打仗	*v.*	dǎzhàng	fight in a battle
大臣	*n.*	dàchén	court official; minister
大惊失色		dàjīng-shīsè	be fluttered
大权	*n.*	dàquán	great power; authority
大帐	*n.*	dàzhàng	central military camp
带领	*v.*	dàilǐng	lead; command
担任	*v.*	dānrèn	hold (a post)
担忧	*v.*	dānyōu	worry about
耽误	*v.*	dānwu	delay
胆子	*n.*	dǎnzi	courage
瞪	*v.*	dèng	stare; glare
敌人	*n.*	dírén	enemy; foe
抵抗	*v.*	dǐkàng	resist
地盘	*n.*	dìpán	territory
地势	*n.*	dìshì	terrain
雕像	*n.*	diāoxiàng	effigy; statue
毒箭	*n.*	dú jiàn	poisoned arrow
对抗	*v.*	duìkàng	resist; oppose
对峙	*v.*	duìzhì	confront each other

恩情	*n.*	ēnqíng	kindness
发丧	*v.*	fāsāng	release an obituary and mourn the dead
放肆	*adj.*	fàngsì	presumptuous; rude
飞扬	*v.*	fēiyáng	fly upward
肥沃	*adj.*	féiwò	fertile
愤怒	*adj.*	fènnù	angry; indignant
锋利	*adj.*	fēnglì	sharp
缝	*v.*	féng	sew; stitch
服	*v.*	fú	be convinced
腐败	*adj.*	fǔbài	corrupt
副手	*n.*	fùshǒu	assistant
嘎吱嘎吱	*onom.*	gāzhī gāzhī	creak
干柴	*n.*	gānchái	dry wood
告示	*n.*	gàoshì	official notice
割	*v.*	gē	cut
各显神通		gè xiǎn shéntōng	each one showing his special prowess
弓箭	*n.*	gōngjiàn	bow and arrows
攻打	*v.*	gōngdǎ	attack; assault
宫殿	*n.*	gōngdiàn	palace
古琴	*n.*	gǔqín	*guqin*, a seven-stringed plucked instrument in ancient China
刮	*v.*	guā	scrape
关	*n.*	guān	strategic pass
观赏	*v.*	guānshǎng	view and enjoy
跪	*v.*	guì	kneel
汉朝	*n.*	Hàncháo	Han Dynasty (206 BC-220 AD)
和睦	*adj.*	hémù	harmonious
荷花池	*n.*	héhuāchí	lotus pool
后代	*n.*	hòudài	descendant; offspring
胡子	*n.*	húzi	beard
慌张	*adj.*	huāngzhāng	flustered; frantic
皇帝	*n.*	huángdì	emperor
皇室	*n.*	huángshì	royal family
皇叔	*n.*	huángshū	uncle of the emperor
恍然大悟		huǎngrán-dàwù	suddenly realize
回报	*v.*	huíbào	requite; repay
回合	*n.*	huíhé	round; bout

活捉	*v.*	huózhuō	capture alive
火爆	*adj.*	huǒbào	hot-tempered
火攻	*n.*	huǒgōng	fire attack
祸	*n.*	huò	disaster; great misfortune
击退	*v.*	jītuì	beat back; repel
嫉妒	*v.*	jídù	envy; be jealous of
计谋	*n.*	jìmóu	scheme; stratagem
祭祖	*v.*	jìzǔ	worship one's ancestors
嘉奖	*v.*	jiājiǎng	commend
假装	*v.*	jiǎzhuāng	pretend
奸臣	*n.*	jiānchén	wicked minister
奸污	*v.*	jiānwū	rape
奸贼	*n.*	jiānzéi	conspirator
兼并	*v.*	jiānbìng	annex; amalgamate
剑	*n.*	jiàn	sword
将军	*n.*	jiāngjūn	general
将领	*n.*	jiànglǐng	general
将士	*n.*	jiàngshì	generals and soldiers
交战	*v.*	jiāozhàn	fight; battle
酒馆	*n.*	jiǔguǎn	pub
酒宴	*n.*	jiǔyàn	banquet
救	*v.*	jiù	save; rescue
局面	*n.*	júmiàn	situation
决一死战		juéyìsǐzhàn	fight to the death
军队	*n.*	jūnduì	army; troops
军阀	*n.*	jūnfá	warlord
军棍	*n.*	jūngùn	rod of birch used for corporal punishment in an army
军纪	*n.*	jūnjì	military discipline
军师	*n.*	jūnshī	military counselor
军心	*n.*	jūnxīn	morale of troops
军营	*n.*	jūnyíng	barracks; military camp
看作	*v.*	kànzuò	regard…as
抗击	*v.*	kàngjī	fight against
控制	*v.*	kòngzhì	control
捆	*v.*	kǔn	bind; tie
困境	*n.*	kùnjìng	plight

蜡烛	*n.*	làzhú	candle
狼狈不堪		lángbèi-bùkān	in a very awkward position
劳累	*adj.*	láolèi	tired
擂鼓		léi gǔ	beat drums
礼服	*n.*	lǐfú	ceremonial robe or dress
联合	*v.*	liánhé	unite; ally with
联军	*n.*	liánjūn	allied troops; united army
廉相	*n.*	lián xiàng	upright and incorruptible prime minister
粮草	*n.*	liángcǎo	army provision
龙	*n.*	lóng	dragon
龙卷风	*n.*	lóngjuǎnfēng	tornado
路	*n.*	lù	route
路口	*n.*	lùkǒu	road junction; crossroads
埋伏	*v.*	máifú	ambush
茅庐	*n.*	máolú	thatched cottage
美德	*n.*	měidé	virtue
美梦	*n.*	měimèng	happy dream
猛烈	*adj.*	měngliè	strong; violent
密探	*n.*	mìtàn	spy
密信	*n.*	mìxìn	confidential letter
灭亡	*v.*	mièwáng	perish
名义	*n.*	míngyì	name
名震天下		míngzhèn-tiānxià	become well-known all over the world
命令	*v.*	mìnglìng	command; order
莫名其妙		mòmíngqímiào	be baffled; be perplexed
谋反	*v.*	móufǎn	conspire against the court
目瞪口呆		mùdèng-kǒudāi	be struck dumb with astonishment
呐喊	*v.*	nàhǎn	shout loudly
能言善辩		néngyán-shànbiàn	be eloquent
尿	*n.*	niào	urine
叛乱	*v.*	pànluàn	revolt
炮	*n.*	pào	gunfire
佩服	*v.*	pèifú	admire
披散	*v.*	pīsǎn	(of hair) hang down loosely
皮肉	*n.*	píròu	skin and flesh
匹	*m.w.*	pǐ	(for horses, mules, etc.)
平定	*v.*	píngdìng	pacify

奇才	*n.*	qícái	rare talent
奇妙	*adj.*	qímiào	wonderful; marvelous
骑兵	*n.*	qíbīng	cavalrymen
旗帜	*n.*	qízhì	flag; banner
钱财	*n.*	qiáncái	money; wealth
枪	*n.*	qiāng	spear; pike
强盛	*adj.*	qiángshèng	powerful and prosperous
抢	*v.*	qiǎng	rob; grab
擒	*v.*	qín	capture
青梅	*n.*	qīngméi	green plum
清心寡欲		qīngxīn-guǎyù	have a pure heart and few desires
情义	*n.*	qíngyì	friendship; brotherhood
庆祝	*v.*	qìngzhù	celebrate
求情	*v.*	qiúqíng	beg for leniency
扰乱	*v.*	rǎoluàn	disturb; disrupt
仁义	*adj.*	rényì	amiable and upright
忍心	*v.*	rěnxīn	have the heart to
僧人	*n.*	sēngrén	Buddhist monk
傻	*adj.*	shǎ	stunned
山谷	*n.*	shāngǔ	canyon; gorge
烧	*v.*	shāo	burn; set fire
少数民族	*n.*	shǎoshù mínzú	ethnic minority group
射	*v.*	shè	shoot at
神医	*n.*	shényī	miracle-working doctor
声望	*n.*	shēngwàng	reputation; fame
圣人	*n.*	shèngrén	sage
胜仗	*n.*	shèngzhàng	victorious battle
尸体	*n.*	shītǐ	corpse
失误	*v.*	shīwù	make a mistake (out of negligence)
石壁	*n.*	shíbì	cliff
试探	*v.*	shìtàn	test; probe
收服	*v.*	shōufú	subdue; bring under control
收获	*n.*	shōuhuò	harvest
首领	*n.*	shǒulǐng	leader; head
树林	*n.*	shùlín	woods; grove
树枝	*n.*	shùzhī	branch
衰落	*v.*	shuāiluò	decline

水井	*n.*	shuǐjǐng	well
水寨	*n.*	shuǐzhài	naval camp
说客	*n.*	shuìkè	lobbyist
死罪	*n.*	sǐzuì	capital offence
寺庙	*n.*	sìmiào	temple
谈判	*v.*	tánpàn	negotiate
弹琴	*v.*	tánqín	play stringed musical instrument
逃跑	*v.*	táopǎo	escape; flee
讨伐	*v.*	tǎofá	send a punitive expedition against
挑战	*v.*	tiǎozhàn	challenge in battle
铁	*n.*	tiě	iron
铁环	*n.*	tiěhuán	iron hoop
统一	*v.*	tǒngyī	reunify
投降	*v.*	tóuxiáng	surrender
土坑	*n.*	tǔkēng	pit
退	*v.*	tuì	retreat
退兵	*v.*	tuìbīng	retreat
托孤	*v.*	tuō gū	(of an emperor) entrust his young sons to the care of his ministers
危急	*adj.*	wēijí	critical
温和	*adj.*	wēnhé	moderate; mild
文官	*n.*	wénguān	civil official
雾	*n.*	wù	fog
犀牛皮	*n.*	xīniúpí	rhino hide
下棋		xià qí	play chess
贤明	*adj.*	xiánmíng	wise and able
险要	*adj.*	xiǎnyào	strategic and inaccessible
陷入	*v.*	xiànrù	be caught in
献给	*v.*	xiàn gěi	give; present sth. to sb.
相貌堂堂		xiàngmào-tángtáng	handsome; elegant in appearance
香	*n.*	xiāng	incense
香炉	*n.*	xiānglú	censer; incense burner
小妾	*n.*	xiǎoqiè	concubine
孝顺	*v.*	xiàoshùn	be filially pious; be dutiful
效劳	*v.*	xiàoláo	serve; work for
心服口服		xīnfú-kǒufú	be sincerely convinced
心事	*n.*	xīnshì	something weighing on one's mind

形成	*v.*	xíngchéng	form
血	*n.*	xuè	blood
严肃	*adj.*	yánsù	serious
仰慕	*v.*	yǎngmù	admire
野人	*n.*	yěrén	wild man; savage
野兽	*n.*	yěshòu	wild animal; beast
野心	*n.*	yěxīn	ambition
遗憾	*adj.*	yíhàn	regretful
遗志	*n.*	yízhì	deathbed behest
遗嘱	*n.*	yízhǔ	will; testament
以防万一		yǐfáng-wànyī	be prepared for the emergency
义女	*n.*	yìnǚ	adoptive daughter
英俊	*adj.*	yīngjùn	handsome
英雄	*n.*	yīngxióng	hero
映	*v.*	yìng	reflect
油	*n.*	yóu	oil
右臂	*n.*	yòu bì	right arm
羽扇	*n.*	yǔshàn	feather fan
元旦	*n.*	Yuándàn	New Year's Day
怨	*v.*	yuàn	blame; resent
晕船	*v.*	yūnchuán	be seasick
运输	*v.*	yùnshū	transport
葬礼	*n.*	zànglǐ	funeral
扎营	*v.*	zhāyíng	encamp
窄	*adj.*	zhǎi	narrow
占领	*v.*	zhànlǐng	occupy
战乱	*n.*	zhànluàn	turmoil of war
召集	*v.*	zhàojí	call together; rally
遮天蔽日		zhētiān-bìrì	blot out the sun and the sky
争夺	*v.*	zhēngduó	contend for
征兵	*v.*	zhēngbīng	recruit soldiers; conscript
支援	*v.*	zhīyuán	assist; aid
知遇之恩		zhīyùzhī'ēn	gratitude for someone who is apprecia-tive of one's ability
治病	*v.*	zhìbìng	treat an illness
智慧	*n.*	zhìhuì	wisdom
中……计谋	*v.*	zhòng…jìmóu	be caught in (a scheme)

忠诚	*adj.*	zhōngchéng	loyal
肿	*adj.*	zhǒng	swollen
重伤	*v.*	zhòngshāng	be seriously wounded
诸侯	*n.*	zhūhóu	dukes or princes under an empire
柱子	*n.*	zhùzi	pillar
子子孙孙		zǐzǐsūnsūn	descendants; offspring
奏折	*n.*	zòuzhé	memorial to the emperor
阻挡	*v.*	zǔdǎng	obstruct; stop
左臂	*n.*	zuǒ bì	left arm

项目策划：韩　颖　刘小琳
责任编辑：杨　晗
英文翻译：薛彧威　闫传海
英文编辑：吴爱俊
英文审订：卢　敏
设计指导：战文庭　卞　淳
设计制作：isles studio

图书在版编目（CIP）数据

三国演义 / 史迹，黎明主编 ；马郡等编．— 北京 ：华语教学出版社，2018.12
（“彩虹桥”汉语分级读物）
ISBN 978-7-5138-1646-5

Ⅰ．①三… Ⅱ．①史… ②黎… ③马… Ⅲ．①汉语－对外汉语教学－语言读物 Ⅳ．①H195.5

中国版本图书馆 CIP 数据核字（2018）第 262470 号

三国演义
罗贯中　原著
史迹　黎明　主编
*

华语教学出版社有限责任公司出版
（中国北京百万庄大街24号　邮政编码 100037）
电话：(86)10-68320585　68997826
传真：(86)10-68997826　68326333
网址：www.sinolingua.com.cn
电子信箱：hyjx@sinolingua.com.cn
北京京华虎彩印刷有限公司印刷
2019年（32开）第1版
2019年第1版第1次印刷
（汉英）
ISBN 978-7-5138-1646-5
定价：59.00元